Martin Luther,

the Bible,

and the

Jewish People

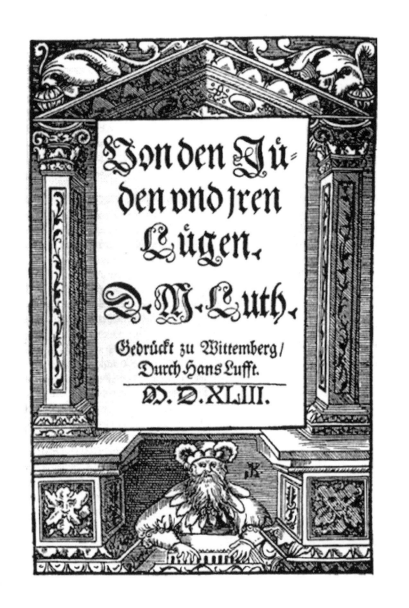

Von den Ju-
den vnd jren
Lügen.

D. M. Luth.

Gedruckt zu Wittemberg/
Durch Hans Lufft.
M. D. XLIII.

Martin Luther, the Bible, and the Jewish People

A READER

Edited by Brooks Schramm and Kirsi I. Stjerna

Fortress Press

Minneapolis

To our children

Ben, David, Kiki, and Kristian.

MARTIN LUTHER, THE BIBLE, AND THE JEWISH PEOPLE
A Reader

Copyright © 2012 Fortress Press. All rights reserved. Except for brief quotations in critical articles or reviews, no part of this book may be reproduced in any manner without prior written permission from the publisher. Visit http://www.augsburgfortress.org/copyrights/contact.asp or write to Permissions, Augsburg Fortress, Box 1209, Minneapolis, MN 55440.

Images on pages 2 and 16 courtesy of the Kessler Reformation Collection at Pitts Theology Library, Candler School of Theology, Emory University. Images on pages 36, 38, and 40 courtesy of the Klau Library at Hebrew Union College-Jewish Institute of Religion, Cincinnati. Held by the Bayerische Staatsbibliothek, Munich.

Cover image: Title page of *Von den Jüden und Iren Lügen* (*On the Jews and Their Lies*), 1543.
Cover design: Laurie Ingram
Book design and typesetting: Josh Messner

Library of Congress Cataloging-in-Publication Data
Luther, Martin, 1483-1546.
[Selections. English. 2012]
Martin Luther, the Bible, and the Jewish people : a reader / edited by Brooks Schramm and Kirsi I. Stjerna.
         p. cm.
Includes bibliographical references and index.
ISBN 978-0-8006-9804-1 (pbk. : alk. paper) — ISBN 978-1-4514-2428-7 (ebook)
1. Jews. 2. Christianity and antisemitism. 3. Antisemitism. 4. Christianity and other religions—Judaism. 5. Judaism—Relations—Christianity. 6. Bible—Sermons. I. Schramm, Brooks, 1957– II. Stjerna, Kirsi Irmeli, 1963– III. Title.
BR333.5.J4L8813 2012
261.2'6—dc23   2012008043

The paper used in this publication meets the minimum requirements of American National Standard for Information Sciences—Permanence of Paper for Printed Library Materials, ANSI Z329.48-1984.
Manufactured in the U.S.A.
16 15 14 13 12 1 2 3 4 5 6 7 8 9 10

Contents

Preface

The difficult subject matter of the present volume has been a common scholarly and human interest of both writers for many years. The momentum to launch the project derives from two "Luther and the Jews" seminars jointly taught at the Lutheran Theological Seminary at Gettysburg (LTSG) in the fall semester of 2007 and the spring semester of 2009. We are beneficiaries of the aid, support, and counsel of numerous people and institutions, and our work was made possible by three financial resources: (1) a summer research scholarship (2009) jointly administered by the Evangelische Kirche in Deutschland (EKD) and the ELCA Wittenberg Center; (2) an ATS/Lilly Joint Research Grant (2010–2011) administered by the Lilly Theological Research Grants Program; (3) sabbatical leave and funding (June 2010—January 2011) granted by LTSG, as well as faculty globalization funds (2009).

Instrumental discussions and networking with colleagues have occurred through several venues: the Luther Colloquy at LTSG; the North American Luther Forum; the Society for Sixteenth Century Study Conference; the American Academy of Religion: Martin Luther and Global Lutheran Traditions Group; the monthly meetings of the Harrisburg, Pennsylvania, area Jewish-Christian Dialogue; and most importantly, the ATS Grant Recipients' Seminar (Pittsburgh, February 2011).

The resources of several magnificent libraries, at home and abroad, supported our primary research: A. R. Wentz Library, LTSG (thank you to library director and dear friend Briant Bohleke, and the three angels—Susann Posey, Roberta Brent, and Karen Hunt); the Library of Congress (2009–2011); Herzog August Bibliothek, Wolfenbüttel, Germany (Summers 2009/2010); Leucorea and Augusteum, Lutherstadt Wittenberg, Germany (Summers 2009/2010); Pitts Theology Library, Candler School of Theology, Emory University (thank you to M. Patrick Graham for generous assistance in finding images). The bulk of assembling and writing was accomplished at the guest house of the University of Erfurt, Germany (Summer 2011), and we thank Professor Christoph Bultmann, Dr. Claudia Bergmann, and Pastor Scott Moore for making this unforgettable summer possible for us.

We extend heartfelt gratitude to colleagues who either read and critiqued portions of the manuscript or who offered strategic advice: Dean Phillip Bell, Stephen Burnett, Guy Carter, Rabbi Carl Choper, Eric Crump, Rabbi Eric Cytryn, Hans

Hillerbrand, Leonard Hummel, Denis Janz, Debra Kaplan, Robert Kolb, Jon Levenson, Carter Lindberg, Kevin Madigan, and Nelson Strobert. Claudia Bergmann played an indispensable role regarding obscure points of *Lutherdeutsch*. A special thank you is due to our faculty secretary, Danielle Garber, for multi-level assistance throughout the course of the project. Any factual errors in the presentation of the material are solely our own responsibility.

We are indebted to our editors at Fortress Press: to Michael West, who encouraged and adopted the project, to Susan Johnson and Will Bergkamp, who saw it through to completion, and to Josh Messner, Sally Messner, and Marissa Wold for copyediting, proofreading, and project management.

We regret that two important new books on Luther and the Jews appeared too late in the process for us to utilize: Eric W. Gritsch, *Martin Luther's Anti-Semitism: Against His Better Judgment* (Grand Rapids: Eerdmans, 2011), and Thomas Kaufmann, *Luthers "Judenschriften": Ein Beitrag zu ihrer historischen Kontextualisierung* (Tübingen: Mohr, 2011).

For the text selections from Luther, we have opted to use the translation from the American Edition of Luther's Works when available. For Luther texts not in the American Edition, we have drawn from alternate sources or provided our own translation. In order to address adequately the issue of the prevalent "he-language" in the existing English translations, the text would have become unavoidably cluttered and would have distracted from the focus of this study. In anticipation of forthcoming gender-inclusive translations, such revisions have not been made here but left to the reader's imagination. Finally, the reader should also note that, for reasons of page limitation, endnotes have been kept at an absolute minimum.

We dedicate this book to our children: Ben, David, Kiki, and Kristian.

Brooks Schramm
Kirsi Stjerna
April 19, 2012 (*Yom Ha-Sho'ah*)
Gettysburg, Pennsylvania

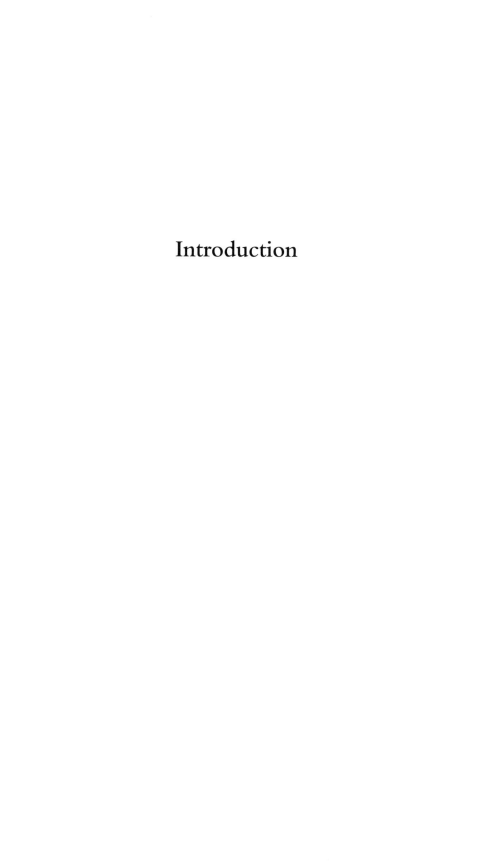

Introduction

An anti-Jewish image from Johannes Pfefferkorn, *Mirror of the Jews [Speculum adhortationis iudaice ad Christum]* (Cologne: Martin von Werden, 1507).

Martin Luther, the Bible, and the Jewish People

Brooks Schramm

On October 31, 2017, the city of Lutherstadt Wittenberg and Lutherans throughout the world will commemorate the five-hundredth anniversary of the posting
of Martin Luther's *Ninety-Five Theses* and the beginning of the Protestant Reformation. The years leading up to this commemoration have been designated by the
Evangelical Protestant Church in Germany as the Luther Decade. This date will
mark a significant milestone for Lutherans specifically and for Protestants in general.
It is also an opportune moment to revisit a grim problem at the heart of Lutheran
(and Protestant) origins, that of *Luther and the Jews*.

Why This Book?

The place, significance, and influence of Martin Luther in the long history of Christian anti-Jewish polemic has been and continues to be a contested issue. The literature on the subject is substantial and diverse. While efforts to absolve Luther as
simply a man of his times—as one who merely passed on and perpetuated what he
himself had already received from his cultural and theological tradition—have generally been jettisoned, there still persists even among the educated public the percep-
tion that the truly problematic aspects of Luther's anti-Jewish attitudes are confined
to the final stages of his career. To be sure, one can speak of an intensification of
anti-Jewish rhetoric toward the end of his life—especially with regard to the question of what should be done about the Jews—but Luther's *theological* evaluation of
Judaism and the Jewish people remains essentially unchanged from the earliest stages
of his career. This has been bluntly articulated by Oberman: "The basis of Luther's
anti-Judaism was the conviction that ever since Christ's appearance on earth, the
Jews have had no more future as Jews."[1]

Related to this static aspect of Luther's thought is the significance of it. When one
reads Luther with a careful eye toward "the Jewish question" (and without a predis-
position to exonerate him), it becomes apparent that, far from being tangential, the

Jews are rather a central, core component of his thought and that this was the case throughout his career, not only at the end. If this is in fact so, then it follows that it is essentially impossible to understand the heart and building blocks of Luther's theology (justification, faith, salvation, grace, freedom, Law and Gospel, and so on) without acknowledging the crucial role played by "the Jews" in his fundamental thinking.

Luther was indeed constrained by ideas, images, and superstitions regarding the Jews and Judaism that he inherited from medieval Christian tradition, but the engine in the development of his theological thought as it relates to the Jews is his biblical hermeneutics, in particular his Old Testament hermeneutics. It is not commonly appreciated that Luther the university professor lectured far more on the Old Testament than he did on the New. Just as "the Jewish question" is a central, core component of his thought, so biblical interpretation—and especially Old Testament interpretation—is the primary arena in which essential claims about the Jews and Judaism are formulated and developed. To a degree, this sets him apart from much of the theological tradition that had preceded him. Luther's anti-Judaism is predominantly biblically based and biblically driven, rather than culturally or socially based, and this aspect of his thinking vis-à-vis the Jews has had no small impact on subsequent Lutheran biblical interpretation.

No contemporary study of the history of Christian attitudes toward and teaching about Judaism can avoid its own post-Holocaust context. It affects the questions we ask of historical documents, persons, and events, as well as why we ask them. It may even contribute to why we are interested in certain historical matters at all. The Holocaust has forever changed the rules of engagement for all matters Jewish-Christian. On the other hand, a developed historical consciousness also reminds us that there are no straight lines in history. History is too complex—and too capricious—to tolerate the imposition of arguments of historical inevitability. Luther, for example, did not make the *Führer* inevitable. But history can teach broad lessons, and especially the history of Christian Europe. When seen in this light, Luther takes his place alongside that legion of Christian thinkers and leaders—both before and after him—that forcefully advocated and participated in the expulsion or deportation of Jews. Over the course of his career, Luther came to the conclusion that Christian and Jewish coexistence could not be achieved, nor should it be. In addition, no reasonable reading of Luther can avoid the conclusion that his statements and beliefs about the Jews further contributed to their dehumanization by Christians, both in thought and in practice. Despite the revolutionary religious, social, and political character of "Luther's Reformation," it did nothing to make matters any better for the lives of actual European Jews. In terms of Luther's immediate legacy in the late sixteenth and early seventeenth centuries, Kaufmann has gone so far as to say: "At the level of confessionally distinct identities, 'Lutheran' could be the same as 'anti-Jewish.'"[2] Contemporary Lutheran Christians, and indeed any Christian who has been positively affected by Luther's courageous articulation of the gospel, have a moral obligation to reckon with how Luther sounded—and sounds—to Jewish ears.

With the above issues in mind, and with a desire to participate in the broader ongoing and constructive conversations on the roots of different faith traditions and the relevance of the teachers of yesterday for today's world, this volume is offered as a textbook for theological and religious education. For the sake of accountability and honest exploration of matters that matter, this book is intended to assist students in diverse settings, especially in seminary contexts and departments of religion, to begin to come to terms with material that is difficult but timelessly pertinent, as it invites re-exploration of the basic tenets of Christian faith. It is also offered out of the conviction that such re-exploration is integral to formation in ministry and to the identity of the church and its believers. The explicit focus on Luther is warranted for many reasons, but it is perhaps stated most poignantly by Oberman: "The terrible tragedy of the relationship between the Jews and Christians in world history can be studied in concentrated form in the history of this one man."[3]

What Luther Knew and Thought of Judaism

There are few subjects historically that Christians have written more about—and known less about—than Judaism, and perhaps nowhere is this clearer than in the case of Martin Luther. He had neither Jewish conversation partners nor Jewish friends. His knowledge of Judaism was primarily dependent on what he read, and those readings were dominated by overtly anti-Jewish treatises, some of which were written by Christians and some by Jewish converts. Though classical Jewish texts were becoming widely available to Christian scholars during the time of Luther's academic career, by his own admission he was not in position to handle these texts for himself. Thus his descriptions of Judaism and Jewish thought are partial truths and caricatures, though there is no reason to suspect that he himself did not regard them as factual. Ironically, if Luther had learned more about Judaism, it likely would have made no real difference to him. For example, when in 1530 the Jewish convert Anthonius Margaritha translated substantial portions of the Jewish daily liturgy into German, Luther found in these prayers confirmation for his own unflinching anti-Jewish stance.[4]

Where the Jews are concerned, Luther sees a rupture between the Judaism of biblical times and that of post-biblical times, that is, the time prior to the coming of the Christ and the time during and after his coming. The significance of this crucial distinction is captured on the first page of Bornkamm's classic study: "Luther's quarrel with the Judaism of his day must not be treated as a repudiation of the Old Testament. To do so would prevent any understanding of what the Old Testament meant to him. Luther made a clear and sharp distinction between the two. No one who has even superficially looked into [Luther's] writings can doubt his passionate opposition to the Jews as blasphemers of Christ on the one hand, and his deep love for the Old Testament on the other. He had no difficulty maintaining both, as paradoxical as this may appear to some people today."[5]

The watershed moment for Luther—that is, that which brings about the distinction—is the overwhelming and ongoing no of the Jews (the Old Testament people of God) to Jesus as the Christ. Few Christian thinkers have been more genuinely troubled, even tormented, by this no than was Luther. Over his entire career he struggled to find a plausible explanation to account for how it could be. Like most before him, he regarded the Roman destruction of Jerusalem and the temple in 70 CE as the strict judgment of God visited on the Jews for the crucifixion of Christ, and the interminable exile of the Jews, which by Luther's time was approaching 1,500 years, became for him definitive proof that God had cast them off and that they were—obviously—no longer the people of God.

Though he never tires of taunting[6] the Jews in his writings with the "1,500 years" argument, it is not difficult to perceive that Luther himself was terrified by what he knew of Jewish life in the European diaspora. Being landless, always vulnerable to persecution and expulsion, and lacking any clear word from God regarding the end of their exile—all of these embodied for Luther what it looks like to live life under the wrath of God. It was *unthinkable* to him that the promises of the biblical prophets could have remained unfulfilled for so long, as the Jews claimed, because this contradicted his most basic convictions about the nature of God. Luther certainly believed that God on occasion punishes God's own people, even severely; the biblical record is too clear on this issue. But God would not—*could not*—punish the Jews in the way they are being punished if they were still God's own people. The only tenable explanation for him was that the promises of the prophets had passed to another people. Otherwise God would be a liar.

Luther was honestly baffled by how the Jews could continue to deny the reason for their miserable 1,500-year exile, especially when the witness of Scripture was so evident to him. Over the course of his career, he would come to the conclusion that the only thing, finally, that could explain it was that they had been handed over by God to the Devil. Thus their resistance to the gospel—and their resistance to admitting *the* reason for their exile—was willful and unforgiveable. Though it was not typical of Luther, this thoroughgoing demonization of the Jews led late in his career to the dredging up and repeating of scurrilous accusations, to the effect that it was in the nature of Jews to want to kill Christians. A particularly repulsive example comes from his 1544 Lenten lectures on Isaiah 53. Commenting on Isa. 53:8, the verse that speaks of the death of the Servant of the Lord, Luther (echoing the centuries old blood-libel accusation) states: "The Jews still kill Christ daily, not in the sense that they merely desire to do so, but rather in fact. For they slaughter many Christian infants and children. In short, they are killers forever."[7]

Of all of the theological charges that Luther levels against the Jews, the most consistently recurring one has to do with the issue of chosenness, that is, the Jewish claim to be the chosen people of God based upon physical descent from Abraham. Luther readily grants that the Jews are indeed Abraham's physical descendents but that they have consistently misconstrued the nature of God's promise to Abraham. For Luther, the promise to Abraham's seed was in reality the promise of the Seed, that is, the Messiah/Christ (Gen. 3:15). The physical seed of Abraham, the Jews, were God's chosen instrument in Old Testament times to bear that promise. But Abraham's true descendents/seed, even in Old Testament times, were always those who believed in the promise of the Messiah and not those who relied on their physical descent. This is the fundamental error, and sin, of the Jews, who trust as it were that they have been born into grace, that they are bound to God by birth, and thus that God owes them God's benevolence. For Luther, this constitutes a theological obscenity, because the grace and benevolence of God can *only* be accessed by faith, and it has never been otherwise. The only thing the human being (the Jew included) is born into is sin. The human being has nothing of its own that can be held up to God, and certainly not its own birth. God owes the human being nothing. The Jewish claim of chosenness, therefore, becomes the quintessential example of what Luther means by "boasting in the flesh," and it is at the root of his understanding of Judaism as a purely carnal religion that knows nothing of the spiritual or the eternal.

This boast of the Jews then carries with it two corollaries that Luther pursues with vigor. The first is the completely exclusive character of Jewish chosenness. If the Jews are God's chosen people, then it follows that everyone else is damned, Luther included. The second corollary follows immediately from the first: If the Jews claim salvation exclusively for themselves, then they are by definition despisers of the rest of humanity, and ultimately μισάνθρωποι (misanthropes).[8] The misanthropic character of Jewish life and hope crystalizes for Luther around Jewish messianic expectation, which, as he understands it, longs for the messianic annihilation of all the Gentiles, and such longing is illustrated by the love the Jews have for the book of Esther, a book that he particularly detested.

These are of course radically serious charges, but Luther was equally radical in his conviction of their veracity. To be fair to him, Luther was not making these charges up out of thin air. Since at least the twelfth century there had indeed developed in European Jewish circles a strident anti-Christian literature, which satirized Christian beliefs, attacked Christian exegesis, and longed for the destruction of the enemies of the Jewish people.[9] Aspects of this anti-Christian polemic had filtered down to Luther, and he was acutely offended by it. But beyond the offense he experienced, Luther came to believe—and teach—that the most extreme anti-Christian positions articulated by Jews (in the wake of the Crusades, no less!) were definitive of Jewish thought as such, and this without regard to the increasingly desperate situations that had contributed to the rise of this type of literature in the first place. Pertinent here is the argument of Alex Bein: "With regard to Luther's accusation (and that of many later enemies of the Jews) to the effect that the Jews ridiculed among themselves—both orally and in numerous writings—Jesus and Mary or insulted them with shameful names, it can be said—in spite of the contrary claims of Jewish apologists past and present—that the accusation is in principle true. But how could it have been otherwise, given the polarity of the respective views and given the inhuman treatment that the Jews had received from 'Christian love-of-neighbor'"?[10]

The picture of the Jew and of Judaism that thus emerges in Luther's thought is not a pretty one. While other leading sixteenth-century reformers also wrote against the Jews, Luther outpaced them all both quantitatively and "qualitatively." Though no single explanation can account for this phenomenon, the sheer fact itself highlights the centrality of the Jew in Luther's mind. Thus Kaufmann can write that "[t]he Jews represented for Luther the opposite of what it meant to be a Christian or what it ought to mean."[11] Kaufmann's words are consistent with the equally broad claim made by Maurer in his landmark study of over a half-century ago: for Luther, "[t]he post-biblical Jew is the archetype of the human being standing in opposition to God."[12] If the Jew is archetypal of the human condition vis-à-vis God, then it follows that the ultimate human problem that Christ and the gospel have to remedy is the Jew inside us all. Thus for Luther, and this is the case throughout his career, the Jew—and Judaism—represent the negative religious standard against which all other negative religious phenomena are finally measured.[13]

One does not have to read far in Luther to encounter his unholy threesome of "the Jew, the Pope, and the Turk" as the prime enemies of the gospel. Given the frequency of the recurrence of this phrase, and especially given the similarity of language that Luther uses to attack all three members of the group, the criticism is occasionally made that attempts to isolate the question of "Luther and the Jews" are misguided and that the "Jewish question" therefore should not be privileged.[14] Without minimizing Luther's anti-Papist or anti-Turkish language, we follow that line of Luther scholarship that nevertheless argues for a qualitative distinction where the Jews are concerned, which for us turns on three points. The first has already been made above, in regard to the archetypal or prototypical role that the Jews play in Luther's thought. The second is similar. For Luther, the Jews were the first enemies of the gospel, and their hostility has never ceased. The current Popes, and certainly the Turks, are relative late-comers in the battle against Christ and the gospel. In Luther's view of church history, the gospel has its sworn enemies in every generation, and he did come to believe that the Pope and the Turk were in fact the final apocalyptic enemy, the Antichrist. But the Jews are once again distinct, because they and they alone have the character of being the *perennial* enemies of the gospel.[15] In this regard, they share that role only with the Devil himself.

There is a third point, however, that is decisive for us, and that is the question of social location. The Pope was the most religiously powerful person in Europe. Luther's rhetorical attacks against him took true courage, placed his life in real jeopardy, and resulted in a strict geographical confinement for most of his career. The Turk had a mighty army, and though the threat to Germany was genuine, it nevertheless remained at a distance. Luther's writings against him did not have the slightest effect upon him. But for the Jews of Germany and neighboring lands, Luther was "a player." Both through his writings and his personal influence on Protestant princes, Luther helped to make the lives of his Jewish contemporaries more precarious and influenced the imaginations of subsequent generations of Lutherans toward Jews in numerous deleterious ways.[16] The issue at stake is not whether Luther was the most virulent anti-Jewish Christian writer ever—he wasn't. Nor is it whether he said equally repulsive things about other groups—he did. It is rather about the precariousness of the Jewish social situation. All three of these points when taken together warrant an explicit focus on *Luther and the Jews*.

In light of the derogatory and hostile views described above, there may seem to be a contradiction with what is often referred to as the "Jew-friendly" side of Luther, as expressed most notably in his treatise of 1523, *That Jesus Christ Was born a Jew*.[17] But it is only a seeming contradiction. At no point in his career does Luther ever express hope for the Jew as Jew. Judaism is a dead religion, and Luther makes no distinction between Judaism and those who practice it, the Jews.[18] What he says about one applies to the other. What he does express, in varying degrees, is a hope for the Jew to become a Christian. The phrase "Jew-friendly Luther" only makes sense if it refers to the degree of openness to or optimism about Jewish conversion to Christianity. Even as early as his lectures on Romans (1515–1516), he expresses skepticism about readings of Romans 11 to the effect that all Jews would convert at the end of time, and by the end of his career he would reject this reading altogether. In the early 1520's, however, he does go through a period when he manifests significant optimism toward the prospect of the conversion of a number of Jews. But this optimism was to be short-lived, and already by the mid-1520's it disappears and never returns. What does remain roughly consistent is his conviction, expressed most noticeably in his commentary on the *Magnificat* (June 1521), that there will always be Christians, however few, among Abraham's seed, and that therefore, in so far as possible, Christians should treat Jews in a kindly manner.[19]

Ironically, it is the period of Luther's greatest optimism regarding Jewish conversions that also highlights his thoroughgoing negative evaluation of Jews and Judaism. While in hiding on the Wartburg and virtually at the same time as he wrote his *Magnificat* commentary, he also wrote a commentary on *Psalm 68* (May 1521). The latter was motivated by the liturgical use of portions of the psalm during the festivals of Ascension and Pentecost. Within the space of one month, the same person who wrote that the Jews should be treated in a kindly manner in hopes of their conversion also wrote the following about Ps. 68:21, "But God will shatter the heads of his enemies, the hairy crown of him who walks in his guilty ways":

> It is known well enough that the Jews have at all times been Christ's greatest enemies, their claim to be God's most loyal friends notwithstanding. It is undeniable that this verse chronicles their fate: their head is shattered; they no longer have a kingdom, a government, a priesthood. Soon after Christ's ascent they lost that head and never regained it, which is the result of but one crime, namely, their hostility to Christ and their refusal to let Him be God.... All this is the consequence of their refusal to believe in Him who takes away both sin and death, and of their persistence to remain in their guilty ways, as our text declares. To be sure, they are not aware of their sin or of the reason for their total destruction. In times past they had experienced repeated captivity; but still they had always retained their head and government, or at least a prophet or priest. Never before have they been shorn as bald as after Christ's ascension.[20]

Luther's unrelenting negativity toward Judaism and those who practice it, the Jews, never changed. His legacy in this regard is summarized by Osten-Sacken: "Luther's anti-Jewish writings belong . . . in the front row of treatises, speeches, and sermons delivered against the Jews in all of church history."[21]

The Roots of Luther's Anti-Judaism
Luther and the Old Testament

The corpus of Luther's collected works reaches beyond one hundred large volumes and is still not complete. The size of the collection and its numerous literary genres can have the effect of obscuring what was at the heart of Luther's life-work, namely, his academic lectures on books and portions of books of the Bible at the University of Wittenberg, which spanned a thirty-two-year period of time. Though Luther's academic title was *Professor in Biblia*, he devoted only three or four years to lectures on New Testament books (Romans, Galatians [twice], and Hebrews) while the remainder were completely given over to the Old Testament. The course of the lectures was as follows:[22]

1513–1515	First Psalms Lectures (*Dictata super Psalterium*)
1515–1516	Romans
1516–1517	Galatians
1517–1518	Hebrews
1518–1521	Second Psalms Lectures (*Operationes in Psalmos*)
1523–1525	Deuteronomy

1524–1526	The Twelve Minor Prophets
1526	Ecclesiastes
1528–1530	Isaiah
1530–1531	Song of Songs
1531	Galatians
1532–1535	Psalms 2; 45; 51; 90; 120–134
1535–1545	Genesis
1543/1544	Isaiah 9
1544	Isaiah 53

While so much of what Luther wrote was dictated by ecclesiastical and political circumstance, these biblical lectures represent his own free choices, and thus reveal something essential about his own theological orientation as intently focused on the Old Testament and its interpretation.

His engagement with the Old Testament, however, was not limited to the lecture hall. He preached sixty-two sermons on Genesis (1523–1524), sixty-five on Exodus (1524–1526), thirty-two on Leviticus and Numbers (1527–1528), and seventeen on Deuteronomy (1529). He wrote numerous commentaries or expositions on Psalms and collections of Psalms, and several of his polemical treatises are centered on Old Testament texts or themes. And last but not least was the Old Testament translation project that involved Luther and his team of translators ("The Wittenberg Sanhedrin") for twelve years (1523–1534) and then on to the end of his life as the translation was subsequently revised.

By any estimation, therefore, the Old Testament and its proper interpretation were at the core of Luther's thought. For our purposes, however, the crucial issue was noted by the great Jewish scholar, Salo Baron, in stating that "Luther's lifetime preoccupation with the Old Testament made him, on the whole, less rather than more friendly to contemporary Jews."[23] Why this was the case is directly anchored in the way Luther insisted that the Old Testament should be read by Christians. By way of initial orientation to the question, one would be hard-pressed to find a more precise yet concise description than that offered by Christopher Brown:

> Luther's sharp theological condemnation of contemporary Judaism and severe practical proposals for expulsion of Jewish "blasphemers" cannot be separated from the long history of Christian-Jewish relations. But for Luther, the conflict was made all the more bitter—but also redirected from traditional avenues—by the distinctive features of his theology. The significance of exegetical disagreements was magnified by Luther's own very high theological estimation of the Hebrew Scriptures—his own *métier* as a professor—and his belief that Christianity came not as a replacement for an incomplete or false religion contained in

the Jewish Old Testament, but as the continuation and full manifestation of the Gospel of the promised Seed that had been preached and believed by all the patriarchs and prophets throughout the Hebrew Scripture.[24]

Old Testament Interpretation

Luther inherited from his medieval forebears the tradition of interpreting biblical texts, and especially Old Testament texts, according to a fourfold meaning (literal, allegorical, tropological, anagogical), which, theoretically, tended to correspond to the historical meaning, the meaning for the church, the meaning for the individual, and the eschatological meaning. This fourfold meaning was actually an elaboration upon the ancient church's twofold distinction between the literal and the spiritual, with the spiritual now being subdivided into three levels. In both the ancient and medieval church, the term allegory could be used in a general way to refer to any nonliteral reading of a text. The relationship between Luther and medieval exegesis, as he developed as an interpreter, is exceedingly complex. Though it has often been portrayed as a rupture, that is clearly too strong as evidenced by the fact that he continued to use allegory throughout his career.

What he did do, however, was seek to simplify the interpretation of the Bible. This is seen most directly in his conviction, already evident by 1518–1519, that biblical texts rightly ought to have one proper or legitimate meaning.[25] As long as there was agreement on this proper or legitimate meaning as the foundation, Luther had no problem whatsoever in bringing other interpretations to enhance or illustrate it. But in addition, the proper or legitimate meaning served to limit other readings, that is, readings that he regarded as utterly fanciful or in no way related to the legitimate meaning. Thus simplification and limitation are important terms for understanding Luther's approach to biblical interpretation vis-à-vis his forebears.[26] On the other hand, Luther was actually quite flexible when it came to the issue of the "application" of a text to the present day. Because he was convinced that Scripture, when properly understood, was a living thing, it could speak in concretely different ways in different times and places. He never made any claim to have exhausted the potential applications of Scripture.

In terms of the relationship between the Old Testament and Judaism, three aspects of Luther's thought are all-determinative. The first has to do with the most basic of all Christian theological claims: the messiahship of Jesus. Or, Jesus *Christ*. More precisely, it is the conviction that the Christ proclaimed in the New Testament is the same Christ promised in numerous passages in the Old Testament, and—in addition—that this equivalence of the one promised and the one proclaimed can be *proven* by the proper interpretation of these key Old Testament texts. In this regard there is nothing new or unique in Luther, as his primary proof-texts are essentially the same as those used by Justin Martyr and Tertullian already in the second century and which were consistently used by Christians against the Jews ever since. What is characteristic of Luther, however, is his seeming need to argue this point against the Jews over and over and over again. Why? A reasonable answer is that Luther perceived in Jewish readings of the Old Testament a genuine threat. Precisely because this was for him the most basic of all theological issues—that Jesus *is* the Messiah promised in the Old Testament—it had to be sustained otherwise the entire edifice would collapse. From Luther's perspective, Jewish interpretation represented an assault on the very foundations of Christianity itself. This also helps to explain why he was so harsh toward his Christian contemporaries who were making use of Jewish readings of the Old Testament, because he was convinced that these Christian interpreters were sawing off the limb on which they themselves were sitting. For Luther, there could be no compromise on this most basic of all theological issues. Jewish interpreters, and Christians who interpreted like Jews, had to be attacked and defeated on the Old Testament battlefield, because *everything*, from a religious point of view, was at stake.[27]

The second aspect flows directly from the first. For Luther, the Old Testament—properly understood—is a Christian book, and the two volumes of the Christian Bible, therefore, constitute a theological unity. This is what enables him to speak of the church as being present already in the Old Testament and to speak of certain Old Testament characters as Christians. What binds the two volumes of the Christian Bible together is the promise of the coming of the Messiah and faith in that promise. For Luther, the faith of the Old Testament and the faith of the New Testament are the same, and thus the criteria for determining who are and are not the people of God are also the same. The only significant distinction is that Old Testament Christians trust in the One who *will* come, while New Testament Christians trust in the one who *has* come. Luther can even say that Old Testament faith was actually superior to New Testament faith, because the saints of the Old Testament trusted, contrary to all appearances, in a *pure* promise. Once one recognizes Luther's understanding of the Old Testament as a Christian book—not by adoption but in its essence—then another claim of his, which on the surface seems quite peculiar, makes sense. This is his idea that when a Jew converts to Christianity the Jew is actually *returning* to the faith of his/her forebears, that is, to the faith of the Old Testament. And this in turn is consistent with his broader understanding that the New Testament and Christianity represent theological continuity with the Old Testament, while rabbinic Judaism and rabbinic texts are in complete theological discontinuity; in fact they are an utter aberration.

The third aspect has to do with Luther's use of Old Testament curse and judgment language. Aside from the strictly christological proof-texts, it is in these areas where much of his anti-Jewish polemic emerges. The Old Testament itself does in fact place strong emphasis on the infidelity and disobedience of ancient Israel over

against God, as well as the judgment that such behavior incurs. But it also emphasizes, by way of counter argument, God's eternal love for and fidelity toward Israel.
In Luther's treatment of Old Testament judgment language, he seeks, on the one
hand, to discern which passages apply to Israel in its ancient historical context, and,
on the other, which are genuinely prophetic and thus apply to Israel at the time of
the coming of Christ, and beyond. Once this distinction has been made, then anything that falls into the latter category can be used against the Jews as condemnation for their rejection of Jesus as Messiah. Though this area of Luther's thought still
requires significant scholarly attention, one thing is clear: in theological terms much
of the worst of what Luther had to say about the Jews occurs in the context of his
wrestling with Old Testament judgment language, for it was precisely there that he
found the shocking possibility that God can cast off God's own people.

The Problem of the Hebrew Bible: "The Rabbis"

An obvious problem for Luther, and indeed for anyone who wants to argue for the
theological unity of the Christian Bible, is the fact that the Old Testament is written
in a language wholly unrelated to the Greek New Testament. As a young scholar,
Luther made himself a student of biblical Hebrew, and he continued to work with
the language until the end of his life. He was an expert Latinist and he also had fine
Greek skills, but by his own admission his competence in biblical Hebrew did not
approach that of his Greek and much less his Latin. This did not deter him, however,
from often making very bold theological claims based on his (faulty) understanding
of certain nuances of the Hebrew language.

An even more significant problem for Luther was his discovery of the Jewish interpretive tradition. What he actually knew of rabbinic interpretation, and
how he knew it, has still not been resolved satisfactorily. From early to mid-career,
Luther's primary conduit into rabbinic learning (essentially Rashi [1040–1105]) was
the biblical commentaries of Nicholas of Lyra (1270–1349), as well as the "Addi-
tions" to Lyra by the Jewish convert, Paul of Burgos (1351–1435). In late career,
Luther had access to Sebastian Münster's diglot Hebrew-Latin Bible with annota-
tions (1534/1535), a work of immense learning that drew on numerous medieval
Jewish commentators not well represented in Lyra or Burgos. Though the Wittenberg translation team had available to it a copy of the *Second Rabbinic Bible* (1525),
there can be no question of Luther reading Hebrew and Aramaic rabbinic texts for
himself in systematic fashion. His own firsthand engagement with this literature was
selective at best.[28] Be that as it may, Luther was convinced that he knew more than
enough about rabbinic interpretation, and over the course of his career he developed a visceral antipathy toward "the rabbis." Already by the mid-1520's, he had
concluded that they were the central instruments of the ongoing Jewish resistance
to the gospel, and his *Genesis Lectures* (1535–1545) are saturated with anti-rabbinic

polemic. His most consistent critique of the rabbis is that while they can be helpful to Christians in matters of Hebrew grammar, they know nothing of theology, that is, the subject matter of the text. For example, in 1536 while lecturing on the story of Cain and Abel, he states:

> [T]he rabbis distort the meaning of Scripture almost everywhere. Therefore I am beginning to hate them and to advise that those who read them read with careful judgment. Although they had in their possession certain facts through tradition from the patriarchs, they nevertheless corrupted these facts in various ways. Consequently, they often deceived Jerome too. The poets have not filled the world with their fabrications to the extent to which the ungodly Jews have filled Scripture with their silly opinions. Hence it causes us much work to keep our text free from their misleading comments. . . . The reason for their going astray is that they are indeed familiar with the language but have no knowledge of the subject matter; that is, they are not theologians. Therefore they are compelled to twaddle and to crucify both themselves and Scripture. How is it possible to judge correctly about things that are unknown?[29]

For Luther, the strict corollary of such anti-rabbinic polemic is the folly of Christian interpreters who allow themselves to be influenced theologically by the rabbis. The sixteenth century was the age of the birth of Christian Hebraism, that intellectual movement within Christianity that sought and eventually gained expertise not only in biblical Hebrew but also in the Hebrew and Aramaic of classic rabbinic sources and in their systems of thought, as well as in the great medieval Jewish biblical commentators. Luther's scholarly career spanned the beginnings of this movement, and he himself benefited from it and, to a limited extent, contributed to it. But when it came to matters of theology, Luther adopted a rigidly antagonistic stance. In his infamous anti-Jewish treatise, *On the Ineffable Name* (March 1543), he makes his position crystal clear:

> On pain of losing divine grace and eternal life, it is forbidden for us Christians to believe or regard as right the scriptural interpretations and glosses of the rabbis. We are, however, permitted to read them in order to see what kind of damned Devil's work they're up to, and so protect ourselves from it. For thus says Moses in Deut. 28{:28}: "God will strike you with madness, blindness, and frenzy of heart." Moses did not say this about the cursed Goyim but rather about his circumcised saints, the noble blood, the princes of heaven and earth, who call themselves Israel. Thereby all of their interpretations, glosses, and exegesis of Scripture are damned by God himself as nothing more than pure madness, blindness, and frenzy. God himself regards and judges all of their labor over Scripture these past 1500 years as not only false and lies, but also pure blindness and a frenzied, mad thing.[30]

In February of 1537, while on a trip to Smalcald, Luther was ill with a terrible bout of kidney stones, in fact so ill that he thought he was dying. Among the several statements that were recorded at his bedside, one reveals something vital about Luther's own self-understanding: "I'll be and I'll die an enemy of all the enemies of my Christ."[31] As the 1543 statement above shows, not only the rabbis but also those Christian interpreters who follow them in matters theological are high on the list of those regarded by Luther as "the enemies of my Christ."

Woodcut of a Jewish money-lender from the title page of Luther's sermon on usury, *Eyn Sermon von dem Wucher*, 1520.

The Jew in Luther's World

Kirsi Stjerna

What did Martin Luther know and think about the Jews? What did he mean with the words "Jew" and "Jewish"? What were his sources? What do we know about the lives and conditions of Jews in sixteenth-century Europe, and what can we gather particularly about their place in Christian imagination, rhetoric, beliefs, on the one hand, and in legislation and daily lives, on the other? With these questions in mind, this introduction is designed as an orientation and expansion of our horizons beyond those of Luther, whose perceptions and perspectives we will examine and seek to comprehend.

The following pages will not exhaust all that Jewish lives, traditions, and experiences in the early modern period were about but will offer some basic observations. Most importantly, Jews should not be seen solely as the objects of Christian hatred, as if without any agency of their own. The contrary is the case. Regardless of the varied regulations, Jews lived rich lives of their own and actively developed their communal and religious identity and traditions in different locations—often even in quite amicable, natural relations with their Christian neighbors. Even if they were few in number in comparison to Christians, Jews were important participants in early modern European societies.

That said, to expose Luther's inherited bias and framework, this introduction focuses intentionally on the negative expressions of Christians' often-latent animosity and fears toward Jews that erupted from time to time, locally and institutionally. The intent is not to reduce Jewish experience to that of expulsions, persecutions, and subjection, nor to suggest that all private Christians were Jew-haters or had no personal relations with their Jewish neighbors. As argued in recent Jewish scholarship, the "negative history" of laws and restrictions can serve as a mirror to the other side of the reality: the regulations indicate how much human interaction between Christians and Jews was actually a regular, normal occurrence, just as the recurrence of expulsion orders reveals how Jews continued to be an integral part of European life. The evidence indicates how Jews could find ways to exist and even thrive under the harshest circumstances.

Thanks to recent scholarship, the lachrymose history-telling is giving way to celebrating the Jewish people's positive presence, integral contributions, and the dignity of their own agency in the sixteenth-century world and beyond.[1] In light of that framework, the following account seeks to highlight the dark side that shaped Martin Luther's imagination.

Distorted Images

"The Jew" is often present in Luther's sermons, tracts, letters, and biblical commentaries. He speaks about the Jewish people and their faith and practice with an air of authority and with a conviction that suggests not only that Jews are frequently around Luther himself and wherever he mingles but also that Jewish beliefs and practices are quite familiar to him. He writes to his fellow Christians as if he knows, with insider knowledge, what Jews believe and pray and do in their households and synagogues, what their intentions are in regard to Christians, and even what their eternal fate is in the eyes of God. In many ways, however, Luther's information on Jewish beliefs and practices was not based on actual knowledge but largely reflected the Christian prejudices developed since the New Testament. Working from these prejudices, whether deliberately or not, Luther would come to demonize the Jews.

Luther's demonization of the Jews reflects false or incomplete information, hearsay, and inherited anti-Jewish delusions, all of which have centuries-old roots in Christian imagination. The air he breathed since his childhood was poisoned with anti-Jewish laws, fears, jokes, and slander. The church in which he frequently preached, the Marienkirche in Wittenberg, featured its own *Judensau*, an image found on many European churches from the thirteenth century onward: a sandstone relief of a large sow with Jewish children sucking and a male Jew staring intently into the sow's behind.[2] This image, in a most grotesque way, mocked the Jews in the plain sight of Christian worshippers.

The image of Jews portrayed in art and print was similarly negative, a slandering caricature. Such prejudice, rooted in a triumphalist theology, was also depicted in the contrasting images of church and synagogue. For example, the sculptures of the same on the south entrance of the Strasbourg cathedral proclaim that "God has rejected the Jews!"[3] Typically in Christian art, the Jew was recognizable from particular clothing (such as a cloak or a pointy hat) or the use of a particular color (yellow, red, or white), Hebrew letters, money bags (a symbol of moneylending and greed), or particular physical characteristics (large nose, full lips); that these indicators were missing from most Jewish art is noteworthy. In time, the symbols that Christians used to indicate Jewishness, that were intended to tarnish the Jew thoroughly in the Christian imagination, came to be associated with foul play and conniving, bad smells, feces, and lust; a Jew and Jewishness could be associated with sin and anti-social behavior. The power and intentionality of these well-known images is evident in the ensuing Protestant practice of using similar imagery in their critique of the abuses in the Roman Catholic Church.

Then as now we cannot overestimate the power of the printed or sculpted image in shaping people's minds. We should not assume that Luther was immune to the power of such visual propaganda nor that he himself did not become a generator of it.[4] We can appreciate the impact of the works he read—professionally and for leisure—that included not only imagery ridiculing the Jews but also stories and jokes to the same effect, and most of it plainly false information. Likewise, we must acknowledge the influence of the portraits of the Jews coming from respected preachers and widely read authors.

Widely circulating stories employed stereotypes prevalent in medieval vernacular writing and accused Jews of being enemies of Christian society, blasphemous, blind "Christ killers" who engaged in host desecration and ritual murder. This, combined with randomly flaring critiques of local Jews practicing usury—without the benefit of fully appreciating the central role Jewish moneylenders played in the development of the credit system in the Holy Roman Empire, or that this was a respectable profession for a Jew—only added to Christian suspicions and fears toward their Jewish neighbors and business associates.[5] The linking of Jews with feces (especially from the thirteenth century onward), filth, and smell enforced the sentiment that Jews contaminated Christian society. In the context of late medieval and early modern social and economic problems, anti-Jewish literature denounced Jews as a danger to Christians who, therefore, found it therapeutic to mock and scapegoat them (just as Christians found ritualized ways to mock the devil and death and corrupt clergy).[6]

Fraenkel-Goldschmidt observes that "[t]he entire society believed in the wickedness of the Jews and that they were the children or tools of Satan, just as they believed in the evil and satanity of witches."[7] Thus in this distorted Christian imagination. Jews were capable of virtually anything, from blaspheming God (the most outrageous transgression that could bring God's punishment upon all) to ritualistic physical harming of Christian children and poisoning wells. Some of these fears were fueled further in the telling of the Miracle Stories—of Christian martyrs who died presumably at the hands of Jews and subsequently worked miracles. Similarly damaging were the annual Passion Plays where the killing of Christ was explicitly blamed upon the Jews. Both genres, beloved by Christians, explicitly incorporated the most negative stereotypes of Jews and frequently stirred Christian mob violence, which was prone to erupt especially at Easter time (thus the imperially ordered restrictions on Jews appearing in public on Good Friday).[8]

In addition to accusations of host desecration and blasphemy, the charge that brought the most extreme danger to Jews was that "Jews murdered Christian children for their blood to be used in the Passover celebration and in various magical activities."[9] Such cases could be brought to trial, even in Luther's time, and the most famous cases could be debated in public, with the participation of famous theologians, such as Johann Eck, wishing to prove the legitimacy of the horrific accusations.[10] The idea of Jewish ritual murder has roots long before the Reformation. From Norwich around 1144 comes a story about a missing boy named William who was found dead and buried. Ten years later rumors circulated that he had been captured by Jews on Good Friday and crucified or hung on a cross before being killed. Later, the monks in Norwich testified that the body was causing miracles. After this first recorded accusation about the attempt of Jews to repeat the passion of Christ on Good Friday by murdering Christian children, similar rumors and accusations would spread also to France and Germany.[11]

From the thirteenth century onward, the story included a religious rationale: because Jews needed blood for their rituals for Passover and for healing, they deliberately killed Christian children. Martyr cults that developed around some of these stories created a popular following, supported by the publication of the Miracle Stories.[12] While the stories of murdered miracle-causing children could bring spiritual comfort to Christians at a time of trial, they also nurtured Christian rage and latent animosity toward Jews at times when a scapegoat was needed. Of the many illustrations of this, one is the "Beautiful Mary" church and pilgrimage site in Regensburg that like many other Marian pilgrimage sites promoted anti-Jewish violence in its own way.[13]

In an age when life was precarious and catastrophes could visit a community at any time, the Christian mob did not need much kindling to react violently toward an individual or a group deemed to be the scapegoat; the Jew was a most vulnerable, convenient target. Any individual could raise a suspicion, with little or no hard evidence required. Whether the charge was a child murder, blasphemy, host desecration, or a conflict in a money matter (often the hidden cause), once a trial process began it almost inevitably led to the expulsion or death of the accused. Religiously fueled trials regularly led to the punishment of an entire Jewish community, regardless of the nature of the often-forced confession or fabricated proof of guilt.[14]

Jews were a significant bargaining tool in the game of profit from the local level and up. If a particular constituency in a town or village saw financial profit through expulsion or trial of Jews, then secondary accusations of crimes of a religious nature could effectively sway the opinion of even those initially hesitant—for instance the rulers and territorial authorities, who were in a position to offer concrete protection to the Jews but who were also most interested in securing their own cash flow, in the form of high Jewish taxes. Regardless of the actual accusation or motives that led to the trial or the expulsion act, only rarely would anyone rise for the accused Jews' public defense.[15]

Early on Luther did not participate publically in discussions on assumed blood crimes of the Jews, but occasionally he would comment on the stupidity of such accusations and advocate treating Jewish persons with Christian mercy. For years he did not touch upon the outrageous anti-Jewish stories and legends, as his preoccupation was elsewhere, in the Bible and its interpretation. Later in his career, however, he would invoke some of the worst Christian gutter-talk; just like his archenemy Johann Eck, the reformer had swallowed the negative caricature that Christian believers had developed about the Jews over the centuries. Like his medieval forefathers and foremothers, and like the majority of both Catholic and Protestant leaders, Luther came to see the continued Jewish presence in Germany (regardless of repeated expulsions) as a problem that required political action. While Luther was not one to provoke pogroms, the option (or the necessity, as he came to see it) to rid Christian lands of Jews for good to prevent harm against Christians, whether physical or spiritual, was something he did come to address with frightening fury. His primary mirror in this was not the blood libels and legends of Jewish religious crimes but, first, how he constructed reality from what he read in his Bible and, second, the legal expulsions of the past that spoke their own language about what generations of Christians before him had thought was good for them and theirs.

Fragile Communities

Luther was born into a world where major expulsions of Jews had taken place and where frequent and random expulsions and acts of violence toward Jews still continued. Major expulsions had taken place in France in 1182, in 1290, 1306, 1322, 1394, in England in 1290, and in Spain in 1492. Between 1390 and 1391 Strasbourg expelled its Jews (after a major pogrom and expulsion in 1348).[16] Similarly, Jews were expelled from Geneva in 1491. Austria expelled its Jews in 1421.[17]

The Reformation era and especially the following "age of confessionalism" (when Protestant identities were solidified with written confessions and defended in ecclesiastical and political arenas, in order to establish firmly the new faith) witnessed an intensification of efforts to purge the Holy Roman Empire of its remaining Jews and heretics, just as the Catholic church was trying, in vain, to rid western Christendom from the "Protestant heretics." This was true also in the Reformation heartland, including those few areas in Germany where Jews had been able to establish residence and business after the mass expulsions of the medieval period in the west. Local smaller as well as larger scale expulsions and acts of violence toward the Jews took place already centuries before the Protestant reformation, and only continued in the fifteenth and sixteenth centuries. As Debra Kaplan observes (particularly in Strasbourg), "Christians' increasing need for confessional definition led to a greater rift between them and Jews. As Christian authorities cracked down on the contact between different Christian confessions, they also sought to limit relations between Jews and Chrstians."[18] Expulsions were part of this effort at distancing. Luther, well abreast of world news, was hardly oblivious to all of this.

The list of expulsions is long and covers all areas of the German-speaking territories.[19] This does not mean that all Jews left and never returned. There was often significant back and forth in the matter, as authorities, churchmen, and local people debated the Jews' right to stay, and as Jewish families found ways to relocate, return, and stay present and involved.[20] During interims and times of relaxed ordinances, Jews could return, even if doing so in smaller numbers.

For example, in Hesse, Jewish communities had persisted regardless of several expulsion orders. After Philip of Hesse extended their right to stay for another six years after an expulsion edict, the lot of Jews was heavily debated in 1538. As a result, a stricter *Judenordnung*[21] was introduced in 1539 to control the lives of Jews remaining in the area.[22] Similarly in Braunschweig: Jews were expelled after a host desecration trial in 1510, before being allowed to return six months later, only to be expelled again in 1546.[23] Luther's own territory of Saxony also expelled Jews on several occasions: In 1349 and 1432 Jews had been forbidden from living or traveling in Saxony. The rules were about to be tightened again in 1536–1537, but (with the influence of Josel of Rosheim and the princes' meeting in Frankfurt in 1539) the restrictions were relaxed in 1539, allowing Jews to return and travel in the area, with restrictions. The 1543 electoral decree forbade once again any Jewish presence in the land.[24]

Based on what we know about the demographics and expulsions, the reality of Jewish presence in Luther's world is quite different from what his fantasizing words might suggest; it is also different from what recorded numbers and expulsion orders seem to indicate. Extant residence records that list Jewish households and communities are illuminating, while ambiguous, in this regard. On the one hand, it is clear that Jews were always a minority in late medieval and early modern towns and villages, even apart from the expulsions. On the other hand, life in the countryside or around smaller towns offered more peaceful conditions for tradition-building purposes and possibilities for the existence of even (at least temporarily) larger Jewish communities, when Jews were pushed to leave cities and towns.[25]

Records portray a complex picture of Jewish presence/absence, while revealing the Jews' integral role in the society. Namely, Jewish families sought ways to remain or operate for business in the vicinity of or even within the urban centers. They managed to do so either under the radar screen or under special arrangements and exceptions to the general rulings of the territorial lords and with the acceptance of Christian citizens who saw this as beneficial. Amidst expulsion orders and limitations, as Kaplan points out in the case of Strasbourg, "[t]he myriad contacts between Jews and Christians and the evolving limits to those contacts illustrate that at the onset of the Reformation, the Jews actively participated in various urban experiences, specifically in the marketplace and the municipal court system." While official rulings proved, thus, ineffective in reality, obviously "Jewish participation in urban life and its culture was not unfettered" but both "social and economic contact" became increasingly regulated.[26]

It is important to remember, regardless of Luther's perceptions, that the number of Jewish residents was generally speaking very small. Sometimes only a handful, or even a single Jew, can be found in registers. Only a few cities recorded Jews in several hundreds or even thousands; Worms and Frankfurt boasted the largest numbers in Germany.[27] Still, the number of Jews residing in Germany was significantly higher in comparison to major neighboring countries in the west that had already undergone mass expulsions. With a push toward the east, many a Jewish family and community had tried to establish a home in Germany, or in the Netherlands, Poland, Lithuania, and other eastern European regions, and considered it their right to stay.

According to Bell, at the beginning of the sixteenth century, Germany had about 7,000 Jewish families, consisting of 25,000–30,000 individuals.[28] The numbers fluctuated greatly due to expulsions and the significant amount of moving around characteristic of Jewish life in Europe. A considerable part of Jewish history is that of migration. Mobility in itself was a significant part of Jewish identity and preserving tradition: in addition to academic migration and traveling for business and trade— as certain trades that were available for Jews required traveling, such as traveling merchants—traveling was necessary for establishing spousal contracts and for religious celebrations for which a certain quota was needed.[29]

While medieval Germany had had some 1,100 Jewish settlements, by the eighteenth and nineteenth centuries only 9 percent of those settlements had survived. In Germany between 1399 and 1520, the recorded 765 Jewish settlements dropped to 230 by 1520, until by 1600 only about 0.2 percent of the German population was Jewish (35,000–40,000 in all). On the other hand, between 1350 and 1519, for instance, the cities of Worms and Frankfurt am Main had 11 percent of its population Jewish; these were significant urban centers for Jewish life.[30] In Hesse, a place most welcoming to Jews for a time, over eighty Jewish communities could be found. The city records of Braunschweig note that one hundred Jews lived there in 1546 before a new wave of expulsions.[31] Densely populated areas, like the Middle Rhine and Franconia, attracted Jews, while only a few urban communities continued to exist, in cities like Frankfurt am Main and Worms (as well as Friedberg and Fulda).[32] The further east or south, the better were Jewish chances to establish long-term communities. While Germany had a larger Jewish population in comparison to other countries, some of the largest populations were outside Germany. Prague remained a significant urban center for Jewish life, regardless of expulsion orders there as well; and Ferrara, Italy, was one of the few safe havens.[33]

In Saxony, the Reformation center, Luther's town of residence, Wittenberg, had few if any Jews during Luther's lifetime: Jews had been expelled already in 1304, with a small community reentering before the end of the century.[34] There is evidence of an occasional Jew traveling or small communities residing in the larger area of Saxony, as indicated by the elector's need to adjust repeatedly the order regarding Jewish rights (1536, 1539, 1543). Earlier, while still a student and a monk in Erfurt, Luther must have known (whether he cared about it or not) that he walked the very streets that had been a prominent Jewish quarter until the pogrom of 1349 and final expulsion in 1458.[35] The most Jews Luther might have ever seen in person were in his birthtown of Eisleben. Without contact with a living Jewish community but rather with the tradition's preconceived memories of the Jews, Luther, thus, carried with him an image of the Jew that did not have roots in regular real-life encounters.

Since in Luther's personal daily surroundings any normal interaction between Christians and Jews was nonexistent, chances for encounters with Jewish persons for Luther came mostly at the university or in conversation with Jewish converts. On his many travels he could possibly get a glimpse of a Jew or even a Jewish community's whereabouts. Should these glimpses occur, awareness of Jewish presence in numbers filled him with anxiety, as attested, for example, by his letters to his wife, Katharina, from his final trip to his birthplace of Eisleben, a town that still had a considerable Jewish community at the time. As Luther's anxious words manifest, finding a Jewish community of any size within or in the vicinity of a town, while not at all unheard of or unacceptable to all, could be quite unsettling for those eager to implement fully orders for Jews' departure from their midst. From Luther's standpoint, Jewish communities such as the one he countered in Eisleben were like a "blast from the past," a problem previous generations had already tried—but failed—to settle with their expulsion orders.

Limiting Rules

In late medieval and early modern Christian societies, lives were structured such that Jews should remain separate, marginalized, and subject to Christian overlords. Efforts were made to limit and control Christian association with Jews, as specified by local regulations covering everything from daily business relations to family and neighborly matters, the right to live and reside in an area, the right to practice a trade, to build a synagogue and maintain religious traditions. In addition to basic ordinances relating to daily life, various prohibitions were issued forbidding: marriage and sexual relations between a Jew and a Christian (fourth century); Jews hiring Christians in servant positions (sixth century); Jews holding public office (sixth century); Christians using the services of Jewish doctors; Christians living in Jewish homes (eleventh century). Through the Middle Ages, Jews were forbidden from debating Christians about faith matters or building new synagogues, or dining and bathing with Christians (eleventh and thirteenth centuries). Mandates were given for Jews to live in segregated areas and to wear distinguishable clothing (thirteenth century). Jews' practice of their trades—such as moneylending—were strictly regulated. Finally, Christian conversion to Judaism was punishable as heresy, as was re-conversion of a baptized Jew.[36] That these behaviors were addressed by law implies that these were the kinds of relations that Christians and Jews regularly engaged in with one another. Kaplan notes that the simultaneous "animosity" and "intimacy" between Jews and Christians, who over the centuries had found comfortable and workable ways to live side by side, with familiarity with one another's cultures, and through many dimensions of interaction, had a mutual impact on each others' lives.[37]

In a world where regulations pertaining to Jewish lives and livelihoods varied greatly from area to area and from time to time, ultimate authority belonged, at least theoretically, to the emperor and the imperial law. As is well-known, the power struggle between the emperor and the German princes made many an imperial decision moot, or at least seriously challenged in the German-speaking areas of the empire. The same is true regarding imperial rulings about the Jews and their rights. Regardless of how effective the imperial wishes may have been, and how they factored in with the rulings of the local lords who, guided by their own interests, negotiated matters pertaining to the daily lives of citizens, it is of significance that the only "universal" law did include the Jewish people under its umbrella. In the absence of uniform and consistent policies throughout the vast empire and with the lack of consistent rights of all citizens, it was significant that emperor considered the Jews personally and directly subject to his throne. Because the Jews paid taxes directly to the emperor, it was to the emperor's financial advantage to formulate favorable policies toward his Jewish subjects.

This is an area in which considerable bargaining took place, between different authorities and interested parties. For example, local authorities lobbying for the expulsion of Jews—often for the purpose of eliminating Jewish competition in business—could encourage the emperor to renegotiate pro-Jewish policies based on promises to secure imperial income apart from Jewish taxes. While there was no consistent imperial law or mechanism that secured protection of the Jews in the empire, the so-called *Landenfriede* covered, at least theoretically, all the subjects of the emperor, who saw it as his duty to promote peace and control violence for the benefit of all. Most important for the Jews was the chance to be heard at the imperial diets where major issues were negotiated, including the rights of the Jews. At these diets it was also possible for Jewish complaints and greavances to be heard.[38]

Another recourse available to Jews was the protection of territorial lords, the *Schutzherren*. These rulers, in the interest of protecting their income and subjects, could use their authority on behalf of "their Jews" over whom they had judicial rights and for whom they could issue rights. With so-called *Schutzbriefe,* they could give Jews (albeit temporary and limited) permission and protection to stay in areas where Jews otherwise had been expelled. In this regard, in Protestant states the princes in charge could have become powerful protectors of Jews on a larger scale had they considered it their "Christian duty," and some indeed tried to be such. Typically in Protestant territories the so-called *Kirchenordnungen* (church orders) addressed the rights and responsibilities of the Jews just as any other matters. In addition, rulers could issue their own special *Judenordnungen* (Jewish laws), specifically deciding on Jewish rights and responsibilities in the area.[39] As much as these laws were restricting for Jews, they also served as real protection. In addition to written ordinances, other mechanisms of intervention in Germany included the *Hofjuden* (court Jews) and the *Landjudenschaften*, the regional Jewish organizations caring for local Jewish needs and organizing for them.[40] Then there were communities and individuals who sought to protect the Jews of their area with their own means; a most extraordinary intervener throughout Germany was Rabbi Joseph (Josel) of Rosheim (1478?–1554).

Money was a consistent factor in most cases when the monarchs—be it the emperor or the territorial lords and ladies, regardless of their religious persuasion—decided on the lot of the Jews. Monetary gain was far more important than any religious issues that could be raised on the side. Sometimes it was possible for Jews to buy themselves out of a dangerous situation; high enough taxes and special fees could put roadblocks in the way of expulsion efforts. But in both Protestant and Catholic territories, once the German territorial lords became more autonomous and powerful, especially in relation to the emperor, rule over the Jews fell mostly into their hands. From the Jewish perspective this was turn for the worse.[41]

A powerful reminder of the emperor's institutional intervention on behalf of the Jews, in opposition to both Catholic and Protestant lords—and a reminder as well that things could have been different had theologians provided a theological rationale to their own princes for more pro-Jewish legislation—is the imperial ruling from 1544. On April 3, Charles V signed a special charter of rights for the Jewish people (already promised at the Diet of Speyer that year), with unprecedented privileges. In addition to decreeing against the closing of synagogues or schools and attacks against Jews or their expulsions, forbidding charges of ritual murder and allowing Jews to bring charges to the diet, the emperor issued protection for Jews to travel on sea and land and removed the requirement to wear distinguishing clothes or the badge. Furthermore, they were given the right to practice moneylending, and even with higher than usual rates (as they also paid higher taxes).[42] Josel of Rosheim had been observing the events around the diet and most certainly can be credited for significant influence in this historic imperial move.[43]

While many of these rights were soon lost as imperial power faded, the document, in stark contrast to voices like Luther's, stands as an important reality check on "what was" and "what could have been," and "what eventually happened," raising the appropriate question of Luther's particular role in what unfolded. One particular issue having to do with Jewish rights, that of usury, was also explicitly addressed by Luther.

The Specter of "Usury"

In Christian anti-Jewish slander, *Wucherei* (usury) had by Luther's time become a synonym for a Jew and Jewish business, in a negative sense. Regardless of how Christians understood the term or the practice, they generally lacked any sympathy for what most Jews were confronted with in the attempt to secure a livelihood for their families. The numerous restrictions placed on Jews dramatically limited their options, and the constantly changing circumstances and power dynamics made it nearly impossible for Jews to establish homes or professions with any security of permanence. In order to assure their inferior status, Jews were forbidden to engage in crafts or professions where they might hold a superior status to Christians. This extended as well to serving in public office or having Christian servants. Prohibitions against engaging in common professions that required permanence, such as cultivating the land—not to mention the privilege of owning land—compelled Jews to engage activities shunned by or prohibited to Christians, such as moneylending, small businesses, or traveling merchants. Being exempt from the church's laws against usury, and with the Talmud not forbidding lending money at interest to non-Jews, Jews could practice this trade. (The topic was, however, deliberated by medieval Jewish rabbis in Europe).[44] Sometimes, by demand, Jewish businesses may have been pushed to even riskier lending practices, Christians being the clear beneficiaries of it. With the rise of Christian banking systems, generally speaking, Jewish moneylenders' business naturally suffered in this regard.[45]

In a world where moneylending and banking was still in its infancy and the need for credit was increasing, Jewish moneylenders had provided an important service. But with the rise of the first large German banking houses, such as the Fugger house, competition led to the driving of Jews out of the business for which they had been shunned in the first place. Bolstered by Protestant preachers' anti-usury preaching, Jews could be accused of shady business, taking advantage of poor Christians, and demanding unacceptably high interest for loans (accusations that were true in some cases, just as with Christian businesses). The very idea that Christians could owe substantial amounts to Jewish lenders was found irritating.[46] Interestingly enough, in Luther's numerous writings against usury he mainly addressed Christian usurers who should be excommunicated; Jewish usurers were not especially targeted by him, as noted by Carter Lindberg.[47]

The other side of the coin was that any Jew could lose the right to their profession, their residence, or even the right of overnight passage without much warning. The flow of income could be interrupted on any given day for any number of insignificant reasons, even if unrelated to the person in question. While Jews were at the mercy of rulers and the mood of the locals, moneylending businesses provided some degree of security. When the economic situation in a given location changed, and the revenue drawn from Jews in the form of fees and taxes could be replaced through other means, Jews could find themselves unneeded and thus homeless. In fortunate cases they could take their business with them, and practice it in a new place, even in anticipation of possible new expulsions that occurred with the random regularity of thunderstorms.[48]

Sicut Judaeis

Looking at the late medieval and early modern European scene as a whole and the varied regulations for Jewish life, the most significant symbolic protection came from the two most powerful offices: emperor and pope. The ecclesiastical counterpart to imperial efforts to offer institutional protection for the Jews came from the head of the Catholic Church, the pope.[49] Even if papal power in many ways was seriously compromised by the German princes in German-speaking territories in the reformation century, nevertheless, the centuries-old papal position toward the Jews is significant, keeping the big picture in mind. Amidst manifold anti-Jewish violence committed by Christians, it is poignant to observe that at the official level, the medieval church maintained steady opposition against such violence and, especially, against forced baptism. Over a period of four centuries, twenty medieval popes since Calixtus II (1119–1124) and especially with the influence of Innocent III (1187–1216) continued to issue a special "Constitution for the Jews." The document has become known for its initial words, *Sicut Judaeis* ("And thus to the Jews"), words already used by Gregory the Great (590–604), an inspiration behind the bull that became incorporated into canon law in the thirteenth century.[50] The bull addresses obviously recurring violence, and it reveals the kinds of dangers Jewish people lived with on a regular basis. Most poignantly, it argues against forced baptism, reminding Christians of the rationale and effectiveness of baptism when rightly performed, while cautioning against its mechanical use as a miracle tool. In light of the papal document addressing the entire church, neither forced baptism nor violence are to be used in the conversion of Jews, and Jews should not suffer injury at the hands of Christians.

The text of the bull speaks for itself in terms of what could have been:

> *Although in many ways the disbelief of the Jews must be reproved, since nevertheless through them our own faith is truly proved, they must not be oppressed grievously by the faithful, as the prophet says: 'Do not slay them, lest these be forgetful of Thy Law [Ps. 58 (59):12] as if he were saying more openly: 'Do not wipe out the Jews completely, lest perhaps Christians might be able to forget Thy Law, which the former, although not understanding it, present in their books to those who do understand it.*

We, out of the meekness of Christian piety, and in keeping in the footprints or Our predecessors of happy memory, the Roman Pontiffs Calixtus, Eugene,

Alexander, Clement, admit their petition, and We grant them the shield of Our protection. For We make the law that no Christian compel them, unwilling or refusing, by violence to come to baptism. But, if any one of them should spontaneously, and for the sake of the faith, fly to the Christians, once his choice has become evident, let him be made a Christian without any calumny. Indeed, he is not considered to possess the true faith of Christianity who is recognized to have come to Christian baptism, not spontaneously, but unwillingly. Too, no Christian ought to presume, apart from the juridical sentence of the territorial power, wickedly to injure their persons, or with violence to take away their property, or to change the good customs which they have had until now in whatever region they inhabit. Besides, in the celebration of their own festivities, no one ought disturb them in any way, with clubs or stones, nor ought any one try to require from them or to extort from them services they do not owe, except for those they have been accustomed from times past to perform. In addition to these, We decree, blocking the wickedness and avarice of evil men, that no one ought to dare mutilate or diminish a Jewish cemetery, not, in order to get money, to exhume bodies once they have been buried. If anyone, however, shall attempt, the tenor of this degree once known, to go against it—may this be far from happening!—let him be punished by the vengeance of excommunication, unless he correct his presumption by making equivalent satisfaction. *We desire, however, that only those be fortified by the guard of this protection who shall have presumed no plotting for the subversion of the Christian faith."* So signed by Pope Alexander III, with *introduction* and *ending* from Innocent III, in 1199.[51]

This papal document, in its many manifestations, states the church's official position toward the Jews. It would, however, come to be interpreted in light of certain exceptions: Jews were not be hurt, unless—a clause added by Innocent III (1199)—they are found guilty of plotting against Christian faith.[52] "Plotting against Christian faith" came to include Jewish proselytizing of Christians, which was deemed severely punishable, as well as Christian conversion to Judaism, which was regarded as heresy.[53] These would also become Luther's deepest concerns. Toward the goal of preventing Christians from converting to Judaism, the irreversibility of Christian baptism was clarified, and ordinances against the forced baptism of any people were enacted. At the same time, the church enforced the same rules as the secular authorities: forbidding Jews from comingling with Christians, demanding Jews to wear distinguishable clothing, forbidding Jews from holding certain offices, and so on. Thus, officially, the church voiced concern and made efforts to defend Jews who were continuously vulnerable to angry Christian mobs, but on occasion, the church also authorized book burnings and, especially in the connection with the Crusades, in many ways took an active part in anti-Jewish crimes.[54]

Echoes of the powerful *Sicut Judaeis* were heard in Luther's time, as violence toward Jews continued. Christian teachers like Johann Eck and Martin Luther operated in the spirit of the "papal clause": when Jews were found blaspheming Christian faith, Christian love was no longer pertinent but rather a drastic weeding out was required. The Jewish crime of blasphemy specifically would "entitle" Luther to speak forcefully in favor of expulsion, and his own arguments in this regard reveal his dark place on the continuum of the worst expressions of Christian beliefs and actions toward their Jewish contemporaries.

Reality and Interaction, Ghetto and Badge

What we read in the laws is not always an accurate reflection of what "was" but more of "what should or could have been." We can presume that when we read about laws forbidding certain acts and deeds, and recurrently so, that these kind of activities continued to be engaged in by significant numbers of people. Personal Jewish-Christian interaction was one of these areas.

The many rules limiting Jewish lives indicate a reality behind the legal codes. Under peaceful conditions, in towns and villages where Jews were allowed to reside or engage in business, natural associations and business relations and also friendships were formed. While the records indicate efforts to keep Jews and Christians separate, the reality was always more complex. Jews and Christians did interact in various ways, especially through business relations, in addition to many daily, human interactions.[55] Amidst local diversity and fluctuation of Jewish rights in German territory, there were regular indicators of the permanent status of the Jew as "other." The notorious institutions known as the ghetto and the badge were efficiently used to maintain walls between Christians and Jews.

Before Luther's time, in the Middle Ages, Jews and Christians typically lived in physical separation from one another, even if residing within the same city walls. Already from the twelfth century on, towns would have separate sections for Jews. In accordance with the ruling of the III Lateran Council of 1179 that Jews and Christians should live in physical separation from one another, in medieval German cities Jews typically lived in Jewish quarters or streets, named accordingly (*Judengasse, Judenstrasse*). The ghetto institution as such, however, with the requirement for Jews to live in a designated area, is an early modern phenomenon. Its origins are typically dated to 1516 Venice, when the old quarry area already designated for Jewish residents was walled in. By the second half of the sixteenth century, most European Jews lived in ghettoes, after the model of Venice or Rome, where it was established in 1555 by papal order. The purpose of the arrangement was segregation and presumed protection of Christians from all the ills that Jews might present, physical or spiritual, and most of all, control of Jewish people's lives and comings and goings.

In a more positive light, the ghetto system did enable particular organization of Jewish life and the maintenance of a distinctive identity and traditions and kinship, all of which may have opened up structured and safe venues for social and business relations between Christians and Jews. As David B. Ruderman writes, "the closure paradoxically opened up new opportunities for cultural dialogue and interaction."[56] The positive aspects of the medieval ghetto arrangement, however, are inevitably overshadowed by the tyrannical uses of the ghetto in the modern era, when the system that had been more or less abolished in the eighteenth and nineteenth centuries (beginning with Napoleon) was most brutally reemployed by the Nazis. The same is true with the other most famous segregation mechanism: the badge.

The requirement for Jews to wear the badge, like the ghetto arrangement, dates from the twelfth century. The IV Lateran Council in 1215 decreed that Jews (and Muslims) were to wear a particular piece of clothing as a visible indicator of the special status of Jewish people and as a way to secure the following of segregation rules. Throughout Europe Jews were expected to wear either the badge or another form of clothing to signal their Jewishness. The marker could be a white, red, or yellow circle, or another symbol, a red cloak, a green dress, or a pointy hat, or bells attached to Jewish women's dresses (as in Salzburg 1418) to announce their arrival, and so on until more uniform policies were developed by state and church. For Christians this meant that it was easier to avoid interaction with a Jew, but when such interaction did occur, there was undeniable awareness of identities.

The notorious yellow badge in the shape of the Star of David thus has long roots in history. Other types of badges were used over time, and before that, Jewishness was indicated with particular clothing, and in line with the "sumptuary laws" (that regulated lower and middle class people against excess in food and clothing). As Mark R. Cohen states, the first known secular mandate to use a distinctive dress for Jews comes from England in 1217 when King Henry III ordered that Jews were required to wear a white linen or parchment sign of two tables on their outer garment.[57] While in England the indicator for Jews could be white cloth patches (tables of laws) sown on outer garments, in Germany the equivalent was the "rota," *Judenringel*, or *Judenfleck*, typically either white or yellow, or, as an alternative, a larger red circle. This practice was also reflected in church law. The Fourth Lateran Council (1215) mandated that Jews in the Holy Roman Empire wear particular clothes with particular colors to distinguish them from Christians. For centuries there was significant local variety in the following of this rule, depending on the territorial lords' decisions on what kind of identification was required and how firmly the order was to be followed (if at all).[58] Here the court theologians and clergy would have considerable influence.

In the Holy Roman Empire, it was not until the fifteenth century that the church's law about the garment came to be applied more universally. Prior to that Jews wore other distinctive garments, such as foot-length vestments, long coats, and hoods, or they could wear particular caps or hats, typically of particular color and material.[59] The so-called *Judenhut* (Jewish hat) that developed in the Middle Ages was always of a bright color, white or mostly yellow. The "vile" color of yellow became the signature color for Jews (known already from eighth-/ninth-century art). In the fifteenth century Jews were typically required to wear on their clothes a yellow wheel, the "forerunner of the infamous Nazi 'Jewish badge.'"[60] Before the twentieth-century Nazi resurrection of the badge, the use of a clothing indicator for Jewishness continued in various European countries as late as the eighteenth century.

"Friends of Jews"

In Luther's world, Christians were not supposed to be friends with Jews, and vice versa; or so the regulations indicated. Those who voluntarily associated themselves with Jews beyond what was considered acceptable, or who went as far as to defend Jewish believers in public, easily became a target of suspicion themselves. Christians with the unwelcome label of "Jew Friend" encountered resistance and ridicule. There was the fear that Jewish proselytizing could lead to Christian conversions to Judaism; both actions were against the imperial law and counted as reasons for heresy charges. Even willingness to learn the Hebrew language and Jewish sources was problematic, as became evident during the Reuchlin-Pfefferkorn affair.[61]

In the wake of his 1523 treatise, *That Jesus Christ Was Born a Jew*,[62] Luther himself earned the reputation of being a friend of the Jews, and contemporary Jewish sources indicate that the German Jewish community looked upon Luther's movement with a degree of optimism as well. Luther made it clear in *Against the Sabbatarians*[63] that this reputation was not welcomed. In this 1538 treatise, he goes to great lengths to demonstrate that his 1523 words had been misunderstood and misused. In this regard Luther was hardly unique in comparison to his fellow reformers, all of whom applied traditional anti-Jewish stereotypes to a significant degree. Generally speaking the reformers promoted friendly treatment of Jewish people, while their track records show ambiguity and inconsistency, both in regard to their views about what to do with the Jews of their time and in regard to how they thought about the Jews, Judaism, and Jewish biblical interpretation theologically.[64]

Luther's collaborator, Andreas Osiander (1498–1552) of Nuremberg, stands out as an example of this ambiguity.[65] As with the other reformers, his main concern was Jewish conversion to Christian faith, coupled with his interest in Christian access to the Jewish languages to enrich their proper understanding of biblical texts ("There is no language more useful to the Holy Spirit than Hebrew").[66] Although Osiander never wrote a particular treatise on how Christians should deal with the Jews, he had cultivated personal relations with Jewish communities, and responded positively when asked for intervention in the face of looming expulsions. Even if he considered the Jews guilty of killing Christ, the bottom line for him was that there were "no people on earth more meek or frightened than the Jews."[67] Influenced by his personal relationships with Jews, Osiander came to their defense in an anonymously published treatise, *Whether It Is Credible that Jews Secretly Kill Children and Make Use of Their Blood* (1529). This work provoked the Catholic Professor Johann Eck of the University of Ingolstadt to write a viciously anti-Jewish counterattack, *Refutation of a Jew Book* (1541), a publication that can be characterized as "the absolute nadir of anti-Jewish polemic in the early-modern period."[68]

Apart from Osiander, Protestant ranks included few recognizable friends of the Jews, with the exception of Philip of Hesse, a prominent Protestant leader (until his personal downfall with bigamy charges) who considered it his duty as a Christian ruler to be hospitable to the "noble race" of the Jews. He also endured an embarrassing public battle on the matter, in his case with his court theologian, Martin Bucer, and a commission of preachers who demanded harsher measures against the Jews in Hesse, seeking to rescind earlier anti-Jewish regulations.[69]

The Many Faces of the "Jew" for Luther

For all practical purposes, the Jews of his time remained strangers to Luther. Like so many of his contemporaries, he missed the most powerful opportunities for learning and correction: through personal relationships. The only Jews whom Luther engaged with any regularity (as far as we know) were converts such as Bernardus Hebraeus (Rabbi Jacob Gipher)[70] and those involved at the university in particular, who hardly found it beneficial, or safe, to promote Jewish faith to Christians whose piety could be measured by their level of hatred of the Jews (as infamously uttered by Erasmus of Rotterdam). Some converts, predictably, went to the extreme in this and did their best to argue, in print, for the superiority of Christian faith over against Judaism by presenting "insider information" on Jewish life and practice. Most important of these informers for Luther was the convert, Anthonius Margaritha, whose book, *The Whole Jewish Faith* (1530/1531), further enhanced the worst fears of contemporary Christians about Jews and their secret religious customs. His work also highlighted Jewish anti-Christian attitudes and arguments, something that existed to be sure. At the same time, Margaritha's book pioneered in making available to Christian readers like Luther valuable information on Jewish life, rituals, and translations of prayers. In Margaritha, Luther found a Jewish source he trusted, or wanted to trust.[71]

The key source, however, for Luther in regard to the Jews and Jewish faith was the Bible. There he found a Jew he loved, the one he felt he knew, the model of good faith he embraced. Similarly, there he also found the model for living with the gospel, as well as the warning example against living under the law. In the Bible he found the good Jew and the bad, just as he found the good Christian and the bad, and, most of all, examples of the right and the wrong understanding of God's word. In that company, he identified himself with the good Jews.

Luther's words over the course of his career reveal both how loaded his texts are with references to Jews and how complex the word "Jew" is for him. Chronology is of little significance here. It does not matter that much whether we are reading the young or the old Luther, whereas what makes a difference is whom and what he is talking about and with what intent and in what situation. Most of all, it matters what meaning the word Jew has for him in each instance. The following six categories for the word Jew may prove helpful in assessing Luther's complex rhetoric:

First, the contemporary Jew: While not that interested in his contemporary Jews as persons and not wishing for personal relations, Luther has no ill will toward Jewish human beings per se. Especially in situations when addressing human suffering, Luther can react pastorally and with empathy, yet not consistently so. In this regard his words do sharpen toward the end of his life to a degree that we can talk about a change.

Second, Jews as a political entity: Regarding the Jews as a political entity and a "group" within the Christian state, here Luther's ambiguous views develop later, as he becomes a political force in his context. Once he begins to lose all hope for the conversion of the Jews who, to his annoyance, continue to live in Christian lands and could thus bring about calamities on Christians, Luther entertains, in public, thoughts of Jews as a political entity that should be dealt with through secular means of power. Luther does this more toward the end of his career. His sharpened attitudes and practical proposals regarding the expulsion of the Jews and their "blasphemous" faith practices do not make Luther a modern racial anti-Semite; his basic problem remains religion, not race.

Third, the dangerous Jew: In Luther's imagination, those who practice Jewish faith put everybody's salvation in jeopardy. While his hopes for Jewish conversion as a solution to this danger oscillated over the course of his career, he had no appreciation for Judaism as religion or faith. His opinion of the danger of this "poison" never changed. Theologically and spiritually, this Jew was the most threatening to Luther, and the least known to him in reality.

Fourth, the biblical Jew of the Old Testament: Luther reveres the matriarchs and the patriarchs of the Old Testament as his foremothers and forefathers. They are the models of true faith for Christians who now exemplify saving faith and who are the inheritors of the promise originally given to Abraham. Biblical Jews are the only Jewish friends Luther loved, seeing himself in a familial continuity with those in a lasting covenant with God.

Fifth, the Jew as the old Adam/Eve: As a specifically theological category, Luther uses the word Jew as the embodiment and the symbol of a sinner who is found in every human being in the grip of original sin. Those who instinctively rely on their own efforts and works' righteousness make Christ's work unnecessary and act blasphemously by insulting Christ with their unbelief. Blasphemy was the major offense, worthy of God's wrath, from which only Christ could save. This "inner Jew" needs to be conquered through conversion and the gospel. The tension of law and gospel, one of Luther's central theological perspectives, has at its roots Luther's caricature of a Jewish believer and his solution as to how that believer is to be transformed in the direction of saving faith, that is, to convert to Christian faith.

Conversion of the Jews to Christian faith was of profound interest to Luther. Any changes in his ways of talking about the Jews would have to do with how realistic he saw this possibility and his eventual loss of all hope in this regard. The very expectation indicates an important point: Jewishness per se had no positive value for Luther; Jewishness as race hardly mattered to him. His first and foremost concern was to lift up the gospel about Jesus Christ as the saving Messiah, and spell it out for Jews and Christians alike. The all-consuming passion of his intent is good to keep in mind when attempting the difficult task of understanding his thoughts on the Jews and the Bible. Neither can be appreciated fully without the other.

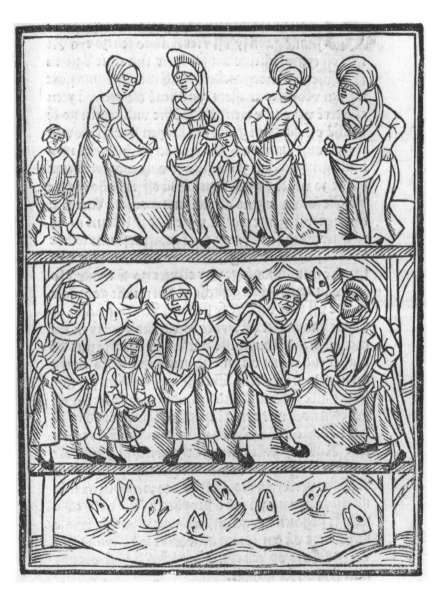

Tashlikh ceremony from the first day of *Rosh Ha-Shanah.* "You will cast all their sins into the depths of the sea" (Micah 7:19) From Johannes Pfefferkorn, *The Confession of the Jews* [*Ich heysß eyn buchlijn der iuden beicht*] (Cologne: Johannes Landen, 1508), depicting aspects of Jewish religious practice—with significant inaccuracies.

The Texts

Kapparot ceremony prior to *Yom Kippur:* symbolic transfer of sins to a fowl (top). Food preparation (bottom left). *Seder, Shabbat,* or festive meal (bottom right, above). Immersion in a *Mikveh* (bottom right, below). From Johannes Pfefferkorn, *The Confession of the Jews* [*Ich heysß eyn buchlijn der iuden beicht*] (Cologne: Johannes Landen, 1508), depicting aspects of Jewish religious practice—with significant inaccuracies.

The Text Selections

L uther's references and allusions to Jews, Judaism, synagogue, rabbis, and so on run into the many thousands. The format of a book such as this requires that numerous difficult decisions be made. The guiding principle throughout has been that the text selections, when taken as a whole, will serve as an orientation for students into a challenging subject matter and as an invitation to further study. In working through the selections, students will gain a strong sense of the breadth as well as something of the depth of the problem. The texts are presented chronologically rather than thematically, from the beginning of Luther's career to just days before his death. This chronological presentation reinforces the reality of the Jew as a persistent element in Luther's thought and by no means restricted to his late treatises against the Jews.

In terms of the actual selection of texts and the respective parts thereof, the attempt has been made to present fundamental aspects of Luther's thinking on the Jews. Rather than seeking to elucidate his familiar theological principles per se, the texts in this volume introduce readers to key aspects of Luther's hermeneutics and theological imagination through a specific albeit disorienting lens: The readings have been chosen with an eye toward highlighting how his thought regarding the Jews is so often anchored in the interpretation of concrete biblical texts.

In so far as possible, enough material is provided for each selection so that readers can follow for themselves Luther's mode of thought on the specific issue at hand. Where we have found it helpful to call attention to Luther's glosses, or to clarify a passage by specifying a verse not included in the original text we have used the distinct bracket. Though selections are made from different genres of Luther's writings, the exegetical works, and especially those relating to the Old Testament, are clearly privileged. These texts, of primary importance to Luther as a believer and a scholar, offer a logical and authentic starting point for observing how he thinks and argues with the "Jewish Question" in mind, be it in terms of his biblical interpretation, his theological reflection, or his pastoral and political advice. The only non-Luther text presented is the letter of Rabbi Josel of Rosheim to the Strasbourg City Council, Text #25.

The issue of the Jew in the context of Luther's sermons is complex and rightfully deserves its own treatment. It is noteworthy, however, that a standard locus for Christian anti-Jewish rhetoric—the Holy Week sermon—is notably absent in Luther.

Especially in the Middle Ages, the Holy Week sermon was an annual opportunity for renewing blame against the Jews for the crucifixion of Christ. Though Luther was clearly capable of referring to Jews as Christ-killers, his own Passion sermons show him moving strongly away from traditional recitations of the sufferings of Christ and the anti-Jewish diatribes that naturally followed therefrom.[1]

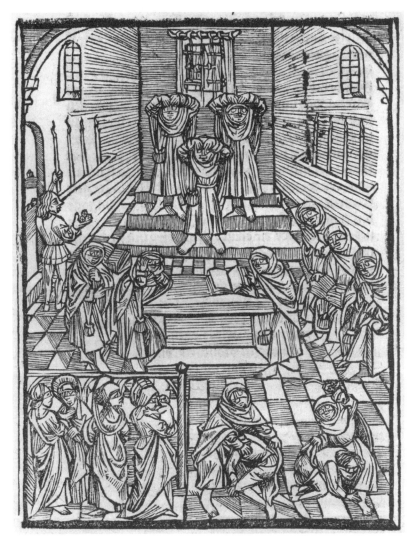

Dukhan (priestly blessing) ceremony (top). Women's gallery (bottom left). Public flogging (bottom right). From Johannes Pfefferkorn, *The Confession of the Jews* [*Ich heysß eyn buchlijn der iuden beicht*] (Cologne: Johannes Landen, 1508), depicting aspects of Jewish religious practice—with significant inaccuracies.

Text #1

First Psalm Lectures (1513–1515)

Language: Latin
Critical Edition: WA 55/1; 55/2 (replaces WA 3; 4)
English translation: LW 10; 11

As a new professor at the University of Wittenberg, Luther chose the Psalms for his first lectures on the Bible, that is, the book that was his most consistent theological and spiritual companion. Presented in the traditional academic style of Glosses (brief grammatical/philological remarks) and Scholia (expansive interpretive remarks), and utilizing the traditional medieval method of fourfold interpretation (literal, allegorical, tropological, anagogical), the lectures are preserved in Luther's own hand (though they were not published). The reader of these lectures *in toto* will note how pervasive is the polemic directed against either the Jews or the synagogue, so pervasive in fact that it rises to the level of a central characteristic of the lectures. While Luther was both an heir to and a purveyor of an already protracted Christian anti-Jewish rhetorical tradition, nevertheless one can speak here of both an *intensification* of such rhetoric and of the creation of *new polemic* in Psalms interpretation where it had not occurred before.[1] Especially noteworthy, however, is the complete absence of traditional accusations of host desecration, well poisoning, and ritual murder. Luther's battle against the Jews, rather, is exegetically and theologically based, that is, it is driven by his understanding of the christological meaning of actual Psalms texts.[2] In his Preface to the Glosses, Luther states the exegetical principle that drives his reading of the Old Testament in general and of the Psalms in particular: "If the Old Testament can be interpreted by human wisdom without the New Testament, I should say that the New Testament has been given to no purpose. So Paul concluded that 'Christ died to no purpose' if the Law were sufficient (Gal. 2:21)."[3]

Because the Jews are the prime example of those who would interpret the Old Testament apart from the New, this principle would set him on a career-long collision course with Jewish interpretation and with those in the Christian community who would read the Old Testament in a "Jewish" manner.

Presented here are excerpts from Psalms 1 and 78. Psalm 1, which Luther regarded as a preface to the entire Psalter, sketches the distinction between the righteous and the wicked. Key polemical themes that emerge in Luther's treatment are: (1) the twofold (and unforgiveable) sin of the Jews, who not only crucified Christ but refuse to confess the sin of having done so; (2) the Jew as negative example and warning to Christians not to behave likewise; (3) the ongoing Jewish crucifixion of Christ via distorted and treacherous interpretation of Scripture;[4] (4) the linking of Christians with righteousness and Jews with sinfulness.

Psalm 78 is an historical Psalm that narrates the fidelity of God and the rebelliousness of Israel during the deliverance from Egypt, the years in the Wilderness, and the entry into the Promised Land. Luther regarded the Psalm as a sermon of Christ to the synagogue, and in his "spiritual" reading the plagues against the Egyptians become plagues against the Jews, and the driving out of the Canaanites becomes the driving out of the Jews. Here we encounter a classic displacement theology, with the spiritual church (*verus Israel*, true Israel) trumping the carnal synagogue. The final excerpt is one of the stranger things one will encounter in Luther: an extended scatological description of Jewish malice and treachery.

Psalm 1
{LW 10:11–13}[5]
The first psalm speaks literally concerning Christ thus:

1. *Blessed is the man.* He is the only blessed One and the only Man from whose fullness they have all received (John 1:16) that they might be blessed and men and everything that follows in this psalm. He is "the firstborn among many brethren" (Rom. 8:29), "the firstfruits of those who have fallen asleep" (1 Cor. 15:20), so that He might also be the firstfruits of those who are awake, namely, in the Spirit.... He is a "man" in a threefold sense: first, because He is a man of manly virtue; second, because He is not a boy to be educated but is manly in grace; third, because He has a bride. This is the Man whom a woman has embraced, because as a bridegroom He went forth not only after but also from His chamber (cf. Ps. 19:6), having His own bride from the beginning. *Who has not walked in the counsel of the ungodly*, that is, He did not consent to the designs of the Jews, who afterwards crucified Him. This is the first stage in which all kinds of sins are included. For in whatever kind of sins one sins, one departs from God into the counsel of the ungodly. Ungodliness is against God and also against His worship, which is godliness. The addition of the word "counsel" denotes the vice of the will, because such people do evil on purpose and willingly, deliberately and advisedly, not out of ignorance. Some indeed act in an ungodly manner advisedly, from an evil will, while others depart into this their counsel by consenting to it ignorantly and because they are led astray. *Nor has stood in the way of sinners.* The way of sinners is the very life of the ungodly, which has already been mentioned,

a way upon which those who become ungodly enter. But this second stage is worse. It commits the first sin twofold, and now they are not simply ungodly, but what is more, they are sinners. The word "sin" is quite frequently used in Scripture for idolatry. But this is a double sin, to stand, to defend, to withstand one who tries to correct and recall, to refuse to agree, like Saul, in 1 Sam. 16{:15}, to turn the heart to words of evil for the purpose of excusing the excuses for sins, to justify oneself after he has sinned, and thus to confirm his iniquity against God and His righteousness, that is, to repudiate God and fashion an idol for oneself, the work of his hands, to refuse confession and glory to God. This is what the Jews did against Christ then and are still doing until now. Therefore they are already not merely ungodly, involved in a simple sin, but they are also sinners in a twofold sense. Thus Jeremiah, Lam. 1{:8}, says: "Jerusalem sinned grievously, therefore she became unstable." He says she "sinned a sin," that is, she doubled a simple sin. In chapter 2 of the same prophet (Jer. 2:13) we read: "My people have committed two evils." This is why he said in the following, "I have not sinned" (cf. Jer. 2:23), although, of course, the people had sinned. [Prov. 30{:20}: "This (namely, as follows) is the way of an adulteress: she eats, and wipes her mouth, and says (that is, excusing herself), 'I have done no wrong,'" that is, the synagog.] Hence Is. 55{:7} promises: "Let the wicked forsake his way . . . and the Lord will have mercy on him." But Amos 2{:6} says concerning them: "For three transgressions of Israel and for four I will not convert him." The "three transgressions" are all sins, namely, sins of weakness against the Father, sins of ignorance against the Son, and sins of evil or concupiscence against the Holy Spirit. But the "four transgressions" means to add to the sins already mentioned excuses with regard to them and to refuse to confess them. These cause the person to "stand in [his own] way" with a very stiff neck. And therefore he is not converted and cannot be converted, because he directly shuts the door of mercy to himself and resists the Holy Spirit and forgiveness for himself. Therefore for three crimes they might well be converted, but not for three four at the same time. And this second stage is the last in itself, than which none can become worse. Then follows the third which already reaches to others; to others, I say, to corrupt them with the same plague and to draw them along into the same destruction, so that he who in the first stage committed all evils against God in the second rejected all grace of forgiveness and now in the third teaches others to do the same. Upon this follows *nor has sat in the chair of pestilence*. Ungodliness did not have a place to go to within itself, except to set itself up as righteousness. Therefore, behold, it had to go beyond itself now and proceed also to others. So the apostle says, 2 Tim. 3{:13}: "Evil men and impostors will go on from bad to worse, deceivers and deceived." This is that horrible thing that Hos. 6{:10} saw in the house of Israel. Therefore the chair is the public ruling office, while pestilence is that death-dealing doctrine by which the Jews corrupted, stained, and killed themselves and their own against Christ. For Christ sits in the chaff of salvation and of costly ointment of spikenard (Mark 14:3). This is therefore truly a spiritual pestilence which kills souls by a continuous slaughter. But the force of this sickness is hidden. And this is what they prophesied about themselves when they said, "And the last fraud will be worse than the first" (Matt. 27:64). For to deny that it is a sin to have crucified the Lord is worse than to have perpetrated the sin itself, that is, to do the crucifying. Therefore the last error and the last sin are unforgivable. Oh, what a horrible example that wrath is for us! Cursed be every pride that imitates that error to the present day!

{LW 10:17-19}

. . . {2b.} *And on His law he meditates day and night.* Meditating is an exclusive trait of human beings, for even beasts appear to fancy and to think. Therefore the ability to meditate belongs to reason. There is a difference between meditating and thinking. To meditate is to think carefully, deeply, and diligently, and properly it means to muse in the heart. Hence to meditate is, as it were, to stir up in the inside, or to be moved in the innermost self. Therefore one who thinks inwardly and diligently asks, discusses, etc. Such a person meditates. But one does not meditate on the law of the Lord unless his delight was first fixed in it. For what we want and love, on that we reflect inwardly and diligently. But what we hate or despise we pass over lightly and do not desire deeply, diligently, or for long. Therefore let delight be first sent into the heart as the root, and then meditation will come of its own accord. It is for this reason that the ungodly do not meditate on the law of the Lord, since as false plants they did not take root. Yet they meditate on other things, namely, on things in which their delight is rooted, things they themselves desire and love, such as gold, honor, and flesh. But the Jews meditate on vanities and false frenzies according to their own ideas about the Scriptures, as has been prophesied concerning them in a variety of ways. But David prays (Ps. 119:36): "Incline my heart to Thy testimonies and not to gain!" All of the following do not meditate on the Law, but outside the Law: the greedy, the carnal, and the arrogant. Or they meditate on glosses of the Law, or dross and hulls.

. . . .

Here, too, there are some perverted people (as in the first part of the verse) who in a similar way twist and pervert this word of the Holy Spirit. Their meditation is not on the law of the Lord, but rather, to the contrary, the law of the Lord is in their meditation (which is a horrible situation). They are the ones who twist the Scriptures to their own understanding and by their own fixed meditation compel the Scriptures to enter it and agree with it, when it ought to be the other way around. In this way, then, the law of the Lord is in their meditation, and not their meditation on the law of the Lord. They do not want to agree with their adversary on the way (cf. Matt. 5:25), but they want the adversary to agree with them. They do not want to be holy with the holy, but they want the holy to be profane with them.

Such were the heretics. Such are all who seek to approve their own empty opinion by the authority of Scripture, Judaizing with Jewish treachery.

. . . Hence the Lord complains through Malachi (cf. Mal. 3:8) that evil and perverse interpreters stab Him and do violence to Him. Indeed, their own sayings are like goads and nails, says Eccl. 12{:11}, whereby, when the truth is forbidden, the Lord is pierced, so that the truth may not freely move and be seen. Thence, in line with this image, the Lord remained crucified to the Jews, and He never appeared to them again, except to the remnant of Israel. To this very day they crucify Him within themselves, as the apostle accuses them (Heb. 6:6), because they keep the truth pierced through and continue to stab it with their extremely hard iron lies (which are their goads). Thus to this day they do not know what they are doing, just as they did not know then. They scourge, stone, and kill the prophets and scribes in the same way as did their fathers. And just as the fathers did it literally, the Jews now do the same mystically. For a prophet is killed when his sermons are choked as to the living sense which the Holy Spirit intends. See how much learning there is in this one verse! Therefore we must take the utmost care that we do not quickly believe our own idea and that we must expound Scripture in all humility and reverence, because Scripture is the stone of offense and rock of scandal for those who are in a hurry. But Scripture turns that rock into pools of water (cf. Ps. 114:8) for those who meditate on the law of the Lord. Therefore the Lord also reproves those who seek Him thus, but Is. 65{:1} tells us that those who did not seek Him in that way find Him . . .

{LW 10:24}

5. *Therefore the ungodly will not rise in the judgment.* He did not say "in the day of judgment," but "in the judgment." The judgment of the world is going on even now, although it has not yet been revealed what will happen on the day of judgment. Therefore the Lord is already judging the peoples in fairness, by His graces distinguishing the good from the bad, and He transfers them out of darkness into His marvelous light (1 Pet. 2:9), separating light from darkness. In this judgment a man rises in the first resurrection according to the soul. The image and cause of this resurrection is the resurrection of Christ, as the apostle theologizes in many places. But the Jews do not rise in that judgment. Why not? Because they do not want to, because they excuse themselves for their sins and justify themselves, and thus resist. It is, however, a multiple judgment. (1) It is a passive judgment, in which we are judged by the Lord, namely, by His separating us from the midst of the evil. This takes place according to the body through discipline and chastisement and according to the soul through grace. Thus the apostle says (1 Cor. 11:32): "When we are judged by the Lord, we are chastened so that we may not be condemned along with the world." (2) It is a judgment by which we judge ourselves. This takes place when we accuse ourselves and confess our sin, and thereby we acknowledge that we are

worthy of punishment and death. Thus we read Rom. 2{:3, 1}: "You judge those who do such things, etc.," and again, "You are doing the same things which you condemn," that is, you acknowledge and discern evil deeds and things not to be done. Therefore, when we acknowledge such things in ourselves and impose punishment on ourselves because of them, we are passing judgment on ourselves. Therefore the ungodly do not rise in the judgment. *Nor sinners in the council of the righteous*, that is, Jews in the church of the Christians. These alone are righteous, made thus by our only righteous Lord Jesus Christ . . .

Psalm 78

{LW 11:78–80}

49–51. *He sent upon them the wrath of His indignation, indignation and wrath and trouble, which He sent in by evil angels. He made a way for the pathway of His anger. He spared not their souls from death, and their cattle He shut up in death. And He smote all the firstborn in the land of Egypt, the firstfruits of all their labor in the tents of Ham.* (10) Here the last plague is described, and it includes the fifth one reported in Exodus, namely, the death of the cattle. But he pictures it as having been done by the ministry of evil angels. And that he is speaking rather of spiritual death he shows by saying "the death of their souls." There is a big difference between "wrath" and "wrath of indignation." For the wrath of indignation is that by which He not only inflicts punishment on the body in a physical sense, but also on the soul in a spiritual sense. Therefore, in order to express the greatness of this evil, he thus repeats and doubles wrath and wrath, etc. This is the last plague, by which the Jews have been destroyed. They were the firstborn, because they had received the Law before the Gentiles. But all this according to the flesh. For the last were made first and the first last. Not

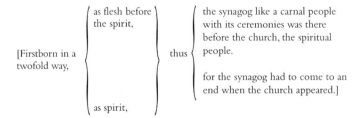

indeed by the election of grace, but by the sequence of nature they were the first for God's people.

[Not what was spiritual, but what was physical was first.][6] Thus, then, God killed all the firstborn, that He might receive something else to be offered as a firstborn, namely, the spirit. The flesh is before the spirit, and the birth of the flesh in wrath is earlier than the birth of the spirit in grace. And by the latter the former is removed and killed. For now it is not those who are sons of the flesh who are born, but those who are sons of the faith and the promise. Therefore to kill the firstborn is to reject and cast off the people according to physical birth. And whoever does not agree to this rejection is cast forth with it at the same time, as happened to the Jews. Now, the flesh is firstborn before the spirit. And the carnal people are firstborn before the spiritual people (that is, the old before the new). This, then, is that dreadful wrath of God upon them, for God rejected them altogether according to the flesh and killed the standing of the synagog and put the Law to death, in which they nevertheless think they are living, but they are not alive before God. The fact that their sacrifices and ceremonies and works are dead, this God did with the word alone, for He removed them and determined that they should come to an end. But since they were unwilling, the wrath of indignation was sent upon them. For they were punished with endless plagues and given up to the power of evil angels. As the flesh is born before the spirit, which must be reborn, and the firstborn flesh killed by a mystical death, so the carnal people were born before the spiritual. And they, too, had to be killed by a mystical death so that they might be reborn a spiritual people. Therefore the killing of the firstborn of Egypt is nothing else than that the people of the synagog living in the letter come to an end. The letter lives as long as it binds, but it is killed since it has now been fulfilled by Christ, so that it may not bind. Therefore the killed (letter) kills all who cling to it.]

But where our version has "He made a way for the pathway of His anger," the Hebrew has "He built a road for His rage."... The sense [of our text] seems to be that He made this a firm policy, and He punishes them permanently without ceasing, not in passing, like the godly, but over and over again. As a road is usually not made by one passing but by incessant footsteps, so by incessant tracks and signs of God's wrath, which we see in them, He has now, as it were, made a road, a road worn and indeed made firm. Therefore the path of God's anger is the token and work of the divine wrath which appears in them to us and to them. But for this path He made a way, that is, a persistence and duration and well-worn continuity. The paths of God are the works of God. But the paths of God's wrath are God's works of punishment and vengeance. So the prophet threatens. Therefore in this word a perfect and persevering wrath is described.

. . .

{LW 11:86–88}

54. *And He brought them to the mountain of His sanctuary, the mountain which His right hand had purchased.* Thus Is. 2{:3} says: "Come, let us go up to the mountain of the Lord, to the house of the God of Jacob." This is the church, which is the true sanctuary (that is, the mystical temple of God), which His right hand, that is, the Son of God, has acquired. Hence we are called a people of His possession in 1 Peter 2{:9}.

55. *And He drove out the Gentiles before them and by lot divided to them their land by a line of distribution.* This refers particularly to the Jews. They had been made the seed and people of Canaan, and they took possession of the land flowing with milk and honey (that is, Holy Scripture), from which they were cast out. And this land was divided and distributed to the faithful according to the measure of the gift of Christ, as the apostle says. For to each one is given the manifestation of the Spirit in Scripture for profit (1 Cor. 12:7).

. . .

And He made the tribes of Israel dwell in their tabernacles. These are the beautiful tabernacles of Jacob (Num. 24:5), that is, the books of the prophets and Holy Scripture, as above, in which the true Israel dwells now. Then, as I said in the gloss on the text, they are the bodies or cities or souls, in which demons and vices reigned. Now the apostles and saints dwell in them.

56. *Yet they tested and rebelled against the Most High God.* The Jews did this first, and then our heretics. They were made crooked arrows, aiming themselves at an evil sense and detracting from the truth, and in a bold and foolhardy manner attacking it with their arrows. Indeed, even with those who cling to the truth, like the Arians and other heretics.

But with regard to the plagues which follow, as they befell the synagog, so they also befell the heretics, and even the faithful who were led astray, killed, and troubled by the heretics. For they fell by the sword (their wicked word) and were not lamented (v. 64).

65. *And the Lord was awakened as one out of sleep, and like a mighty man that has been surfeited with wine.* The Lord Jesus Christ slept in the grave and arose when He had been roused. And He was drunk with the drained cup of suffering, for He drank the wine in His suffering to the point of total inebriation and extreme excess. But when this wine which had weakened Him had been assimilated, He arose a mighty man.

66. *And He smote His adversaries in the rear and put them to everlasting shame.*[7] These are the scribes and lawyers with their own, the true Philistines, who at the time of Christ had oppressed the faithful people and led them astray and killed them with false teachings. Besides, they had also captured and killed the ark, that is, the body of Christ, which was then handed over into the hands of the enemy. Or, the ark is Holy Scripture in its own true understanding which they crucified in its words as they crucified Christ in the body], which they place next to their idol, Dagon, that is, twist it to their own meaning, when they ought rather bend their own opinion to conform to Scripture. But the ark causes Dagon to be mutilated with hands, head, and feet cut off. For they see that their own opinion has neither works nor words nor any vital meaning. About this elsewhere.

Therefore the Lord struck them in the rear, when He afflicted them in earthly things, and caused them to trust in what the apostle nevertheless teaches should be regarded as dung (Phil. 3:8). The rear parts in spirit are, indeed, the body itself, just as the front parts are the souls. Hence the Lord said to Moses, "You will see My back parts" (Ex. 33:23). Second, they are the earthly things to which our rear is turned, namely, the body, and the front parts are the eternal things toward which our fore-part is turned, namely, the spirit. But at this place what seems to be more expressly denoted is that their *recta*, their innermost bowels, are sticking out through the rear, because the rear is different from the buttocks on which we sit. And there is trouble before me to recognize this. Is it perhaps because the Jews have no definite seat in the world? They are driven like wanderers from place to place.

But since these are our unseemly parts, which we are accustomed to hide, it seems that it may denote the malice and treachery of the Jews, which they per-petrated against Christ, and which is poured out throughout the world with their grief and indignation, so that by this deed they are in disgrace among all nations and without excuse. Yet they make leather seats for themselves, that is, they draw comfort from their physical paternal descent: or from the literal sense of Scripture], on which they rest, sit, and rely, and thus they excuse themselves to the present, though they are unable to deny what was done openly before all. For their *recta* stick out, that is, the innermost feelings of their heart and their desires in opposition to Christ they display to the present. Through these they have then poured out their excrement. Therefore, the *recta* sticking out means that their will to harm and do evil appears, since they are not able to vomit the feces of evils against Him.

But the fact that they offer five golden hemorrhoids and mice to that God whom they do not worship means that they pay riches from themselves to the Christian Caesar. Or the mystery is still hidden for me.

Or, their rear parts are the reputation of their works, which is now rotting and stinking throughout the world, since the Gospel is being revealed. And their *recta* stick out because the Gospel makes known even the innermost evils of their heart, show-ing what kind of people they were inwardly. And this is their everlasting reproach.

Text #2

Letter to George Spalatin (1514)

Language:	Latin
Critical Edition:	WABr 1:23–24 (Nr. 7b)
English translation:	Smith/Jacobs, 1:28–29[1]

A t the time of the writing of this letter, George Spalatin (1484–1545) was in the service of Elector Frederick the Wise in the Saxon court, and among his many duties he served as laison to the University of Wittenberg. Luther and Spalatin developed a lifelong friendship, and over the course of his career Luther would write more letters to Spalatin than to anyone else.

The occasion of this letter centers around a major, long-lasting controversy between the humanist defenders of academic freedom and ancient sources, on the one hand, and the religious defenders of Christian orthodoxy, on the other. A central figure targeted by both sides was Johannes Reuchlin, the father of sixteenth-century Christian hebraism and a distant relative of Philip Melanchthon (who would become Luther's closest colleague). A student of rabbinic texts both for philological reasons and because of his interest in kabbalah, the Jewish mystical tradition, Reuchlin positioned himself as a defender of academic freedom generally and Jewish books specifically, and argued that as Christians gained linguistic competency in Jewish literature this would create the "possibility of bringing the Jews amicably into the bosom of the true faith."[2] Johannes Pfefferkorn, a Jewish convert, published several treatises, some directed specifically against Reuchlin whom he accused of "Judaizing," while himself lobbying with the emperor for the authority to confiscate and even burn Jewish books (especially volumes of Talmud) as harmful for Christian wellbeing. On the grounds that such texts contained lies and blasphemies against Christ and the church and thus served as a major hindrance to desired Jewish conversion to Christianity, Pfefferkorn's cause gained initial support from major faculties consulted and from the emperor, who eventually let the case be resolved and dismissed in secular and papal courts. The debate continued in public, however, and brought Jewish rights in general under consideration.

In this letter, Luther weighs in on the side of Reuchlin but for reasons that Reuchlin himself would not necessarily have recognized. Luther argues that it is a biblically based fact that the Jews will always be blasphemers of Christ, and any attempt to stop Jewish blasphemy (for example, by confiscating their books) actually constitutes working against the Bible and the will of God. Any conversion of Jews can only come from God and not from human effort. This letter is of significance because it demonstrates that "[n]ot the 'late' or the 'middle,' but even the 'youngest' Luther known to us believed that the Jews as Jews had no future."[3]

On the other hand, whether or not Luther knew that the Cologne debate potentially extended from the fate of Jewish books to Jewish lives, it is notable that Luther did take the side of the single man labeled in this major controversy as a "Jew-friend." In addition, he would later remember this debate well when he found himself a target of censorship.

Luther to George Spalatin
{Smith/Jacobs, 1:28–29}
{Jesus}

Peace be with you, Reverend Spalatin! Brother John Lang has just asked me what I think of the innocent and learned John Reuchlin and his prosecutors at Cologne, and whether he is in danger of heresy. You know that I greatly esteem and like the man, and perchance my judgment will be suspected, because, as I say, I am not free and neutral; nevertheless as you wish it I will give my opinion, namely that in all his writings there appears to me absolutely nothing dangerous.

I much wonder at the men of Cologne ferreting out such an obscure perplexity, worse tangled than the Gordian knot as they say, in a case as plain as day. Reuchlin himself has often protested his innocence, and solemnly asserts he is only proposing questions for debate, not laying down articles of faith, which alone, in my opinion, absolves him, so that had he the dregs of all known heresies in his memorial, I should believe him sound and pure of faith. For if such protests and expressions of opinion are not free from danger, we must needs fear that these inquisitors, who strain at gnats though they swallow camels, should at their own pleasure pronounce the orthodox heretics, no matter how much the accused protested their innocence.

What shall I say? That they are trying to cast out Beelzebub but not by the finger of God. I often regret and deplore that we Christians have begun to be wise abroad and fools at home. A hundred times worse blasphemies than this exist in the very streets of Jerusalem, and the high places are filled with spiritual idols. We ought to show our excessive zeal in removing these offenses which are our real, intestine enemies. Instead of which we abandon all that is really urgent and turn to foreign and external affairs, under the inspiration of the devil who intends that we should neglect our own business without helping that of others.

Pray can anything be imagined more foolish and imprudent than such zeal? Has unhappy Cologne no waste places nor turbulence in her own church, to which she could devote her knowledge, zeal and charity, that she must needs search out such cases as this in remote parts?

But what am I doing? My heart is fuller of these thoughts than my tongue can tell. I have come to the conclusion that the Jews will always curse and blaspheme God and his King Christ, as all the prophets have predicted. He who neither reads nor understands this, as yet knows no theology, in my opinion. And so I presume the men of Cologne cannot understand the Scripture, because it is necessary that such things take place to fulfill prophecy. If they are trying to stop the Jews blaspheming, they are working to prove the Bible and God liars.

But trust God to be true, even if a million men of Cologne sweat to make him false. Conversion of the Jews will be the work of God alone operating from within, and not of man working—or rather playing—from without. If these offenses be taken away, worse will follow. For they are thus given over by the wrath of God to reprobation, that they may become incorrigible, as Ecclesiastes says, for every one who is incorrigible is rendered worse rather than better by correction.

Farewell in the Lord; pardon my words, and pray the Lord for my sinning soul.

Your brother, Martin Luther.

Text #3

Lectures on Romans (1515–1516)

Language:	Latin
Critical Edition:	WA 56
English translation:	LW 25; LCC 15[1]

After lecturing through the Psalter, Luther turned next to Romans. The lectures, still in the style of Glosses and Scholia, were delivered from Spring 1515–Fall 1516 but were not published. Long thought to have been lost, Luther's original manuscript was rediscovered in the early twentieth century by Johannes Ficker, the editor of WA 56.

There is no question but that Luther regarded Romans as the single most important book in the Bible, and he vigorously encouraged other Christians to follow his judgment in this matter. In the *Preface to Romans*, which he composed for his German translation of the New Testament in 1522 (and only slightly revised subsequently), he states: "This epistle is really the chief part of the New Testament, and is truly the purest gospel. It is worthy not only that every Christian should know it word for word, by heart, but also that he should occupy himself with it every day, as the daily bread of the soul. We can never read it or ponder over it too much; for the more we deal with it, the more precious it becomes and the better it tastes."[2]

For our purposes it is crucial to note that Luther regarded Romans as the key for how to read the Old Testament properly: "Therefore it appears that [Paul] wanted in this one epistle to sum up briefly the whole Christian and evangelical doctrine, and to prepare an introduction to the entire Old Testament."[3] Behind this conviction stands Luther's own personal experience of being "born again" while studying and meditating on Romans, especially 1:16-17: "For I am not ashamed of the Gospel of Christ, for it is the power of God that saves everyone who believes in it, the Jews first and also the Greeks, since the righteousness that counts before God is revealed in it, which comes from faith in faith; as it is written: 'The righteous will live by his faith.'"[4]

Upon his discovery of forgiveness and justification as matters of grace and faith alone, God no longer appeared to him as a wrathful judge who measures people by their obedience to the law. Reinterpreting the meaning of righteousness and its source from the work of Christ as the fulfillment of the law, Luther had found a new—and in his view, the correct—way of reading Scripture. Looking back on this experience many years later, he would write about Rom. 1:16-17: "Thus that place in Paul was for me truly the gate to paradise."[5]

As most interpreters have recognized, Romans 9–11 plays a central role in Paul's epistle. In these chapters he meditates on the "mystery" of Israel according to the flesh and attempts to account for the conundrum of the Gentile world's receptivity to the gospel while Israel has overwhelmingly rejected it. At the end of this meditation he makes the claim that "all Israel will be saved" (Rom. 11:26). What exactly this means has been a bone of contention for Christian interpreters from the beginning, and remains so today. In his lectures on Romans 9–11, Luther admits to being puzzled by what Paul intends to say, but he nevertheless articulates a guarded optimism with respect to the future of the Jewish people, cautions against Christian maledictions directed toward the Jews, and speaks strongly against attempts to convert the Jews by force. Romans 11:25-26 would be a career-long "discomfort" for Luther, and what he writes here will not be his last word on the subject.

Romans 11:25-36 = Gloss
{LW 25:101–3}

11:25. *Lest you be wise in your own conceits*, by being proud and complacent over against them, *I want you to understand*, for this is necessary in order to curb pride, *this mystery*, this holy secret, *brethren: a hardening* {of unbelief}[6] *has come upon part of Israel*, the people of Israel, *until the full number of the Gentiles*, the completed predestination of the Gentiles, *come in*, into the church of God. 26. *And so all Israel*, all of Israel who are to be saved, *will be saved; as it is written*, Is. 59{:20–21}: *The Deliverer*, as He has done in the case of the rest of the firstfruits, *will come from Zion*, that is, Christ into the flesh, *and He will banish ungodliness from Jacob*, that is, the unbelief of the Jews. He will do this at the end of the world. 27. *And this will be my covenant with them*, namely, a new covenant in faith for both, *when I take away their sins*,[7] through the suffering of Christ; for in this way "He banishes ungodliness." 28. *As regards the Gospel*, because they do not receive what you have received, *they are enemies* of God and of the apostles, *for your sakes*, you Gentiles who have been taken up by God, that is, through you, because you have been accepted as friends; *but as regards election*, by which many of them have been chosen, *they are most dear*, "beloved," *for the sake of their forefathers*, from whom they have been born. 29. *For the gifts and the call of God are irrevocable*, that is, He does not revoke or change what He has predetermined to give and call. Therefore He will give, and He will call, and He will not be changed. 30. *For just as you*, Gentiles, *were once disobedient to God*, that is, you were blinded, while they were enlightened and obedient, *but now have received mercy*, so that you might have what they had, *because of*, that is, "through," or as a result of, not because of, *their disobedience*, 31. *So they have now been disobedient*, that is, they have become unbelieving (and the Word has been taken away from them) while you have become believers, *in order that by the mercy shown to you*, that is, in, or according to, the mercy you have received, *they also may receive mercy*, so that they might have what you now possess. 32. *For God has consigned*, that is, He has testified through His Word that all men are in disobedience, in sin, in unbelief. He has shown that all have been thus consigned and surrounded by sins, *all*, namely, the Jews now and the Gentiles previously (in the Greek it reads "all men"), *to disobedience*, that is, to sin, *that He may have mercy upon all*, that is, so that they might come to faith through His mercy. 33. *O the depths*,[8] the profundity, or the abyss, *of the riches and wisdom*, by which He dispenses all things and rules them, *and knowledge of God*, that is, of His understanding, because He knows, or sees, all things; *How unsearchable are His judgments*, because there is no way to render a judgment over the things which we see done by Him, *and how inscrutable*, that is, how unsearchable, *His ways!* that is, His works. 34. *For who has known*, 1 Cor. 2:11: "No one comprehends the thoughts of God except the Spirit of God," *the mind of the Lord*, that is, His thinking and ideas by learning from Him so that a person might know them, *or who has been His counselor*, by giving Him counsel, so that He might give counsel. 35. *Or who has given a gift to Him*, for He Himself first gives to all whatever they possess, *that He might be repaid* by Him? No one has first given to Him, and the reason is: 36. *For from Him and through Him and in Him* (in the Greek it reads "to Him") *are all things. To Him*, alone, *be glory forever. Amen.*

Romans 11:22, 25-29 = Scholia
{LW 25:428–32}

11:22. *Note then the kindness.* On the basis of this passage we teach that when we see the fall of Jews or heretics or others, we should consider not those who fell but the work of God in them, so we may learn to fear God by the example of the misery of others and in no way be proud. For this is the noble teaching of the apostle, who urges us to a consideration more of the one who works by his work than to a comparison of ourselves with others.

In opposition to this many people are proud with marvelous stupidity when they call the Jews dogs, evildoers, or whatever they like, while they too, and equally, do not realize who or what they are in the sight of God. Boldly they heap blasphemous insults upon them, when they ought to have compassion on them and fear the same punishments for themselves. Moreover, as if certain concerning themselves and the others, they rashly pronounce themselves blessed and the others cursed. Such today are the theologians of Cologne, who are so stupid in their zeal, that in their articles, or rather their inarticulate and inept writings, they say that the Jews are accursed.

Why? Because they have forgotten what is said in the following chapter: "Bless and do not curse" (Rom. 12:14), and in another place: "When reviled, we bless; when slandered, we try to conciliate" (1 Cor. 4:12-13). They wish to convert the Jews by force and curses, but God will resist them.

25. *I want you to understand.* On the basis of this text it is commonly accepted that the Jews at the end of the world will return to the faith, although the text is so obscure that unless one is willing to follow the authority of the fathers who explain the apostle in this way, no one would seem to be convinced of this purely on the basis of the text. But the Lord also agrees with this idea of the apostle in Luke 21{:23–24}, when He says: "For great distress shall be upon the earth, and wrath upon this people; and they will fall by the edge of the sword and be led captive among all nations; and Jerusalem will be trodden down by the Gentiles, until the times of the Gentiles are fulfilled," that is, as he says here: *until the full number of the Gentiles come in.* And Moses in Deut. 4{:30–31}, when he had prophesied that they must be led through all nations, followed by saying: "In the latter days you will return to the Lord your God and obey His voice, for the Lord your God is a merciful God." Likewise we read in Hos. 3{:4–5}: "For the children of Israel shall dwell many days without king or prince, without sacrifice or pillar, without ephod or teraphim. Afterward the children of Israel shall return and seek the Lord their God and David their king; and they shall come in fear to the Lord and to His goodness in the latter days." Again in Hos. 5{:12}: "I am like a moth to Ephraim, and like dry rot to the house of Judah." And again (5:15): "I will go and return to My place, until you are consumed and seek My face." Again, the Lord says in Matt. 23{:38–39}: "Behold, your house is forsaken and desolate. For I tell you, you will not see me again until you say, 'Blessed be he who comes in the name of the Lord.'" According to this interpretation, therefore, the meaning of the apostle is: "I want you to understand this mystery, brethren," that is, "Do not be proud; it is a holy secret why the Jews fell, a secret which no man knows, namely, that the Jews who are now fallen shall return and be saved, after the Gentiles according to the fullness of their election have entered. They will not remain outside forever, but will return in their own time."

A very clear figure of this is Joseph, the symbol of Christ, who was sold by his brothers into Egypt (Gen. 37:28) and there elevated to the position of a ruler and in the end recognized unexpectedly by his father and brothers, as Genesis so beautifully puts it near the end of the book. So also the Jews who threw Christ out to the Gentiles, where He now has the position of ruler, will finally come back to Him, drawn by hunger for the Word, and they will receive Him among the Gentiles.

The apostle indicates this when he cites Isaiah in connection with the statement: *And so all Israel will be saved* (v. 26). In our version Isaiah reads thus in chapter 59{:20}: "And there shall come a redeemer to Zion, and to them that return from iniquity in Jacob." But they will not return from iniquity unless they are in it, as the

Jews now are. For "impiety" or "iniquity," the Greek ἀσέβεια does not signify just any kind of sin, but a sin against the worship of God, that is, against faith, through one's own self-righteousness. In Hebrew this is called רֶשַׁע as in Eccl. 8{:8}: "God-lessness will not save the ungodly," that is, one's own righteousness (as he thinks) will not save a person, because it is not righteousness but ungodliness.

Furthermore, he adds the expression *when I take away their sins* (v. 27), which is not in Isaiah but is added by the apostle or brought in from other prophets. And this indicates the difference between the two testaments. For the former testament was one in which we increased sin. But the New Testament is the one under which God takes away sin. Therefore he is trying to say: "This is the testament of the remission of sin," in which "He will banish ungodliness from Jacob," just as the other is the testament of the commission of sin, under which men were turned to ungodliness. Therefore Christ has not yet come to the Jews, but He will come, namely, at the Last Day, as the writers cited above show. Thus it is necessary that we interpret the apostle as speaking of the mystical coming of Christ to the Jews. In other places this word of Isaiah is clearly fulfilled in the physical coming of Christ. Therefore I said that the apostle speaks in an unclear way and we could not determine his meaning from the text if we did not believe the interpretation of the fathers. Thus in our time "a partial blindness has befallen Israel," but in that future day not a part but all Israel shall be saved. Now only in part are they saved, but then all shall be.

Corollary

This term "mystery" is taken at this point in an absolute sense, indicating that which is unknown, but not in the ordinary sense in terms of the "figurative" or "literal" meaning, as when, for example, we speak of the "mystical sense," where there is one meaning on the surface and another in the depth. But this is a mystery in the absolute sense, because it is hidden to all, namely, that the fullness of the Gentiles is going to come in while certain Jews fall. He says the same thing elsewhere, as in Rom. 16{:25}: "According to the revelation of the mystery which was kept secret for long ages." And also in Col. 1{:26}.

For this entire text has the purpose of persuading his people to return. Therefore in order that the apostle may be understood correctly, we must understand that his remarks extend over the whole mass of the Jewish people and refers to the good among them, both past, present, and future. Although some among them are lost, yet the mass of them must be respected because of the elect. Just as any community must be honored because of the good citizens, even though they are less in number than the wicked ones. Hence this one rule applies regarding the interpretation of Scripture, namely, that it speaks at the same time about the good and the wicked who exist in the one mystical body—for thus the Jewish people are a "holy mass" because of the elect, but "broken branches" because of the lost; thus they are a "fulfilling" and a "lessening"; likewise they are "enemies because of the Gentiles" and at the same time "the well-beloved because of the fathers"—the Scripture speaking all the time about the same people because of the diversity found among them. This sounds as if the apostle wished the same people to be considered both his personal friends and personal enemies, while he still distinguishes between persons, but asserts that they belong to the same mass. Therefore he uses the term "mass," so that he may show that he is speaking not of individual people but of the entire race, in which are many unholy people.

28. *As regards the Gospel.* This term *enemies* in this passage is taken in the passive sense, that is, they are worthy of being hated, and God hates them, and for this reason so do the apostle and all who are of God. This is clearly indicated by the antithesis *but they are beloved,* as if to say, they are hated and yet loved, that is, the mass is loved and hated; hated "as regards the Gospel . . . for your sake," that is, because you have been loved according to the Gospel, and thus they are hated as regards the Gospel; but yet they are beloved *for the sake of their forefathers,* that is, because the election adopts some from among them to this very day; therefore they are beloved because of the forefathers, because they, too, are friends.

29. *For the gifts of God are irrevocable.* This is a remarkable statement. For the counsel of God is not changed by either the merits or demerits of anyone. For He does not repent of the gifts and calling which He has promised, because the Jews are now unworthy of them and you are worthy. He is not changed just because you are changed, and therefore they shall turn back and be led again to the truth of the faith. Hence in the Greek we read ἀμεταμέλητα, that is, "God's gifts are irreversible, etc." Hence it is not a matter of our repentence, but of God, who repents of what He changes and destroys.

Text #4

Lectures on Galatians (1519)

Language:	Latin
Critical Edition:	WA 2: (436), 445–618
English Translation:	LW 27: (ix), 151–409

Luther's third lectures on Bible focused on Galatians and were delivered from October 1516—March 1517, and then with significant revisions published in 1519. It is noteworthy that the Gloss/Scholia format is no longer in use. This is the epistle that Luther would later equate with his beloved wife: "The Epistle to the Galatians is my dear epistle. I have put my confidence in it. It is my Katy von Bora."[1]

Having just discovered in Paul's Romans what was for him an entirely new, faith-centered lens to the Scriptures, these first lectures on Galatians coincide with the most formative period in Luther's life, both theologically and spiritually. By the time the lectures were published, he had already launched his scripturally argued attack on his church's penitential practices (*95 Theses*, 1517) and had challenged the foundations of scholastic theology (*Disputation against Scholastic Theology*, 1517); in 1518 in Heidelberg he had the opportunity to explicate his groundbreaking, and troubling, theological insights to his Augustinian peers (*Heidelberg Disputation*).[2] Luther had found a new face of God in the Scriptures and had begun to see the futility of older constructions of faith and human-made requirements for grace. With Galatians he could explicate his exhilarating discoveries of Christian freedom, Christian knowledge of divine truths, and the overwhelming Christian message of salvation: a restored relationship with God, even to the point of oneness with God, because of Christ. Luther's opponents—be they scholastics, fellow monks, or Jews—were guilty of trusting in their own effort in respect to a gift that only God can choose to give. The freedom of the gospel over against servitude to the law was the theme that Luther would emphasize for the rest of his life, and this was why from his own perspective he was in perennial tension with Judaism.

Paul's allegory of Sarah and Hagar in Gal. 4:21-31 (the only passage in the entire New Testament that contains the term "allegory") has been one of the most influential texts in Christian history for the construal of the relationship, or rather the antithesis, between church and synagogue. Illustrative of this antithesis are the sharp dichotomies that Paul describes:

Abraham
Two Covenants

Isaac	Ishmael
Free	Slave
Sarah	Hagar
Promise	Flesh
Jerusalem Above	Sinai/Jerusalem
Promise-Children	Slave-Children
More	Less
Spirit	Flesh

Luther extends these dichotomies further:
Spirit/Flesh

Gospel	Law
Grace	Sin
Church	Synagogue
New	Old
Christian	Jew
Law of the Spirit	Law of the Letter
Pentecost	Sinai
Eternal	Temporal
Heavenly	Earthly

Characteristic of Luther's reading of Gal. 4:21-31 is his hostility toward Jewish "exclusivism," that is, the Jewish claim to be the chosen people of God. Luther emphasizes in contrast that the Jews are actually Ishmael while Christians are the true children of Abraham. The Synagogue is portrayed as devoid of grace, and Judaism is described as a purely carnal religion, that is, the diametric opposite of what Luther understands the gospel to be. The notion of Judaism as a purely carnal religion is a consistent teaching of Luther's from the beginning of his career until the end.

Galatians 4:21-31
{LW 27:309–324}

21. *Tell me, you who desire to be under the Law, have you not read the Law?. . .* 22. *For it is written that Abraham had two sons, one by a slave and one by a free woman.* 23. *But the son of the slave was born according to the flesh, the son of the free woman through promise.* 24. *Now this is an allegory.*

Not that these statements are to be understood allegorically in Genesis, but the apostle is indicating that what was said there in a literal sense is said by him by way of allegory.

The question arises in what way Ishmael was not also born through promise, since in Gen. 16 so many things are promised by the angel of the Lord to his mother concerning him before he was born. Again, in the seventeenth chapter, many more things are promised to Abraham by God Himself concerning him, now that he had been born. St. Jerome brings up many points and leaves the matter unsettled. It is clear, however, that Ishmael was conceived, not because of the promise of God but because of the command of Sarah, and because of the natural vigor in the young woman Hagar. But Isaac was conceived by a sterile and aged mother through the supernatural strength of Him who gave the promise. For what the angel said to Hagar—"Behold, you are with child and shall bear a son" (Gen. 16:11)—is certainly not the statement of one who is promising that a conception is to take place; it is the statement of one who is predicting what will happen with regard to him who has already been conceived, or even of one who is giving a command. Accordingly, Isaac is the son of the promise—born, however, of the flesh but not conceived by the power of the flesh or according to the flesh.

These women are two covenants. One is from Mt. Sinai, bearing children for slavery; she is Hagar.

Because the Galatians were believers, they could be instructed with allegorical teachings. Otherwise, as Paul says in 1 Cor. 14{:22}: *"Tongues are a sign for unbelievers."* But to unbelievers nothing can be proved by allegorical statements, as St. Augustine also points out in his letter to Vincentius. Or at least the case is this, that out of fatherly concern the apostle intentionally pictures his subject by means of comparisons and allegories for the Galatians, as for people who are rather weak, in order to fit the words to their power of comprehension. For people who are not very well instructed are fascinated (and with pleasure at that) by comparisons, parables, and allegories. For this reason Christ, too, as Matthew says (13:13), teaches by means of parables in the Gospel, so that everyone can understand Him. So let us see how Paul makes use of this allegorical teaching to oppose the righteousness of the Law.

"These," he says, "are two covenants." That is, the two women, Sarah and Hagar, were a figurative example of the two covenants under one and the same Abraham, who represents the heavenly Father.

. . .

{There now follows an extended discourse in which Luther critiques the traditional fourfold interpretive approach as inconsistent and unreliable. He cautions against approaches that obscure "the main and legitimate sense of the text" and sides with Augustine's fundamental distinction between Letter and Spirit. He quotes with approval the formula from Augustine's commentary on Ps. 71 that "the letter is the Law without grace."}

To return to the apostle. "One is from Mt. Sinai, bearing children for slavery." Enough has been said on what that slavery of the Law is into which we are delivered when we receive the Law without grace. For then we keep it either out of fear of threatened evil or out of hope of gain, that is, hypocritically. In both cases we act like slaves, not like free men. But he calls it a "covenant." Hence to understand this one must also see here the sign of the testament. First there is the testament itself, which was the naming of the Land of Promise, as is written in Ex. 3{:8}. The testator was an angel in the Person of God. The legacy that was bequeathed was the land of Canaan itself. The people for whom the testament was being made were the Children of Israel, as Exodus describes all these details. But this testament was confirmed by the death of an animal and by its blood, with which they were sprinkled, as one reads in Ex. 24{:8}, because a sacrifice of the flesh was appropriate for a fleshly promise, a fleshly testament, and fleshly heirs. "She is Hagar," he says; that is, this testament of slavery that gives birth to slaves is an allegorical Hagar, the slave woman.

25. *For Sinai is a mountain in Arabia which is connected with that which now is Jerusalem and is in slavery with her children.*

. . .

Now the allegorical interpretation of the names, according to Jerome. Sarah means "princess" or "lady." For this reason Sarah's sons, the sons of a lady, the sons of a princess, are rightly called the sons of a free woman, while, on the other hand, the sons of the handmaid are sons of a slave woman and of slavery. For the apostle also comes near to expressing Sarah's name when he calls her "free." In Scripture, you see, princes are also called נְדִיבוֹת, that is, free and willing. Hagar, on the other hand, means "journey abroad" or "foreigner," "resident," "sojourn"; and this is rightly contrasted with the citizens and members of God's household (Eph. 2:19). "You are not foreigners and guests," he says. It is as if he were saying: "You do not belong to Hagar; you belong to Sarah. You are not foreigners; you are sons of the free woman and lady." "The slave does not continue in the house forever; the son continues forever" (John 8:35). Now the righteousness of the Law is temporary; but the righteousness of Christ continues forever, because the one serves for pay in this life, while the other is a freely granted inheritance of the life to come. "Arabia" is the sunset or the evening, which verges toward the night, whereas in many passages the church and the Gospel are called the dawn and the morning. Thus the Law and the synagog finally fade away, but grace reigns and takes its ease in the noonday of eternity. What if the apostle is also designating Arabia as a desert? For "Arabia" has this significance too. In fact, in Holy Writ, Arabia is nearly always understood to refer to the Arabian Desert. For Arabia Felix is called by the name Saba, as well as by the names of other parts of it; Arabia Petraea is called Cedar, Amon, Moab, and by many names. Arabia, therefore, seems to be so called because it is a wasteland, in order to signify the sterile and barren synagog, or the righteousness of the Law in the sight of God. While the church, on the other hand, is fruitful in God's sight, even though it is a desert in the sight of men. According to St. Jerome, "Sinai" means "trial," that is, the unrest and the disturbance of peace that we have from the Law. For "through the Law comes knowledge of sin" (Rom. 3:20) and for this reason also the disturbing of one's conscience. "Jerusalem" means "vision of peace," namely, tranquillity of conscience; for through the Gospel we see in the church the remission of sins, which is peace of heart. "Ishmael" means "hearing of God" or "one who hears God," namely, the people who, coming before Christ, heard that He would come after them but did not see Him face to face and clearly. They heard the prophets and read Moses. Yet they did not know Christ as One who was present. They always had Him at their back; they always heard and never saw Him. This is the condition of everyone who wants to be justified on the basis of the Law. He hears of the righteousness of the Law and does not see that righteousness is in Christ. He looks at some things and hears other things; he looks at those things that are in front of him and at his own powers, not at the virtues of Christ. Nevertheless, he always hears himself being driven to righteousness through the Law, but he never comes to it. "Isaac" means laughter; for this is characteristic of grace, which, with its oil, makes glad the face of man (Ps. 104:15). Opposed to this is weeping. This is characteristic of guilt, which comes from the Law. Therefore each name, when compared with its opposites, shows in a beautiful way the difference between Law and Gospel, sin and grace, the synagog and the church, the flesh and the spirit, the old and the new.

26. *But the Jerusalem above is free, and she is the mother of us all.*

Paul would be saying: "The other testament is from the Jerusalem which is above." Meanwhile, however, by giving his attention to the other Jerusalem, he has changed the construction and has resorted to an anacoluthon. But he makes up for this with other words, because the other testament actually began in Jerusalem when the Holy Spirit was sent from heaven to Mt. Zion, as Is. 2{:3} says: "For out of Zion shall go forth the Law, and the Word of the Lord from Jerusalem." And in Ps. 110{:2} we read: "The Lord sends forth from Zion your mighty scepter." But because Jerusalem was indeed the earthly inheritance promised at Sinai by the earlier testament, whereas another inheritance is promised us in heaven—for this reason we also have another Jerusalem which is not adjacent to Mt. Sinai and is not close to or related, so to speak, to the slavery of the Law. But there is also this difference: The Law of the letter was given from Mt. Sinai to those to whom temporal blessings were promised; but the Law of the Spirit was given, not from Jerusalem but rather from heaven on the day of Pentecost. And to this Law heavenly blessings were promised. Consequently, just as Jerusalem is the mother and capital city of all those who, under the Sinaitic Law, are her children and her citizens, so the Jerusalem above is the mother of all those who are her children and her citizens under the Law of heavenly grace. For these taste the things that are above, not the things that are on the earth (Matt. 16:23), because they have the Spirit as a pledge and token of the promise, and as the first fruits of the future inheritance of the eternal city and the new Jerusalem.

27. *For it is written: Rejoice, O barren one that dost not bear; break forth and shout, thou who art not in travail; for the desolate hath more children than she who hath a husband.*

These words are written in Is. 54{:1}, and a strange antithesis and contradiction gives them the nature of a paradox. The barren and widowed rejoices in her many children, while, on the other hand, the one who is married and fertile is without children. Who will be able to understand this? Paul is being allegorical and is talking spiritually by taking a parable from physical generation, in which children are begotten by the man's insemination of the woman. That allegorical man who speaks of women as both married and widowed, as both barren and fruitful, is the Law. This, as St. Augustine says, is expressed more aptly in the Greek, where the Law is called νόμος in the masculine gender; just as it is also θάνατος of which the apostle likewise speaks in the masculine gender as the "last enemy" (1 Cor. 15:26). The Law, I say, the man of the synagog, or of any people whatever that is situated outside the grace of God, does indeed, though to his own grief, beget many children; but they are all sinners, because in their reliance on the wisdom of the Law and on righteousness by the works of the Law they glory in the Law, on the grounds that they have become such people as they are on the basis of the Law, and that in the whole outward appearance of their life they have become similar to their parent, that is, the Law. And yet inwardly, in spirit, they differ far from the pattern of the Law, since in fact by the Law sin rather increases, as I have said. The Law discloses sin but does not take it away, a point which Paul treats at greater length in Rom. 7{:5}: "While we were living in the flesh, our sinful passions, aroused by the Law, were at work in our members to bear fruit for death."

And so that allegorical man inseminates his wife; that is, he teaches the synagog things that are good. But the synagog, forsaken by the spirit of grace, gives birth only to sinners, who pretend to fulfill the Law but, on the other hand, are aroused all the more against the Law, just as in the desert the Jews were against Moses, who was a type of the Law and of this man. From this man the church or any people at all is released through grace, by which it dies to the Law in such a way that it no longer needs the Law with its urging and demanding but of its own accord and freely does everything that belongs to the Law as if there were no Law, because "the Law is not laid down for the just" (1 Tim. 1:9). Thus it comes about that she who was subject to the Law, like a wife fruitful with sinful offspring, is now widowed, without the Law, and forsaken and barren, but with a good and fortunate widowhood and barrenness; for thereby she becomes the wife of another man, namely, of grace, or of Christ. For grace takes the place of the Law, and Christ takes the place of Moses. Endowed by this husband with another kind of fruitfulness, she speaks the well-known word of Is. 49{:21–22}: *"Who has borne me these? I was bereaved and barren, exiled and put away, but who has brought up these? Behold, I was left alone; whence, then, have these come? Thus says the Lord God: 'Behold, I will lift up My hand to the nations and raise My signal to the peoples; and they shall bring your sons in their bosom, and your daughters shall be carried on their shoulders.'"* These things are said because the church's children are instructed, not by the teaching of the letter but by the touch of the Spirit of God, as John 6{:45} states: *"They shall all be taught by God."* For where the Spirit does not touch, there indeed the Law does the teaching; and people in great numbers bring forth issue, but only sinners, as I have said. And it is only the work of man that is carried on there. They produce the kind of people they themselves are, but neither kind is good. The good are produced without the Law, solely by the grace of the Spirit.

. . .

28. *Now we, brethren, like Isaac, are children of promise.*

Paul is applying the allegory. "We, like Isaac"; that is, we are children of the free woman and lady, just as Isaac was. And just as he, through the flesh, was a son, not of the flesh but of the promise, so we are too, because we were promised to Abraham in his offspring, as has been said at greater length above. The Jews, however, are like Ishmael, that is, children of the slave woman, not of the promise but of the flesh. So are all who trust in being justified on the basis of the Law and its works.

29. *But as at that time he who was born according to the flesh persecuted him who was born according to the Spirit, so it is now.*

Gen. 21 does not describe what that persecution was with which Ishmael persecuted Isaac, but one can learn what it was from the words of Sarah. When she saw the son of Hagar, the Egyptian woman, playing with her son Isaac, she said to Abraham: "Cast out this slave woman with her son, for the son of this slave woman shall not be heir with my son Isaac" (v. 10). It is as if she were saying: "I see that he wants to rely on the fact that he is an heir. He despises my son and forgets that he is the son of a slave woman." Moreover, it appears that this "playing" was of such a nature that Ishmael, puffed up by his primogeniture, vaunted it as he ridiculed and insulted Isaac, just as if Ishmael were Abraham's first son. But Sarah, seeing this, maintained the opposite: "The son of a slave woman, I say, will not be the heir." She called Ishmael a slave woman's son by way of derogation. And the Hebrew text supports this meaning. There we have: *"And when Sarah saw the son of Hagar, the Egyptian woman—the son whom she had borne to Abraham—laughing and playing"* (for "with her son" is added in our Latin version of the text). It is as if she were saying: "Hagar bore Ishmael to Abraham. This is why Ishmael was puffed up. This is why he was laughing and exulting in front of Isaac: On this account he, smug concerning the inheritance, was scorning Isaac, the true heir."

The symbolic meaning of the figure as Paul employs it is in harmony with this. For "so it is now," he says, "with Israel, who declare in their snobbery that they alone are the offspring of Abraham, that they alone are the heirs of the promise." But no one persecuted the true children of Abraham more cruelly than those very people, as we read in the Acts of the Apostles. For they are "Ishmael." They hear in the prophets that God will come after them; but when He is set before them, they do not recognize Him. In this they reflect the name, the sentiments, and the character of Ishmael, their father.

Finally, the word "playing" is the same as that from which the name Isaac is formed. This name is translated with "laughter" or "rejoicing," to signify perhaps that Ishmael was a facetious person and that with a sharp taunt he had given the name Isaac a turn which derided him who bore it, as if he considered him a truly laughable heir and a man of no account at all. For it is not for nothing that Scripture makes use of the word "playing" or "laughing" in this way and recounts that so saintly a woman was disturbed by it. The apostle, however, refers to this in order to strengthen the Galatians, lest they stop being men of Isaac's type on account of the persecution of those Ishmaelites, because it has to happen that way. But the result will be that the latter will be cast out, as now follows.

30. *But what does Scripture say? Cast out the slave and her son, for the son of the slave shall not inherit with the son of the free woman.*

Scripture speaks emphatically and says what is altogether contrary to the presumption of the slave woman and her son. "She is a slave woman," it says, "and presumes to be a lady. He is a slave woman's son; he laughs at the son of the lady and mocks him with ironic gibes. But God forbid! Let them rather be cast out." From this one understands again that the slave woman Hagar agreed to this or at least allowed her son Ishmael to laugh at Isaac, since she was hoping for the same thing her son was hoping for, namely, that she would become the lady of the house. Nor does Scripture say: "Cast out your son"; it says: "Cast out her son," asserting that Ishmael was the son of the slave woman, not the son of Abraham. "So it will be now too," says Paul. "The sons of the flesh are not heirs; the sons of the promise are. Accordingly, if you do not want to be cast out with the son of the slave woman, continue steadfastly as sons of the free woman. Scripture will not lie. Even against Abraham's will, yet on the authority of God, it declares that the son of the slave woman must be cast out."

31. *So, brethren, we are not children of the slave but of the free woman.*

Paul makes the application of the story and of the allegory and summarizes with a brief conclusion, which now is amply understood from what has already been said. For to be a son of the slave woman means to be a slave to the Law, to be under obligation to the Law, to be obliged to keep the Law, to be a sinner, a son of wrath, a son of death, alienated from Christ, cut off from grace, with no share in the future inheritance, devoid of the blessing of the promise, a son of the flesh, a hypocrite, a hired servant, to live in the spirit of slavery, in fear, and whatever else he has mentioned here and elsewhere. For the names of this evil are infinite.

. . .

Text #5

Second Psalms Lectures (1519–1521)

Language:	Latin
Critical Edition:	WA 5; AWA 2/2–(3) (Here WA 5:427,19–22; 428,27–429,18)
English Translation:	LW 14:279–349 = Psalms 1–2[1]

Having lectured through the Psalms, Romans, Galatians, and Hebrews in the years 1513–1518, Luther returned again to the Psalms in 1519–1521. The first 15 Psalms were published already by January 1520, but the lecture series would end with Psalm 22 because of Luther's summons to the Diet of Worms in March 1521.

These were decisive times for Luther and the evangelical Reformation. Having already been labeled a "heretic," Luther responded to the Papal Bulls of June 15, which he received on October 10, 1520, by publically burning the bull and other Catholic documents on December 10, 1520. He was then formally excommunicated on January 3, 1521. After appealing to the princes, Luther was summoned to the Diet of Worms on March 6, 1521 to appear before the freshly crowned (October 1520) Emperor Charles V. By then he had already written his programmatic Reformation treatises, *To the Christian Nobility of the German Nation* (August 1520), *The Babylonian Captivity of the Church* (October 1520) and *On Christian Freedom* (November 1520).[2] At Worms, after being questioned (April 17/18, 1521), he declared (May 4, 1521) himself "bound" to the Scriptures and his conscience and, after refusing to recant, he was outlawed by the Edict of Worms (May 8, 1521, with May 26 imperial signature). This placed him and his followers under the imperial ban. By that point, the Elector of Saxony, Frederick the Wise, had already arranged for Luther's "kidnapping," and he was spirited off to the safety of the remote Wartburg Castle in Eisenach, where he would stay from May 4, 1521—March 1, 1522, and, among numerous other writing projects, labor on his famous New Testament translation. Meanwhile, some of his reformation ideas were already being put in practice in Wittenberg by his colleagues and students.

The *Second Psalms Lectures* (*Operationes in Psalmos*) are fundamental for understanding the development that took place in Luther's biblical interpretation. Though he would continue to utilize allegorical readings throughout his career, in the *Operationes* he states definitively that Scripture has only one, literal, legitimate, proper, genuine, pure, simple, constant sense or meaning; any other interpretation that is added to the text must be clearly and directly consistent with the one proper mean-ing.[3] In striking contrast to the *First Psalms Lectures* (*Dictata super Psalterium*) the Jews are not nearly as omnipresent here, and the enemies of God tend to be identified with the godless in general rather than above all with the Jews (although the Jews are certainly included under this rubric). As a result, strictly anti-Jewish statements are much more occasional. A major exception is Luther's treatment of Ps. 18:40-51, which rises to the level of "a kind of brief treatise against the Jews."[4] On the other hand, his treatment of Ps. 14:7 (the relevant portions of which are translated below) is remarkable in its condemnation of the persecution of the Jews and signals as well a phase of optimism toward the Jews on his part which is also reflected in Texts #6 (*Magnificat*) and #7 (*That Jesus Christ Was Born a Jew*). In this regard, Luther's own status at this time as a "hunted man" is no doubt pertinent.

Psalm 14:7[5]

{WA 5:427,19–22; 428,27–429,18}

"Oh, that salvation for Israel would come from Zion. When the Lord reverses the captivity of his people, Jacob will rejoice and Israel will be glad."

The way I see it, based on the understanding of the illustrious fathers, the Jews are to be converted at the end . . .

(The psalmist) adds "out of Zion" to show that no other salvation is given to them or to anyone else except that which is in Christ, which was given in Zion and from there it spread to the whole world; and that therefore the Jews are to be converted to Christ, no matter how irrational they may be toward him now. *"For no 'word' is impossible with God"* [Luke 1:37]. Also Rom. 11[:23], *"God is able to graft them in again."* Therefore damnable is the rage of certain Christians (if they can be called Christians), who think that they can demonstrate their compliance to God by persecuting the Jews with extreme hatred, thinking the worst of them, and with extreme pride and contempt insulting them when they bemoan their misery. Whereas according to the example of this Psalm and of Paul in Rom. 9[:1], one ought with great compassion to be sad and ache for them and pray for them without ceasing. These (people) should certainly pay attention when they hear Paul say in Rom. 11[:18]: *"Do not boast against the branches. If you do boast, it is not you that support the root, but the root that supports you."* And further, [Rom. 11:20]: *"Do not think highly of yourself, rather be afraid."* But these godless people, Christians in name only, cause great harm both to the Christian name and to the Christian people with their tyrannical acts, through which they participate in the ungodliness of the Jews, whom they, by their example of cruelty, drive away from Christianity. What they should be doing instead is attracting them with all kindness, patience, prayers, and care. Supported by the rage of such people, certain extremely tasteless theologians maintain and babble with nauseating pride that the Jews are servants of the Christians and subjects of the Emperor, although they are about as truly Christian as there is truly a Roman Emperor today.[6]

Who, I ask, would come over to our religion, be they of such good-natured or patient disposition, if they see themselves dealt with by us in such a cruel and hostile and not only un-Christian but deadly manner? If hatred of Jews, heretics, and Turks makes Christians, then we raging ones are the most Christian of all. But if the love of Christ makes Christians, then we are without doubt worse than the Jews, heretics, and Turks, for no one loves Christ less than we do. Their irrationality is like that of those fools and children who poke out the eyes of Jews painted on walls, as if they wanted to come to the aid of the suffering Christ. Most of those who mourn the passion of Christ accomplish nothing more than to exaggerate the defiance of Jews against Christ and provoke the hearts of the faithful against them, while the gospel [by contrast] works such that it entrusts to us the love of God and of Christ in this matter utterly and completely; about this those (people) remember not a single word.

Text #6

Magnificat (1521)

Language: German

Critical Edition: WA 7: (538), 544–604

English Translation: LW 21: (xvii), 295–358

Luther's treatise on Mary's "Magnificat" (Luke 1:46-55) was begun in early 1521, but the writing was delayed by his summons to Worms. He completed the work while in hiding on the Wartburg in June 1521, and it was in print by August/ September 1521. The work was quite popular, and it circulated in several editions and translations.

The final portion of the treatise, Luther's treatment of Luke 1:54-55, contains in a nutshell numerous fundamentals in his understanding of the natural seed of Abraham, that is, the Jews, and the proper Christian attitude toward them. The Magnificat is the song of the mother of God, the one who is experiencing in her own body the long-awaited fulfillment of the promise of the Seed, first uttered in Gen. 3:15, and then further clarified in Gen. 12:3 and 22:18. Mary is the Woman spoken of in Gen. 3:15, and her son, to be born outside of the normal physical process, is the Promised Seed. Mary, the virgin mother, is indispensable for Luther's understanding of the gospel. All humanity, by virtue of natural physical conception and birth, is under a curse and condemned. Only one who does not share that curse can redeem humanity from it. This promise of the Seed and belief in it constitute the common faith of both Old and New Testaments; for Luther, Old Testament faith and New Testament faith are fundamentally the same. The natural seed of Abraham, that is, the Jews, were God's chosen vessel to bear this promise. Although natural Israel failed miserably in its mission and the majority have become hardened, only the Jews, and not the Gentiles, have the promise that there will always be Christians, however few, among them. For this reason, Christians should treat Jews in a friendly manner. If Jews reject the gospel, Christians should leave them alone. In all of this, the treatise moves very much in the direction of *That Jesus Christ Was Born a Jew*.[1]

Because of the gravity of the accusations against him, this could quite easily have been Luther's final work. Had that been the case, his words here on the need to treat the Jews in a kindly manner as well as his opposition to forced conversations would have left a significantly different legacy on the question of the relationship between Jews and Christians.

The Magnificat
{LW 21:297, 349–355}
Translated and Expounded by Dr. Martin Luther, Augustinian
Jesus
To his Serene Highness, Prince John Frederick, Duke of Saxony, Landgrave of Thuringia, Margrave of Meissen, my Gracious Lord and Patron
. . .

{*Luke 1:*}*54. He has helped His servant Israel in remembrance of His mercy.*
After enumerating the works of God in her and in all men, Mary returns to the beginning and to the chief thing. She concludes the Magnificat by mentioning the very greatest of all God's works—the Incarnation of the Son of God. She freely acknowledges herself as the handmaiden and servant of all the world, confessing that this work which was performed in her was not done for her sake alone, but for the sake of all Israel. But she divides Israel into two parts and refers only to that part that is God's servant . . .

Now, the Israel that is God's servant is the one whom the Incarnation of Christ benefits. That is His own beloved people, for whose sake He also became man, to redeem them from the power of the devil, of sin, death, and hell, and to lead them to righteousness, eternal life, and salvation. That is the help of which Mary sings. As Paul says in Titus 2{:14}: "Christ gave Himself for us, to purify for Himself a people of His own"; and St. Peter in 1 Peter 2{:9}: "You are a holy nation, a chosen people, a royal priesthood." These are the riches of the boundless mercy of God, which we have received by no merit but by pure grace. Therefore she sings: "He has remembered His mercy." She does not say: "He has remembered our merit and worthiness." We were in need, to be sure, but completely unworthy. That is the basis of His praise and glory, while our boasting aud presumption must keep quiet. There was nothing for Him to regard that could move Him except His mercy, and this name He desired to make known. But why does she say, "He remembered" rather than "He regarded"? Because He had promised this mercy, as the following verse shows. Now, He had waited a long time before showing it, until it seemed as though He had forgotten—even as all His works seem as though He were forgetting us—but when He came, it was seen that He had not forgotten but had continually had in mind to fulfill His promise.

It is true that the word "Israel" means the Jews alone and not us Gentiles. But because they would not have Him, He chose certain out of their number and thus satisfied the name Israel and made of it henceforth a spiritual Israel. This was shown in Genesis 32{:24–28}, when the holy patriarch Jacob wrestled with the angel, who strained the hollow of his thigh out of joint, to show that his children should henceforth not boast of their fleshly birth, as the Jews do. Therefore he also received a new name, that he should henceforth be called Israel, as a patriarch who was not only Jacob, the father of fleshly children, but Israel, the father of spiritual children. With this the word "Israel" agrees, for it means "a prince with God." That is a most high and holy name and contains in itself the great miracle that, by the grace of God, a man prevailed, as it were, with God, so that God does what man desires. We see the same thing in the case of Christendom. Through Christ she is joined to God as a bride to her bridegroom, so that the bride has a right to, and power over, her Bridegroom's body and all His possessions; all of this happens through faith. By faith man does what God wills; God in turn does what man wills. Thus Israel means a godlike, God-conquering man, who is a lord in God, with God, and through God, able to do all things.

That is the meaning of Israel. For שׂר means a lord, a prince; אל means God. Put them together, and they become יִשְׂרָאֵל according to the Hebrew fashion. Such an Israel God would have. Therefore, when Jacob had wrestled with the angel and prevailed, He said to him (Gen. 32:28): "Your name shall be called Israel; for since you have power with God, you shall also have power with men." There would be much more to say on this subject, for Israel is a strange and profound mystery.

55. As He spoke to our fathers, to Abraham, and to his seed forever.

Here all merit and presumption are brought low, and God's grace and mercy alone are exalted. For God has not helped Israel on account of their merits, but on account of His own promise. In pure grace He made the promise, in pure grace He also fulfilled it. Wherefore St. Paul says in Galatians 3{:17} that God gave the promise to Abraham four hundred years before He gave the Law to Moses, that no one might glory, saying he had merited and obtained such grace and promise through the Law or the works of the Law. This same promise the Mother of God here lauds and exalts above all else, ascribing this work of the Incarnation of God solely to the undeserved promise of divine grace, made to Abraham.

The promise of God to Abraham is recorded especially in Genesis 12{:3} and Genesis 22{:18}, and is referred to in many other places besides. It runs thus: "By Myself I have sworn: in your Seed shall all families or nations of the earth be blessed." These words are highly esteemed by St. Paul (Gal. 3:16) and by all the prophets, and well might they be. For in these words Abraham and all his descendants were preserved and saved, and in them we, too, must all be saved; for here Christ is contained and promised as the Savior of the whole world. This is Abraham's bosom (Luke 16:22), in which were kept all who were saved before Christ's birth; without these words no one was saved, even though he had performed all good works. Let us examine them more fully.

In the first place, it follows from these words of God that without Christ all the world is in sin and under condemnation, and is accursed with all its doing and knowing. For if He says that not some but all nations shall be blessed in Abraham's Seed, then without Abraham's Seed no nation shall be blessed. What need was there for God to promise so solemnly and with so mighty an oath, that He would bless them, if they were already blessed and not rather cursed? From this saying the prophets drew many inferences; namely, that all men are evil, liars all, false and blind, in short, without God, so that in the Scriptural usage to be called a man is no great honor, since in God's sight the name "man" is no better than the name "liar" or "faithless" in the eyes of the world. So completely is man corrupted through Adam's fall that the curse is innate with him and become, as it were, his nature and being.

It follows, in the second place, that this Seed of Abraham could not be born in the common course of nature, of a man and a woman; for such a birth is cursed and results in nothing but accursed seed, as we have just said. Now, if all the world was to be redeemed from the curse by this Seed of Abraham and thereby blessed, as the word and oath of God declare, the Seed itself had to be blessed first, neither touched nor tainted by that curse, but pure blessing, full of grace and truth (John 1:14). Again, if God, who cannot lie, declared with an oath that it should be Abraham's natural seed, that is, a natural and genuine child, born of his flesh and blood, then this Seed had to be a true, natural man, of the flesh and blood of Abraham. Here, then, we have a contradiction—the natural flesh and blood of Abraham, and yet not born in the course of nature, of man and wife. Therefore He uses the word "your seed," not "your child," to make it very clear and certain that it should be his natural flesh and blood, such as seed is. For a child need not be one's natural child, as everyone knows. Now, who will find the means to establish God's word and oath, where such contradictory things lie side by side?

God Himself has done this thing. He is able to keep what He has promised, even though no one may understand it before it come to pass; for His word and work do not demand the proof of reason, but a free and pure faith. Behold, how He combined the two. He raises up seed for Abraham, the natural son of one of his daughters, a pure virgin, Mary, through the Holy Spirit, and without her knowing a man. Here there was no natural conception with its curse, nor could it touch this seed; and yet it is the natural seed of Abraham, as truly as any of the other children of Abraham. That is the blessed Seed of Abraham, in whom all the world is set free from its curse. For whoever believes in this Seed, calls upon Him, confesses Him, and abides in Him, to him all his curse is forgiven and all blessing given, as the word and oath of God declare—"In your Seed shall all the nations of the earth be blessed." That is to say: "Whatever is to be blessed must and shall be blessed through this Seed, and in no other way." This is Abraham's Seed, begotten by none of his sons, as the Jews always confidently expected, but born of this one daughter of his, Mary, alone.

That is what the tender mother of this Seed means here by saying: "He has helped His servant Israel, as He promised to Abraham and to all his seed." She found the promise fulfilled in herself; hence she says: "It is now fulfilled; He has brought help and kept His word, solely in remembrance of His mercy." Here we have the foundation of the Gospel and see why all its teaching and preaching drive men to faith in Christ and into Abraham's bosom. For where there is not this faith, no other way can be devised and no help given to lay hold of this blessed Seed. And indeed, the whole Bible depends on this oath of God, for in the Bible everything has to do with Christ. Furthermore, we see that all the fathers in the Old Testament, together with all the holy prophets, had the same faith and Gospel as we have, as St. Paul says in 1 Corinthians 10{:1–4}; for they all remained with a strong faith in this oath of God and in Abraham's bosom and were preserved in it. The sole difference is, they believed in the coming and promised Seed; we believe in the Seed that has come and has been given. But it is all the one truth of the promise, and hence also one faith, one Spirit, one Christ, one Lord (Eph. 4:5), now as then, and forever, as Paul says in Hebrews 13{:8}.

But the subsequent giving of the Law to the Jews is not on a par with this promise. The Law was given in order that by its light they might the better come to know their cursed state and the more fervently and heartily desire the promised Seed; in this they had an advantage over all the heathen world. But they turned this advantage into a disadvantage; they undertook to keep the Law by their own strength, and failed to learn from it their needy and cursed state. Thus they shut the door upon themselves, so that the Seed was compelled to pass them by. They still continue in this state, but God grant not for long. Amen. This was the cause of the quarrel all the prophets had with them. For the prophets well understood the purpose of the Law, namely, that men should thereby know their accursed nature and learn to call upon Christ. Hence they condemned all the good works and everything in the life of the Jews that did not agree with this purpose. Therefore the Jews became angry with them and put them to death as men who condemned the service of God, good works, and godly living; even as the hypocrites and graceless saints ever do, of which we might say a great deal.

When Mary says, "His seed forever," we are to understand "forever" to mean that such grace is to continue to Abraham's seed (that is, the Jews) from that time forth, throughout all time, down to the Last Day. Although the vast majority of them are hardened, yet there are always some, however few, that are converted to Christ and believe in Him. For this promise of God does not lie: the promise was made to Abraham and to his seed, not for one year or for a thousand years, but "for the ages," that is, from one generation to another, without end. We ought, therefore, not to treat the Jews in so unkindly a spirit, for there are future Christians among them, and they are turning every day. Moreover, they alone, and not we Gentiles, have this promise, that there shall always be Christians among Abraham's seed, who acknowledge the blessed Seed, who knows how or when? As for our cause, it rests upon pure grace, without a promise of God. If we lived Christian lives, and led them with kindness to Christ, there would be the proper response. Who would desire to become a Christian when he sees Christians dealing with men in so unchristian a spirit? Not so, my dear Christians. Tell them the truth in all kindness; if they will not receive it, let them go. How many Christians are there who despise Christ, do not hear His Word, and are worse than Jews or heathen! Yet we leave them in peace and even fall down at their feet and well nigh adore them as gods. Let this suffice for the present. We pray God to give us a right understanding of this Magnificat, an understanding that consists not merely in brilliant words but in glowing life in body and soul. May Christ grant us this through the intercession and for the sake of His dear Mother Mary! Amen.

Text #7

That Jesus Christ Was Born a Jew (1523)

Language: German

Critical Edition: WA 11: (307–) 314–336

English Translation: LW 45: (195), 199–229

This treatise was one of the most popular and successful things that Luther ever wrote.[1] After first defending himself against charges made at the Diet of Nuremberg (1522) to the effect that he denied the virginity of Mary—and thus by implication the divinity of Christ, which would have made him a heretic against the decisions of the early councils he so revered—the treatise evolves into a kind of manual on how to deal with the Jews in hopes of converting them. Luther's proposed strategy regarding Jewish conversion involves a two-step process: (1) treat them kindly; (2) teach them how to interpret Scripture (that is, the Old Testament) properly. This strategy is at the same time a frontal assault on the papal church and its reliance on baptism of Jews, often coerced, and on its failure properly to catechize Jewish converts.

Luther's interest is in a genuine/sincere/internal Jewish conversion to the gospel, and for him the most promising approach is to unfold the Christ promised already in the Old Testament, which involved proving the virginity of Mary. Thus the initial task is to convince Jewish readers of the biblical arguments for Jesus as Messiah. Only after this "milk" has been given to them to drink can the larger issue of Christ's divinity be introduced. Especially noteworthy is the lack of any reference to Jewish hardening or stubbornness. The Jews are portrayed rather as victims of dehumanizing treatment and failed catechesis at the hands of Christians, who are not exactly distinguishing themselves with their actions or their lack of proper understanding of Christian faith. The empathetic tone that Luther strikes here was misunderstood already by his contemporaries, who quickly labeled him a "Jew friend." Luther did not want that label any more than the accusation of being a heretic who denied Mary's virginity. In his later vehement anti-Jewish writings, Luther would repeatedly accuse the Jews of misusing his intentions in this treatise.

One of the many ironies of this treatise is that, although Lutherans have often pointed to it as the *exemplum* of how open the younger Luther was to the Jews, it is throughout a sustained critique of Jewish exegesis of Christian proof texts, and it is these very same proof texts that he will draw on in his later bitter anti-Jewish diatribes. That the distance between his arguments in this treatise and those later bitter writings is not large is signaled here by Luther himself when he states that he has more rhetorical ammunition at his disposal, and he is fully prepared to utilize it later on if he needs to.

The treatise falls into two parts, each of which is structured around proof texts:

Part I. Jesus was a born Jew, of the Virgin Mary (Four Proof Texts)

Gen. 3:15	The Seed of the Woman
Gen. 22:18	The Seed of Abraham
2 Sam. 7:12-14	The Seed of David
Isa. 7:14	The Virgin

Part II versus Jewish Messianic Expectation (Two [Four] Proof Texts)

Gen. 49:10-12	*Shiloh*
Dan. 9:24-27	The coming of Jesus coincides with Daniel's 490 years
(Hag. 2:9)	
(Zech. 8:23)	

The selections below deal with treatment of the Jews and with Luther's take on the *Shiloh* passage in Gen. 49:10-11, where he develops at length his "1,500-year argument" against the Jews. This argument—well known to medieval anti-Jewish polemicists—will be the most consistent, and the most persistent, that Luther will utilize in his attacks on the Jews.

That Jesus Christ Was Born a Jew
{LW 45:199–201}

A new lie about me is being circulated. I am supposed to have preached and written that Mary, the mother of God, was not a virgin either before or after the birth of Christ, but that she conceived Christ through Joseph, and had more children after that. Above and beyond all this, I am supposed to have preached a new heresy, namely, that Christ was [through Joseph] the seed of Abraham. How these lies tickle my good friends, the papists! Indeed, because they condemn the gospel it serves them right that they should have to satisfy and feed their heart's delight and joy with lies. I would venture to wager my neck that none of those very liars who allege such great things in honor of the mother of God believes in his heart a single one of these articles. Yet with their lies they pretend that they are greatly concerned about the Christian faith.

But after all, it is such a poor miserable lie that I despise it and would rather not reply to it. In these past three years I have grown quite accustomed to hearing lies, even from our nearest neighbors. And they in turn have grown accustomed to the noble virtue of neither blushing nor feeling ashamed when they are publicly convicted of lying. They let themselves be chided as liars, yet continue their lying. Still they are the best Christians, striving with all that they have and are to devour the Turk and to extirpate all heresy.

Since for the sake of others, however, I am compelled to answer these lies, I thought I would also write something useful in addition, so that I do not vainly steal the reader's time with such dirty rotten business. Therefore, I will cite from Scripture the reasons that move me to believe that Christ was a Jew born of a virgin, that I might perhaps also win some Jews to the Christian faith. Our fools, the popes, bishops, sophists, and monks—the crude asses' heads—have hitherto so treated the Jews that anyone who wished to be a good Christian would almost have had to become a Jew. If I had been a Jew and had seen such dolts and blockheads govern and teach the Christian faith, I would sooner have become a hog than a Christian.

They have dealt with the Jews as if they were dogs rather than human beings; they have done little else than deride them and seize their property. When they baptize them they show them nothing of Christian doctrine or life, but only subject them to popishness and monkery. When the Jews then see that Judaism has such strong support in Scripture, and that Christianity has become a mere babble without reliance on Scripture, how can they possibly compose themselves and become right good Christians? I have myself heard from pious baptized Jews that if they had not in our day heard the gospel they would have remained Jews under the cloak of Christianity for the rest of their days. For they acknowledge that they have never yet heard anything about Christ from those who baptized and taught them.

I hope that if one deals in a kindly way with the Jews and instructs them carefully from Holy Scripture, many of them will become genuine Christians and turn again to the faith of their fathers, the prophets and patriarchs. They will only be frightened further away from it if their Judaism is so utterly rejected that nothing is allowed to remain, and they are treated only with arrogance and scorn. If the apostles, who also were Jews, had dealt with us Gentiles as we Gentiles deal with the Jews, there would never have been a Christian among the Gentiles. Since they dealt with us Gentiles in such brotherly fashion, we in our turn ought to treat the Jews in a brotherly manner in order that we might convert some of them. For even we ourselves are not yet all very far along, not to speak of having arrived.

When we are inclined to boast of our position we should remember that we are but Gentiles, while the Jews are of the lineage of Christ. We are aliens and in-laws; they are blood relatives, cousins, and brothers of our Lord. Therefore, if one is to boast of flesh and blood, the Jews are actually nearer to Christ than we are, as St. Paul says in Romans 9[:5]. God has also demonstrated this by his acts, for to no nation among the Gentiles has he granted so high an honor as he has to the Jews. For from among the Gentiles there have been raised up no patriarchs, no apostles, no prophets, indeed, very few genuine Christians either. And although the gospel has been proclaimed to all the world, yet He committed the Holy Scriptures, that is, the law and the prophets, to no nation except the Jews, as Paul says in Romans 3[:2] and Psalm 147[:19-20], "He declares his word to Jacob, his statutes and ordinances to Israel. He has not dealt thus with any other nation; nor revealed his ordinances to them."

Accordingly, I beg my dear papists, should they be growing weary of denouncing me as a heretic, to seize the opportunity of denouncing me as a Jew. Perhaps I may yet turn out to be also a Turk, or whatever else my fine gentlemen may wish.

. . .

{LW 45:213–216}

{Having marched through four proof texts that establish Jesus as the son of the Jewish Virgin Mary, he now turns to two proof texts which establish Jesus as the promised Messiah. Presented here are excerpts from the first text, the Shiloh passage in Gen. 49:10-11. Luther develops here his "1,500-year argument" which over the course of his career he will never tire of using against the Jews; indeed he regards it as the most full-proof argument Christians have against the Jews. This entire section is under the rubric of how to convert the Jews.}

This is enough for the present to have sufficiently proved that Mary was a pure maiden, and that Christ was a genuine Jew of Abraham's seed. Although more Scripture passages might be cited, these are the clearest. Moreover, if anyone does not believe a clear saying of His Divine Majesty, it is reasonable to assume that he would not believe either any other more obscure passages. So certainly no one can doubt that it is possible for God to cause a maiden to be with child apart from a man, since he has also created all things from nothing. Therefore, the Jews have no ground for denying this, for they acknowledge God's omnipotence, and they have here the clear testimony of the prophet Isaiah.

While we are on the subject, however, we wish not only to answer the futile liars who publicly malign me in these matters but we would also like to do a service to the Jews on the chance that we might bring some of them back to their own true faith, the one which their fathers held. To this end we will deal with them further, and suggest for the benefit of those who want to work with them a method and some passages from Scripture which they should employ in dealing with them. For many, even of the sophists, have also attempted this; but insofar as they have set about it in their own name, nothing has come of it. For they were trying to cast out the devil by means of the devil, and not by the finger of God [Luke 11:17–20].

In the first place, that the current belief of the Jews and their waiting upon the coming of the Messiah is erroneous is proved by the passage in Genesis 49[:10–12] where the holy patriarch Jacob says: "The scepter shall not depart from Judah, nor a teacher from those at his feet, until the *Shiloh* comes; and to him shall be the gathering of the nations. He will bind his foal to the vine, and his ass to the choice vine. He will wash his garments with wine, and his mantle with the blood of grapes. His eyes are redder than wine, and his teeth whiter than milk." This passage is a divine promise, which cannot lie and must be fulfilled unless heaven and earth were first to pass away. So the Jews cannot deny that for nearly fifteen hundred years now, since the fall of Jerusalem, they have had no scepter, that is, neither kingdom nor king. Therefore, the *Shiloh*, or Messiah, must have come before this fifteen hundred year period, and before the destruction of Jerusalem.

If they try to say that the scepter was also taken away from Judah at the time of the Babylonian captivity, when the Jews were transported to Babylon and remained captive for seventy years, and yet the Messiah did not come at that time, the answer is that this is not true. For during the whole period of captivity the royal line continued in the person of King Jechoniah, thereafter Zerubbabel and other princes in turn until Herod became king. For "scepter" signifies not only a kingdom, but also a hegemony, as the Jews are well aware. Furthermore, they still always had prophets. So the kingdom or hegemony never did disappear, even though for a time it existed outside of its territorial boundaries. Also, never during the captivity were all the inhabitants driven out of the land, as has happened during these past fifteen hundred years when the Jews have had neither princes nor prophets.

It was for this reason that God provided them at that time with the prophets Jeremiah, Ezekiel, Haggai, and Zechariah, who proclaimed to them that they would again be freed from Babylon, in order that they would not think that this word of Jacob was false, or that the Messiah had come. But for these last fifteen hundred years they have had no prophet to proclaim that they should again be free. God would not have permitted this state of affairs to continue for such a long time, since he did not on that occasion permit it for such a short time. He thereby gives ample indication that this prophecy [Gen. 49:10-12] must have been fulfilled.

In addition, when Jacob says here that the scepter shall endure until the Messiah comes, it clearly follows that this scepter not only must not perish but also that it must become far more glorious than it ever was previously, before the Messiah's coming. For all the Jews know full well that the Messiah's kingdom will be the greatest and most glorious that has ever been on earth, as we read in Psalms 2, 72, and 89. For the promise is also made to David that his throne shall endure forever [Ps. 89:4, 29, 36–37]. Now the Jews will have to admit that today their scepter has now been nonexistent for fifteen hundred years, not to speak of its having become more glorious.

This prophecy can therefore be understood to refer to none other than Jesus Christ our Lord, who is of the tribe of Judah and of the royal lineage of David. He came when the scepter had fallen to Herod, the alien; He has been king these fifteen hundred years, and will remain king on into eternity. For his kingdom has spread to the ends of the earth, as the prophets foretold [Ps. 2:8; 72:8-11]; and the nations have been gathered to him, as Jacob says here [Gen. 49:10]. And there could not possibly be a greater king on earth, whose name would be exalted among more nations, than this Jesus Christ.

It is true that some Jews do indeed feel how persuasive and conclusive this passage really is. This is why they hunt up all sorts of weird ways of getting around it. But if you will notice, they only ensnare themselves. For example, they say that in this instance *shiloh* does not signify the Messiah or Christ, and that therefore this passage does not carry any weight with them. It matters not whether he is called Messiah or *shiloh*; we are concerned not with the name, but with the person, with the fact that he shall appear when the scepter is taken away from Judah. No such person can be found except Jesus Christ; otherwise, the passage is false. He will be no mere cobbler or tailor, but a lord to whom the nations will be gathered; that is, his kingdom will be more glorious than the scepter ever was before, as has been said.
. . .

{LW 45:219–221}
{Still treating Gen. 49:10-11: the coincidence of the coming of Jesus and the demise of the kingdom of Israel}

Thus, the kingdom of our Lord Jesus Christ squares perfectly with this prophecy. For there was a hegemony among the Jews until he came. After his coming, however, it was destroyed, and at the same time he began the eternal kingdom in which he still reigns forever. That he was of the tribe of Judah is unquestionable. Because as regards his person he was to be an eternal king, it could not be that he should govern in a temporal and secular sense, because what is temporal will pass away. Conversely, because he had to be David's natural seed, it could not be otherwise than that he should be a natural, mortal, temporal, perishable man.

Now to be temporal and to reign eternally are two mutually contradictory concepts. Therefore, it had to turn out that he died temporally and departed this life, and again that he arose from the dead and became alive in order that he might become an eternal king. For he had to be alive if he were to reign, because one who is dead cannot reign; and he had to die too if he were to shift from this mortal life, into which he necessarily had to enter to fulfill the Scripture which promised he would be the natural blood of David and Abraham.

So now he lives and reigns, and holds the exalted office of binding his foal to the vine and washing his garments in the red wine; that is, he governs our consciences with the holy gospel, which is a most gracious preachment of God's loving-kindness the forgiveness of sins, and redemption from death and hell, by which all who from the heart believe it will be comforted, joyous, and, as it were, drowned in God with the overwhelming comfort of his mercy. The Jews, however, will not listen to this interpretation until they first accept and acknowledge the fact that Christ must have come in accordance with this prophecy. Therefore, we will let the matter rest until its own good time.

On the basis and testimony of this passage [Gen. 49:10-12], another sensible argument is also to be proved, namely, that this *shiloh* must have come at the time our Jesus Christ came, and that he can be none other than that selfsame Jesus. The prophecy says that nations shall be gathered to or be subject to this *shiloh*. Now I ask the Jews: When was there ever such a man of Jewish ancestry to whom so many nations were subject as this Jesus Christ? David was a great king, and so was Solomon; but their kingdom never extended beyond a small portion of the land of Syria. This Jesus, on the contrary, is accepted as a lord and king throughout the world, so that one may consider as fulfilled in him the prophecy from the second Psalm, where God says to the Messiah, "I will give you the Gentiles for your possession, and the uttermost parts of the earth for your inheritance." This had indeed come true in the person of our Jesus since the time when the scepter was taken from the Jews; this is quite apparent and has never yet happened in the case of any other Jew. Because *shiloh* was to come when Judah's scepter was ended, and since that time no other has fulfilled these prophecies, this Jesus must certainly be the real *shiloh* whom Jacob intended.

The Jews will have to admit further that the Gentiles have never once yielded themselves so willingly to a Jew for their lord and king, as to this Jesus. For although Joseph was certainly a great man in Egypt, he was neither its lord nor its king. And even if he had been, Egypt was a mighty small thing compared to this kingdom which everybody ascribes to this Jesus.

Again, neither in Babylon nor in Persia was either Daniel or Mordecai a king, although they were men of power in the government.

It is amazing that the Jews are not moved to believe in this Jesus, their own flesh and blood, with whom the prophecies of Scripture actually square so powerfully and exactly, when they see that we Gentiles cling to him so hard and fast and in such numbers that many thousands have shed their blood for his sake. They know perfectly well that the Gentiles have always shown greater hostility toward the Jews than toward any other nation, and have been unwilling to tolerate their dominion, laws, or government. How is it then that the Gentiles should now so reverse themselves as to willingly and steadfastly surrender themselves to this Jew, and with heart and soul confess him king of kings and lord of lords, unless it be that here is the true Messiah, to whom God by a great miracle has made the Gentiles friendly and submissive in accordance with this and numerous other prophecies?

. . .

{LW 45:229}

{Conclusion}

If the Jews should take offense because we confess our Jesus to be a man, and yet true God, we will deal forcefully with that from Scripture in due time. But this is too harsh for a beginning. Let them first be suckled with milk, and begin by recognizing this man Jesus as the true Messiah; after that they may drink wine, and learn also that he is true God. For they have been led astray so long and so far that one must deal gently with them, as people who have been all too strongly indoctrinated to believe that God cannot be man.

Therefore, I would request and advise that one deal gently with them and instruct them from Scripture; then some of them may come along. Instead of this we are trying only to drive them by force, slandering them, accusing them of having Christian blood if they don't stink, and I know not what other foolishness. So long as we thus treat them like dogs, how can we expect to work any good among them? Again, when we forbid them to labor and do business and have any human fellowship with us, thereby forcing them into usury, how is that supposed to do them any good?

If we really want to help them, we must be guided in our dealings with them not by papal law but by the law of Christian love. We must receive them cordially, and permit them to trade and work with us, that they may have occasion and opportunity to associate with us, hear our Christian teaching, and witness our Christian life. If some of them should prove stiff-necked, what of it? After all, we ourselves are not all good Christians either.

Here I will let the matter rest for the present, until I see what I have accomplished. God grant us all his mercy. Amen.

Text #8

Letter to the Baptized Jew, Bernard (1523)

Language:	Latin
Critical Edition:	WA Br 3:101–102 (Nr. 629)
English Translation:	Smith/Jacobs, 2:185–187[1]

The Bernard of this letter is the former Rabbi Jacob Gipher of Göppingen, who was baptized prior to the summer of 1519 and whose son was baptized in 1523, with Luther present. Bernard, married to Andreas Bodenstein von Carlstadt's maid, occasionally served as both Luther's messenger and as Hebrew instructor at the University of Wittenberg. Having trouble making ends meet, Bernard incurred considerable debts, which compelled him to leave Wittenberg in 1531, during which time Luther and Melachthon took an active role in caring for his children.[2]

The letter to Bernard is written from the same perspective as *That Jesus Christ Was Born a Jew*, and Luther indicates that he has sent a copy of that treatise to Bernard along with the letter. Here he reiterates the same critique of Roman Catholic failure in the conversion and catechizing of Jews, while expressing optimism that the new recovery of the gospel will lead to a significant increase in genuine Jewish conversions, because now Jews have the opportunity to learn about Christianity and see it as it is really supposed to be. Bernard, the former rabbi, represents for Luther what a true Jewish convert looks like. For this reason Luther, feeling special responsibility, showed considerable compassion toward the man.

One area in which Luther distinguishes himself positively with respect to Jewish conversion is that he regards genuine and honest Jewish converts as fully Christian and not second-class citizens. The latter had clearly been the norm in European Christianity where Jewish converts typically encountered ridicule and suspicion from Christians as well as from Jewish communities. For Luther, a Jew who truly and with proper intention converts is a Christian, plain and simple, and ought to be recognized as such by all other Christians.

Given how central the sacrament of baptism is for Luther and his teaching of justification—cherishing baptism as the rite that unites believers with the triune God through a new birth with Christ in their being, while remaining sinners in this life—the issue of the validity of baptism needs to be revisited in the case of

Jewish conversions. Does the sacrament effect saving faith by the mere act properly performed—even by force—or is the rite futile without a faith that receives the benefits promised and effected by God through the Word and water? Luther's answer is complex, but on one thing he is certain: baptism alone, especially if it is forced or nominal, brings no good. Proper and examined faith is needed.

An illustrative example of Luther's deliberation on the validity of and preconditions for baptism of a converting Jew comes from his letter of 1530 to Heinrich Gnesius.[3] Advising about the baptism of a young Jewish girl, Luther emphasizes the importance of the examined faith and intention of the baptized.[4] As for the rite itself, Luther is quite flexible in envisioning the "how" as long as the "why" is correct. He imagines different ways of using towels, linens, and drapes to ensure sufficient coverage for the girl's nudity in the water, out of respect for her and her family's possible sensibilities regarding nudity and Christian practices. Luther wants to accommodate and have a chance to educate. Disturbed by rumors of Jews recently found guilty of deceitfully receiving Christian baptism with an intent to ridicule Christian faith,[5] Luther underscores the urgency of making sure the girl does not pretend her faith and thus receive baptism for her own damnation. On the condition of the girl's faith being found sincere, Luther wishes her grace and perseverance, sending her greetings in Christ's name from himself personally and with his loving service.

Apart from his occasionally frustrated and skeptical quips about the futility of baptisms performed on false premises, Luther consistently underscores the real effectiveness of the sacrament to transform one's life. When addressing the issue of baptism pastorally, Luther seems to appreciate the human difficulty any Jewish convert would face as being suspect in the eyes of both their old Jewish and new Christian communities. Luther thus makes an important theological case to support the "real" Jewish convert as a real Christian. How many such persons he might encounter in his lifetime is a different matter.

{To Bernard, the baptized Jew}

Grace and peace from the Lord. The conversion of the Jews is in bad odor almost everywhere, not only among Christians but also among the Jews. The latter say that no one goes over from Judaism to Christianity in good faith, but that anyone who attempts it is guilty of some crime and cannot stay among the Jews. The Christians say that experience shows that they either return to their vomit [2 Pet. 2:22], or only pretend to have deserted Judaism. Everybody knows the story of what is said to have occurred at the court of the Emperor Sigismund. When a Jew at the Emperor's court desired, with many prayers, to become a Christian, he was at last admitted to baptism, and afterwards was tested, but prematurely and beyond his strength.

For immediately after his baptism the Emperor had two fires built, calling the one the fire of the Christians, the other the fire of the Jews, and bade the baptized Jew choose in which of them he preferred to be burned. "For," said he, "you are now baptized and holy, and it is hardly likely that you will ever become a better man than you now are." The miserable man showed that his faith was either pretended or weak by choosing the fire of the Jews; as a Jew he leaped into it, and as a Jew he burned. The story of the will of the baptized Jew of Cologne is also well known and there are many others.

But I think the cause of this ill-repute is not so much the Jews' obstinancy and wickedness, as rather their absurd and asinine ignorance and the wicked and shameless life of popes, priests, monks and universities. They give the Jews not a single spark of light or warmth, either in doctrine or in Christian life, but, on the contrary, they alienate the Jews' hearts and consciences by the darkness and the errors of their own traditions and by examples of the worst possible morals, and only impart to them the name of Christian, so that you may justly suppose that Christ's word [Matt. 23:15] was spoken to them, "Woe unto you, scribes and Pharisees, who compass sea and land to make one proselyte, and when he is made, you make him twofold more the child of hell than yourselves." They find fault with the Jews because they only pretend to be converted, but they do not find fault with themselves because they only pretend to convert them; nay, they seduce them from one error into another that is worse. What glory is it, pray, nay what madness for a teacher if he gives a bright and promising boy only the most pestilential teaching, then shows him in his own life only the most corrupt morals, and afterwards washes his hands and says he learned nothing good from him? Thus a bawd may teach a girl to be a harlot and afterwards charge her with not living in virginity. That this is the way the Jews are converted and instructed by our sophists and Pharisees, your own experience is witness.

But when the golden light of the Gospel is rising and shining, there is hope that many of the Jews will be converted in earnest and be drawn completely to Christ, as you have been drawn and certain others, who are the remnant of the seed of Abraham that is to be saved by faith; for He Who has begun the work will perfect it [Phil. 1:6], and will not permit His Word to return unto Him void [Isa. 55:11]. I thought it well, therefore, to send you this little book to strengthen and assure your faith in Christ, Whom you have lately learned to know in the Gospel; and now that you are baptized in the Spirit you are born of God. I hope that by your labor and example Christ may be made known to other Jews, so that they who are predestined may be called and may come to their King David, Who feeds and protects them, but Who is condemned among us with incredible madness by the popes and Pharisees, predestined to come into this condemnation. Farewell in the Lord, and pray for me.

Text #9

Lectures on Deuteronomy (1525)

Language: Latin
Critical Edition: WA 14: (489), 497–744
English Translation: LW 9

Luther was occupied with Deuteronomy from 1522–1525. During 1522 he translated the book into German, and in early 1523 he began lectures which were
delivered to a small circle of friends. These lectures covered only the first third of
the book. During 1524–1525 Luther prepared his own notes on the entire book
for publication. His method throughout is to give his understanding of the simple/
literal sense of the text, but then he often adds extensive comments about the alle-
gorical/mystical sense. This latter sense, which he anchors in the simple/literal sense,
is invariably anti-Jewish in character and corresponds closely with much of his anti-
Jewish polemic articulated elsewhere.

Because Deuteronomy is a book of laws and contains numerous exhortations to
be obedient to these laws, Luther had to articulate how to understand Deuteronomy
in light of his fundamental distinction between law and gospel, demand and promise,
death and life, Moses and Christ. It is crucial to recognize in Luther that he does not
equate the Old Testament (the book) with law and the New Testament (the book)
with gospel. For Luther, the law/gospel distinction applies to the entire Bible, and
the Old Testament is saturated with gospel. He does, however, equate the *old covenant* (Moses/Sinai) with law and the *new covenant* (Christ/Pentecost) with gospel.
This issue is complicated, however, by Luther's inconsistent use of the Latin term,
testamentum, and thus *vetus testamentum* (literally "old testament") sometimes refers
to the old covenant (Moses) while at others it means the Old Testament (that is, the
book). The same applies to the phrase *novum testamentum* (literally "new testament").
A classic example occurs in Luther's discussion of Deut. 5:3, *"Not with our ancestors
(did the LORD make this covenant)."*

> Here Moses points out the difference between the New and the Old Testament.
> The New Testament is the older, promised from the beginning of the world, yes,
> "before the times of the world," as Paul says to Titus (1:2), but fulfilled only under

Christ. The Old Testament promised under Moses was fulfilled under Joshua. However, there is this difference between the two: the New is founded wholly on the promise of the merciful and faithful God, without our works; but the Old is founded also on our works. Therefore Moses does not promise beyond the extent to which they keep the statutes and judgments. For this reason the Old Testament finally had to become antiquated and be put aside; it had to serve as a figure of that New and eternal Testament which began before the ages and will endure beyond the ages. The Old, however, began in time and after some time came to an end.[1]

Though Luther uses the term *testamentum* in this passage, he is clearly not referring to the two books of the Christian Bible but rather to the two covenants, and the point he wants to make is that the gospel is eternal and thus also prior to the Law, which is temporal and passes away once the gospel has been revealed in its fullness. This distinction in Luther between Moses/law as temporal and time-bound and Christ/gospel as eternal must always be kept in mind, because it is at the root of his understanding of the fundamental difference between Judaism and Christianity, that is, death and life.[2]

Excerpted below are two passages, one on the distinctiveness of the history of ancient/biblical Israel, and the other on "the prophet like Moses" in Deut. 18:15. In the former passage Luther describes how the history of biblical Israel and God's hidden involvement in that history were utterly different from that of any other people. This was due to Israel's being the divinely chosen vessel to bear the word of God and the name of God. On the one hand, this illustrates Luther's supremely high estimate of the Old Testament and why he was so interested in the Old Testament in the first place, while on the other it also heralds the absolute chasm that Luther believes stands between biblical and post-biblical Israel, between biblical Jews and post-biblical Jews.

Deuteronomy 18:15 was one of *the* central Old Testament texts for Luther, the interpretation of which would remain unchanged throughout his career: the "prophet like Moses" is Christ, and with Christ's coming the ministry of Moses ceases—Moses (death) and Christ (life) are mutually exclusive. This text would also play a key role in his later writings against the Jews, particularly in *On the Jews and Their Lies*.[3]

Lectures on Deuteronomy
{LW 9:32–33}
{Deut 2:}3. *You have been going about this mountain country long enough; turn northward.*

. . .

But note that even though the history of this nation, if viewed according to appearances, seems similar to the histories of the Gentiles—for now they gain victories, now they are defeated; now they have abundance, now they are in want, and whatever wonders are celebrated—nevertheless God so hides Himself that everything appears to be carried out by human prudence and chance. So it doubtless seemed to all those godless Gentiles. Hence they resisted, and they treated them as though there were no God in Israel. Therefore the history of this nation is to be separated from the history of all the Gentiles as far as heaven is from the earth. In the histories of the Gentiles one can see either the greatness or the insignificance of works. But in this account this one thing is to be viewed with admiration and reverence, namely, the Word of God; by its guidance and nod all is carried out and done. In fact, these are truly called sacred histories, not because those things were done by holy men but because they were accomplished according to the holy Word of God, which hallows everything, and by the holy name of God and in His stead. Therefore even though the deeds of all the Gentiles are themselves sheer wonders and acts of God, yet they do not have the testimony of the Word and the good pleasure of God. Hence their affairs and history are only testimonies of His wrath, very terrible signs of the fearful judgment of God. Therefore when the history of the whole world is taken together, it is incomparably less significant than even one most insignificant story of this nation. This is why the proud and carnal are deceived by the simplicity of things in the Scriptures, for they take no notice of the Word of God and value only the things.

{LW 9:176–180}
{Deut 18:}15. *The Lord your God will raise up for you a Prophet like me from among you, from your brethren—Him you shall heed.*

This is the chief passage in this whole book and a clearly expressed prophecy of Christ as the new Teacher. Hence the apostles also courageously adduce this passage (Acts 3:22–23; Acts 7:37). Appropriately, Moses places it here at the end, after he has finished his discourses concerning the priesthood, the kingdom, the government, and the whole worship of God. It is his purpose to show that in the future there will be another priesthood, another kingdom, another worship of God, and another word, by which all of Moses will be set aside. Here Moses clearly describes his own end, and he yields his mastery to the Prophet who is to come. Let us therefore examine his words rather carefully.

First, it is necessary for this Prophet to bring a new word, a word which Moses has not taught, because here God promises that He will put words into His mouth. But if this were not another word, there would be no need to promise that it will be brought by this Prophet; it would have been enough to say: "He shall be a mouth for you," just as is said of Aaron in Ex. 4{:16}, which would mean that the Prophet would teach the words of Moses and his written Law. Now when he says: "Heed Him who will be raised up like me," he teaches plainly that his own word is different from the Word of that Prophet. And this he confirms when he says that the people on Mt. Sinai demanded such a prophet to speak to them, since they had already heard the whole Law through Moses.

But there cannot be another word beyond the word of Moses, unless it is the Gospel, since everything that belongs to the teaching of the Law has been transmitted most perfectly and amply by Moses, so that nothing further can be added. For what could be added to the Decalog, to say nothing of the rest? What loftier thing can be taught than to believe, trust, love, and fear God with one's whole heart, not to tempt God, etc.? Furthermore, what rules can be more just and holy than those which Moses ordains concerning the external worship of God, government, and love for one's neighbor? Therefore the Jews have no cause here to gabble that this Prophet will be one who interprets Moses. Moses interprets himself in this book so well that there is no need of another; nor can another add one jot or tittle to make him clearer or more perfect. Since, therefore, there cannot be another word beyond the perfect teaching of the Law unless it were the Word of grace, it follows that this Prophet will not be a teacher of the Law but a minister of grace. Thus this text clearly forces the Jews to expect from this Prophet something other than what they have in Moses.

Secondly, unless that new Prophet were to bring another word, Moses would not need to compare Him to himself when he says: "The Lord will raise Him up, like me." All the other prophets who taught Moses and did not raise up another word were not like Moses or similar to Moses but inferior to Moses, namely, servants of the word of Moses, teaching what Moses had commanded. Therefore in all of them the people did not hear anyone else or themselves; they heard Moses himself and his words. For Moses speaks in them and puts his words into their mouths, and they are his mouth to the people. This Prophet, however, he does not dare subordinate to himself and put his words into His mouth; but he says that He will be like him in service and obedience, by which he certainly excludes Him from obedience to him and places Him above all prophets who taught on the basis of Moses.

But to exclude Him from obedience to Moses and to prefer Him above all prophets teaching on the basis of Moses is to affirm positively that the ministry of the Law is to be ended and a new one to be set up, since no man is free from the service of the Law but all are subject to the Law. Therefore it is necessary that this

Prophet, who is like Moses—in respect to authority of teaching and commanding, that is, for this is what he means when he says "like me"—be superior to Moses and teach greater things. Unless He were greater than Moses, Moses would not yield obedience and authority to Him. Moreover, unless He taught greater things, He could not be greater. He is not speaking here of similarity between Moses and that Prophet in regard to personal worth but of similarity in authority or office. He is not dealing here with the life, morals, or deeds of Moses and this Prophet but with doctrine, as the text sufficiently proves; for a prophet is a prophet because he teaches and comes to teach, and here the command is to "heed Him."

If, therefore, the doctrine of both is considered, it will be easily apparent from the comparison of their doctrine what He must preach. Moses is a minister of the Law, sin, and death; for he teaches and stresses works, and through the rays of the Law he makes everyone guilty of death and subject to punishment for sin. He demands, but he does not give what he demands. However, since this Prophet finds Moses teaching this and is Himself set up as a Teacher next to him, His Word must teach something else. But He cannot teach anything else than sin, wrath, and death unless He teaches righteousness, grace, and life. Therefore it is necessary that He be a teacher of life, grace, and righteousness, just as Moses is a teacher of sin, wrath, and death. But both teachings must be heard just as they have been raised up by God; for through the Law all must be humbled, and through the Gospel all must be exalted. They are alike in divine authority, but with respect to the fruit of their ministry they are unlike and completely opposed to each other. The sin and wrath which Moses arouses through his ministry that Prophet cancels through righteousness and grace by His ministry. This Prophet, therefore, demands nothing; but He grants what Moses demands.

In this passage we have those two ministries of the Word which are necessary for the salvation of the human race: the ministry of the Law and the ministry of the Gospel, one for death and the other for life. They are indeed alike if you are looking at their authority, but most unlike if you are thinking about their fruit. The ministry of Moses is temporary, finally to be ended by the coming of the ministry of Christ, as he says here, "Heed Him." But the ministry of Christ will be ended by nothing else, since it brings eternal righteousness and "puts an end to sin," as it is said in Dan. 9{:24}. Therefore the Levitical priesthood is wholly ended here and set aside, because it was established to teach Moses. But if the priesthood is ended, the Law is also ended, as it is said (Heb. 7:12): "When there is a change in the priesthood, there is necessarily a change in the Law as well." Thus this Prophet can be none other than Christ Himself.

From all this it follows how completely foreign and even pestilential those teachers in the New Testament are who trouble consciences with laws and works, when this prophecy concerning Christ totally wipes out and does away with that ministry. Even more pestilential are those who weary the earth with their traditions and human laws. If the ministry of this new Prophet does not endure the Law of Moses, which is divine, how will it endure the laws of men in His kingdom? You see, therefore, that by this one text the whole chaos of papistic tyranny, together with its monks, is completely upset.

But here you will say: "You will find commands everywhere in the gospels and the epistles of the apostles. Therefore either our Christ will not be this Prophet, or His doctrine will not differ at all from the Law of Moses." To reply briefly: The commands of the New Testament are directed to those who are justified and are new men in the Spirit. Nothing is taught or commanded there except what pertains solely to believers, who do everything spontaneously, not from necessity or contrary to their own will. But the Law is directed to the old man, who is dead in sin, to urge him on and to show him his sin. This is the true and proper teaching of the Law. Therefore the Law finds man not only unwilling but also unable to do what the Law demands. Thus he says here in the text that on the day of the assembly the people refused and could not hear the voice of the Law, and that therefore they asked for another teacher, one who would speak to them a word they could bear.

The understanding of this matter lies in recognizing and truly distinguishing the Law and the Gospel, that you may know that the teaching of the Law commands only what is to be done by the ungodly and lost, as 1 Tim. 1{:9} says: "The Law is not laid down for the just but for the lawless." But where the godly are, there the Law, which is intended only for the humiliation of the ungodly through the recognition of their sin and weakness, is already abolished. The Gospel teaches from what source you receive the power to fulfill the Law. In this respect it commands nothing; nor does it force the spirit, which hastens of its own accord by faith. It adds some commands, but it does so to kill the remnants of the old man in the flesh, which is not yet justified. From these commands, however, the spirit is free, being satisfied with faith alone. Of this matter we have spoken amply elsewhere.

Now let us look at the words: "The Lord your God will raise up for you a Prophet like me from among you, from your brethren—Him you shall heed." Here he prophesies that Christ will be true man and will come from the blood of the Jews, because salvation is from the Jews (John 4:22). No one has ever arisen from this people who taught a different word from the word of Moses and set up a new ministry except this one Christ of ours. However many prophets there were before Him, they all preserved and taught Moses. This Prophet freed not only the Jews from Moses but all nations throughout the world and gave them the new Word of the Gospel. That He was from the Jews, both the Gentiles and the Jews being witnesses, proves that it is He of whom Moses speaks here, and that this prophecy is fulfilled in Him.

. . .

Text #10

Sermon: How Christians Should Regard Moses (1525)

Language: German
Critical Edition: WA 16:363–393
English Translation: LW 35: (155), 161–74

As part of Luther's long series of sermons on the book of Exodus, this sermon was preached in Wittenberg on August 27, 1525. In revised form it appeared as a separate publication in May 1526, and then shortly after as part of several smaller collections of Luther's writings. In the background of the sermon stand the terrible circumstances surrounding the Peasants' War of January–August 1525, and the execution of Thomas Münzer on May 27, 1525, in Mühlhausen (Thuringia). Shortly before this sermon, Luther had written three harsh treatises about the revolt: *Admonition to Peace: A Reply to the Twelve Articles of the Peasants in Swabia; Against the Robbing and Murdering Hordes of Peasants; An Open Letter on the Harsh Book against the Peasants.*[1]

Throughout the sermon, Luther is fighting against what he regards as the wrongful imposition of Mosaic Law on Christians. In order to make his case, he has to clarify his understanding of the relationship between Moses and Christ, law and gospel, and he does this in the strictest of terms. While the presenting issue is an inner-Christian debate about which Old Testament laws apply to Christian life and about the implications of that debate for a pressing contemporary social and political situation (such as peasants' rights and usury laws), the theological issue at stake for Luther is simultaneously that of Judaism. Thus for him the proper understanding of the antithetical relationship between law and gospel always and unavoidably implies the proper understanding of the antithetical relationship between Judaism and Christianity.

The sermon has two parts: (1) Two public sermons in the Bible: Sinai and Pentecost; (2) Why Christians should read Moses. In part 1, Luther distinguishes sharply between the giving of the law on Sinai, which was intended for the Jews alone, and the announcement of the gospel at Pentecost, which was intended for all the world. Christians should further note that there are two kinds of laws in Moses: (a) those that agree with natural law (that is, the Decalogue, or Ten Commandments) and are binding on all people for all time; and (b) those that are specific to Israel (that is, virtually the remainder of the laws in the Torah). In terms of the latter, Luther boldly states: "Moses is dead." This programmatic claim certainly applies to Christians but also to Jews as well. In part 2 Luther gives three reasons why Christians still need to read and study Moses: (a) Moses provides legal examples that can be freely adopted by Christians, where appropriate; (b) Moses contains promises of the Messiah (for example, Gen. 3:15; Gen. 22:18; Deut. 18:15) that cannot be known by nature; and (c) in the stories of the patriarchs and matriarchs, Moses provides wonderful examples of faith and unbelief.

Excerpted below is all of part 1 as well as the conclusion to the sermon.

How Christians Should Regard Moses
{LW 35:161–66}

Dear friends, you have often heard that there has never been a public sermon from heaven except twice. Apart from them God has spoken many times through and with men on earth, as in the case of the holy patriarchs Adam, Noah, Abraham, Isaac, Jacob, and others, down to Moses. But in none of these cases did he speak with such glorious splendor, visible reality, or public cry and exclamation as he did on those two occasions. Rather God illuminated their heart within and spoke through their mouth, as Luke indicates in the first chapter of his gospel where he says, "As he spoke by the mouth of his holy prophets from of old" [Luke 1:70].

Now the first sermon is in Exodus 19 and 20; by it God caused himself to be heard from heaven with great splendor and might. For the people of Israel heard the trumpets and the voice of God himself.

In the second place God delivered a public sermon through the Holy Spirit on Pentecost [Acts 2:2-4]. On that occasion the Holy Spirit came with great splendor and visible impressiveness, such that there came from heaven the sudden rushing of a mighty wind, and it filled the entire house where the apostles were sitting. And there appeared to them tongues as of fire, distributed and resting on each of them. And they were all filled with the Holy Spirit and began to preach and speak in other tongues. This happened with great spendor and glorious might, so that thereafter the apostles preached so powerfully that the sermons which we hear in the world today are hardly a shadow compared to theirs, so far as the visible splendor and sub-stance of their sermons is concerned. For the apostles spoke in all sorts of languages, performed great miracles, etc. Yet through our preachers today the Holy Spirit does not cause himself to be either heard or seen; nothing is coming down openly from heaven. This is why I have said that there are only two such special and public sermons which have been seen and heard from heaven. To be sure, God spoke also to Christ from heaven, when he was baptized in the Jordan, and on Mount Tabor. However none of this took place in the presence of the general public.

God wanted to send that second sermon into the world, for it had earlier been announced by the mouth and in the books of the holy prophets. He will no longer speak that way publicly through sermons. Instead, in the third place, he will come in person with divine glory, so that all creatures will tremble and quake before him; and then he will no longer preach to them, but they will see and handle him himself.

Now the first sermon, and doctrine, is the law of God. The second is the gospel. These two sermons are not the same. Therefore we must have a good grasp of the matter in order to know how to differentiate between them. We must know what the law is, and what the gospel is. The law commands and requires us to do certain things. The law is thus directed solely to our behavior and consists in making requirements. For God speaks through the law, saying, "Do this, avoid that, this is what I expect of you." The gospel, however, does not preach what we are to do or to avoid. It sets up no requirements but reverses the approach of the law, does the very opposite, and says, "This is what God has done for you; he has let his Son be made flesh for you, has let him be put to death for your sake." So, then, there are two kinds of doctrine and two kinds of works, those of God and those of men. Just as we and God are separated from one another, so also these two doctrines are widely separated from one another. For the gospel teaches exclusively what has been given us by God, and not—as in the case of the law—what we are to do and give to God.

We now want to see how this first sermon sounded forth and with what splendor God gave the law on Mount Sinai. He selected the place where he wanted to be seen and heard. Not that God actually spoke, for he has no mouth, tongue, teeth, or lips as we do. But he who created and formed the mouth of all men can also make speech and the voice. For no one would be able to speak a single word unless God first gave it, as the prophet says, "It would be impossible to speak except God first put it in our mouth." Language, speech, and voice are thus gifts of God like any other gifts, such as the fruit on the trees. Now he who fashioned the mouth and put speech in it can also make and use speech even though there is no mouth present. Now the words which are here written were spoken through an angel. This is not to say that only one angel was there, for there was a great multitude there serving God and preaching to the people of Israel at Mount Sinai. The angel, however, who spoke here and did the talking, spoke just as if God himself were speaking and saying, "I am your God, who brought you out of the land of Egypt," etc., as if Peter or Paul were speaking in God's stead and saying, "I am your God," etc. In his letter to the Galatians, Paul says that the law was ordained by angels. That is, angels were assigned, in God's behalf, to give the law of God; and Moses, as an intermediary, received it from the angels. I say this so that you might know who gave the law. He did this to them, however, because he wanted thereby to compel, burden, and press the Jews.

What kind of a voice that was, you may well imagine. It was a voice like the voice of a man, such that it was actually heard. The syllables and letters thus made sounds which the physical ear was able to pick up. But it was a bold, glorious, and great voice. As told in Deuteronomy 4[:12], the people heard the voice, but saw no one. They heard a powerful voice, for he spoke in a powerful voice, as if in the dark we should hear a voice from a high tower or roof top, and could see no one but only hear the strong voice of a man. And this is why it is called the voice of God, because it was above a human voice.

Now you will hear how God used this voice in order to arouse his people and make them brave. For he intended to institute the tangible and spiritual government. It was previously stated how, on the advice of Jethro, his father-in-law, Moses had established the temporal government and appointed rulers and judges. Beyond that there is yet a spiritual kingdom in which Christ rules in the hearts of men; this kingdom we cannot see, because it consists only in faith and will continue until the Last Day.

These are two kingdoms: the temporal, which governs with the sword and is visible; and the spiritual, which governs solely with grace and with the forgiveness of sins. Between these two kingdoms still another has been placed in the middle, half spiritual and half temporal. It is constituted by the Jews, with commandments and outward ceremonies which prescribe their conduct toward God and men.

The Law of Moses Binds Only the Jews and Not the Gentiles

Here the law of Moses has its place. It is no longer binding on us because it was given only to the people of Israel. And Israel accepted this law for itself and its descendants, while the Gentiles were excluded. To be sure, the Gentiles have certain laws in common with the Jews, such as these: there is one God, no one is to do wrong to another, no one is to commit adultery or murder or steal, and others like them. This is written by nature into their hearts; they did not hear it straight from heaven as the Jews did. This is why this entire text does not pertain to the Gentiles. I say this on account of the enthusiasts. For you see and hear how they read Moses, extol him, and bring up the way he ruled the people with commandments. They try to be clever, and think they know something more than is presented in the gospel; so they minimize faith, contrive something new, and boastfully claim that it comes from the Old Testament. They desire to govern people according to the letter of the law of Moses, as if no one had ever read it before.

But we will not have this sort of thing. We would rather not preach again for the rest of our life than to let Moses return and to let Christ be torn out of our hearts. We will not have Moses as ruler or lawgiver any longer. Indeed God himself will not have it either. Moses was an intermediary solely for the Jewish people. It was to them that he gave the law. We must therefore silence the mouths of those factious spirits who say, "Thus says Moses," etc. Here you simply reply: Moses has nothing to do with us. If I were to accept Moses in one commandment, I would have to accept the entire Moses. Thus the consequence would be that if I accept Moses as master, then I must have myself circumcised, wash my clothes in the Jewish way, eat and drink and dress thus and so, and observe all that stuff. So, then, we will neither observe nor accept Moses. Moses is dead. His rule ended when Christ came. He is of no further service.

That Moses does not bind the Gentiles can be proved from Exodus 20[:1], where God himself speaks, "I am the Lord your God, who brought you out of the land of Egypt, out of the house of bondage." This text makes it clear that even the Ten Commandments do not pertain to us. For God never led us out of Egypt, but only the Jews. The sectarian spirits want to saddle us with Moses and all the commandments. We will just skip that. We will regard Moses as a teacher, but we will not regard him as our lawgiver—unless he agrees with both the New Testament and the natural law. Therefore it is clear enough that Moses is the lawgiver of the Jews and not of the Gentiles. He has given the Jews a sign whereby they should lay hold of God, when they call upon him as the God who brought them out of Egypt. The Christians have a different sign, whereby they conceive of God as the One who gave his Son, etc.

Again one can prove it from the third commandment that Moses does not pertain to Gentiles and Christians. For Paul [Col. 2:16] and the New Testament [Matt. 12:1-12; John 5:16; 7:22-23; 9:14-16] abolish the sabbath, to show us that the sabbath was given to the Jews alone, for whom it is a stern commandment. The prophets referred to it too, that the sabbath of the Jews would be abolished. For Isaiah says in the last chapter, "When the Savior comes, then such will be the time, one sabbath after the other, one month after the other," etc {Isa. 66:23}. This is as though he were trying to say, "It will be the sabbath every day, and the people will be such that they make no distinction between days. For in the New Testament the sabbath is annihilated as regards the crude external observance, for every day is a holy day," etc.

Now if anyone confronts you with Moses and his commandments, and wants to compel you to keep them, simply answer, "Go to the Jews with your Moses; I am no Jew. Do not entangle me with Moses. If I accept Moses in one respect (Paul tells the Galatians in chapter 5[:3]), then I am obligated to keep the entire law." For not one little period in Moses pertains to us.

. . .

{LW 35:173–74}
Conclusion and Summary

I have stated that all Christians, and especially those who handle the word of God and attempt to teach others, should take heed and learn Moses aright. Thus where he gives commandment, we are not to follow him except so far as he agrees with the natural law. Moses is a teacher and doctor of the Jews. We have our own master,

Christ, and he has set before us what we are to know, observe, do, and leave undone. However it is true that Moses sets down, in addition to the laws, fine examples of faith and unfaith—punishment of the godless, elevation of the righteous and believing—and also the dear and comforting promises concerning Christ which we should accept. The same is true also in the gospel. For example in the account of the ten lepers, that Christ bids them go to the priest and make sacrifice [Luke 17:14] does not pertain to me. The example of their faith, however, does pertain to me; I should believe Christ, as did they.

Enough has now been said of this, and it is to be noted well for it is really crucial. Many great and outstanding people have missed it, while even today many great preachers still stumble over it. They do not know how to preach Moses, nor how properly to regard his books. They are absurd as they rage and fume, chattering to people, "God's word, God's word!" All the while they mislead the poor people and drive them to destruction. Many learned men have not known how far Moses ought to be taught. Origen, Jerome, and others like them, have not shown clearly how far Moses can really serve us. This is what I have attempted, to say in an introduction to Moses how we should regard him, and how he should be understood and received and not simply be swept under the rug. For in Moses there is comprehended such a fine order, that it is a joy, etc.

God be praised.

Text #11

Lectures on Zechariah (1525/1526)

Language:	Latin
Critical Edition:	WA 13: (545), 546–669
English Translation:	LW 20: (ix–), 1–152

During the mid-1520's, while heavily involved in translating the Old Testament into German, Luther lectured through the twelve "minor" prophets, Hosea-Malachi. The Latin lectures on Zechariah were not published, although Luther did publish a German commentary on the book in 1527.[1] The German commentary and the Latin lectures are two separate works.

Zechariah 1–6 contains the eight mysterious "night visions" of the prophet Zechariah, who, together with his contemporary prophet, Haggai, was instrumental in the rebuilding of the temple in Jerusalem, 520–515 BCE. Excerpted below are selections from Luther's treatment of the sixth (a flying scroll) and seventh (a woman in a basket/ephah) visions, which he interprets as a prophetic description of the *treachery* of the Jews. With this reference to "Jewish treachery," Luther is invoking language used in the traditional Good Friday Latin liturgy; it was also a standard and favored label for Jews utilized by Christian anti-Jewish polemicists for well over a thousand years prior to Luther.

In light of Texts #5–7, the extreme negativity that Luther expresses toward the Jews here is remarkable.[2] He speaks of their eternal fall, of their being blinded by God, of their being scattered with nowhere to dwell in safety, of their experience as a horrible example for Christians if Christians should behave likewise toward the message of the gospel, of their daily increasing blasphemy for which God blinds them further, and finally—in clear tension with his own earlier statements on Romans 11—an utterly negative claim against Jewish conversion. Regarding this last item, Osten-Sacken has stated: "This may be the most hopeless word which the Reformer ever said or wrote about the Jews."[3]

For the reader's sake, Zech. 5:1-11 is provided prior to the selection from Luther.

Zechariah 5:1-11

Vision 6: The Flying Scroll. Again I lifted my eyes and saw, and behold, a flying scroll! And he said to me, "What do you see?" I answered, "I see a flying scroll; its length is twenty cubits, and its breadth ten cubits." Then he said to me, "This is the curse that goes out over the face of the whole land; for every one who steals shall be cut off henceforth according to it, and every one who swears falsely shall be cut off henceforth according to it. I will send it forth, says the LORD of hosts, and it shall enter the house of the thief, and the house of him who swears falsely by my name; and it shall abide in his house and consume it, both timber and stones."

Vision 7: The Woman in a Basket/Ephah. Then the angel who talked with me came forward and said to me, "Lift your eyes, and see what this is that goes forth." And I said, "What is it?" He said, "This is the ephah that goes forth." And he said, "This is their iniquity in all the land." And behold, the leaden cover was lifted, and there was a woman sitting in the ephah! And he said, "This is Wickedness." And he thrust her back into the ephah, and thrust down the leaden weight upon its mouth. Then I lifted my eyes and saw, and behold, two women coming forward! The wind was in their wings; they had wings like the wings of a stork, and they lifted up the ephah between earth and heaven. Then I said to the angel who talked with me, "Where are they taking the ephah?" He said to me, "To the land of Shinar, to build a house for it; and when this is prepared, they will set the ephah down there on its base."

Zechariah 5
{LW 20:53, 56, 57–58, 59–61}
Saintly writers have treated this chapter in various ways. Let us, however, omit nonsense of this sort and the ideas of men, and let us rather pursue the real message as best we can.

In the earlier chapters the prophet has encouraged and strengthened the prince, the high priest, and the people. This we have explained already in sufficient detail. Then he applied everything to the coming and present kingdom of Christ which, as he had described, would be a kingdom of joy and great calm. Now in this chapter he will speak in the manner of all the prophets. They all have the custom that they not only describe in fullest and sweetest detail the kingdom of Christ but also add the horrible treachery and ruin of Israel, which refused to receive and recognize this King and Savior. So it is with visions, lamentations, and a multitude of prophecies that the prophets declare the eternal fall of that wretched people.

The apostles, too, followed this pattern. Paul and Peter very clearly declare that after the preaching of the Gospel false teachers will come like wolves who will go about at will against the flock of the Lord and will tread underfoot whatever they wish. So also the prophet Daniel says (Dan. 12:10): "All the wicked shall do wickedly." As I have said, Zechariah does exactly the same thing here. When he has made his prophecy about that plummet, he at the same time immediately adds what must happen to these people who are not going to receive this kingdom of Christ. This is the summary of this chapter. It deals directly with Pharisees, Sadducees, and other scribes whom Christ found among His people when He declared that He was King and Savior but whom He also left behind.

. . .

{Sixth Vision: The Flying Scroll}

5:4. *I will send it forth, says the Lord of hosts.* He is saying, "I shall bring forth this scroll," that is, "when they will have sinned enough with that wicked doctrine of theirs, when they have reached the highest point, then I shall declare how all their teachings are wicked thefts and perjuries; I shall declare the wickedness of their doctrine—that, under the pretext of My holy name, they have only destroyed souls by taking My name in vain"; just as He here says that it shall come "into the house of him who swears falsely by My name." The Gospel has accomplished that revelation of wrong, because it came to the house of thieves and of those who swear falsely. That is, it takes revenge on them because of the wrong they have done openly; and just as they have devoured both souls and bodies, so also are they and all theirs going to be devoured. Therefore He says: "I shall not permit it to go unavenged." That this is clearer than the light of noon no one can deny. So wretchedly have the Jews been scattered throughout the world that they do not even have one tiny place where they can live in safety. Blinded by God, they live everywhere as miserable, abject exiles. This is the first vision. The second follows.

. . .

{Seventh Vision: The Woman in a Basket/Ephah}

5:8. *And he thrust her back,* that is, he took away her seat. Thrusting her down from her lofty seat into the cask, he threw her into confusion. Earlier that seat was carrying her above the cask, but now the weight of lead is sent back down onto the mouth of the cask, and she is closed up inside. This means that wickedness indeed is embarrassed by the Gospel and is put to shame. However, the Gospel does not correct it. The hypocrisy always remains and cannot be corrected. In fact, those who have thus given themselves over to hypocrisy become more and more hardened and sink more deeply into their wickedness, even though the Gospel overcomes and confounds them. We see the same thing happening in our time as happened with the Jews. Christ has rebuked them, but they still lie immersed, as it were, in their wrong. They have no hope of coming to the surface. In fact, day by day they are still guilty of further blasphemy. Therefore they become more blinded, because God has cast them down into a very wretched situation. They have no temple, no kingdom, no priesthood, no public schools. If they teach anything, they teach their own topics. If they teach anyone, they teach their own children. This teaching they do in private whispers and in nooks and crannies as they have been pushed down into that cask and closed up therein so that they cannot come forth. The same thing will happen to us who hold the Gospel in contempt. The Gospel will again be taken away, even if human affairs are going to continue to exist still longer.

. . .

5:11. *In the land of Shinar.* Where the location of Shinar is is revealed in Gen. 11. There the sons of Noah are said to have set out to the east, where they found the plain of Shinar. Later the tower of Babel was built there. The plain there is said to have been very broad and pleasant. Then, what we read as *when this is prepared* is more correctly read "when this is let down." Now we shall treat the meaning of this suggested translation of mine. After the ephah was closed up by the lead, the prophet saw it being carried away from his sight upward into the sky. This means that wickedness is not going to remain among this people. Rather, those two flying women will carry it away to a different place. The carrying away is a complete inversion: the Jews were carried away from Babylon to Jerusalem, but the ephah is being transferred from Jerusalem to Babylon. In sum, this means that those whose place the Lord has given to us will be completely uprooted and thrown out of the church—as Paul argues in detail in Romans (Rom. 11). Furthermore, women are carrying it. This signifies the office of teaching. You see, there is no doubt that the two cherubim before Moses and Isaiah indicate the ministry of the Word. At the same time, there is in the middle of them the means of propitiation, that is, Christ, to whom all Scriptures look and whom alone the ministry of the Word treats. The seraphim are winged because the Word flies; it runs swiftly. This is what the poets, too, wanted to picture with their Mercury, the winged messenger of the gods, and that is how his name was chosen, why he should be called "Hermes." So also Vergil described rumor as winged, because there is no other evil which spreads with greater speed. So, just as the righteous ministry of the pure Word, "with wings" means this, so also here in unrighteousness, a wicked ministry of a wicked word is meant. Hence these two winged women signify everything which the Jews or their wicked word teach. These are women who are flying, not married men. That is, all their teaching, all their preaching, all their words, are carnal. There are two women, just as there were two cherubim, because the Word is between speaker and hearer. Similarly Christ also sent out men two by two to preach. The summary, then, of all this is that the suffering and disaster of the Jews is so great that not only are they being held closed up in the ephah so that they are unable to escape but also they are never going to hear the pure Word, that wicked teachers have to be brought together to keep the people from ever hearing the pure Word, locked up as they are in the worst wickedness. So the Lord also threatens in Isaiah (Is. 5:6): "I will also command My clouds that they rain no rain upon it." In such grim terms he describes the hopeless destruction of that people—so hopeless that not even a small remnant of them remains to be restored. They are going to be rejected forever. They will not be converted lest they be saved. Then we must also remember that the flying women are carrying the ephah on high between heaven and earth. This means that their doctrine touches neither heaven nor earth, that is, they do not teach the kingdom of God nor do they compass the kingdom of this world. They no longer have either a spiritual or a physical kingdom. Both administrations have perished—that spiritual one of Joshua the high priest as well as the physical, or political, one of Zerubbabel the prince. In sum, they have lost both their kingdom and their priesthood. Even if the Jews see and know this, they are still so wretched and blind that they cannot recognize their error. So they allow themselves to be carried on high—between heaven and earth. Their stubbornness makes them irreconcilable.

To build a house for it in Shinar. He does not deign to give it its recent name but its original one. He does not say "in Babylon" but "in Shinar." There, he says, a house will be built and prepared for it. There is a question about the place, for it is a matter of comparing the two places, so that there is no need to imagine some definite physical location. Briefly the meaning is this: The people who are now in a double administration, spiritual and political, have been called back from Babylon. They will also be transferred finally into the true Jerusalem. Moreover, the remnant who are destroyed will not remain in Jerusalem but will even be transferred to Babylon, and to a mystical Babylon; that is, to a confused place, to total blindness, to a place where the wrath, judgment, and vengeance of God are present. There there is no peace, no grace, no mercy, no Jerusalem. All this pursues them wherever they may be.

And they will set it down there. The most wretched and terrible thing of all is that this is an irrevocable error; that that rejection lasts forever. And so do the warnings of the Lord everywhere in Scripture sound frightful indeed: "I shall have no more mercy on them"; also: "I shall forget with an eternal forgetfulness" (Hos. 1:6); as one can see everywhere in the prophets. So then, when they have been set down "on their base," that is, on their hardness, obstinacy, and wicked stubbornness so that there is no hope of being called back, they have been broken and cut off from the tree, as the apostle says in Rom. 11[:22–24], etc.

Text #12

Sermon on Jeremiah 23:5-8
(The Visit of Three Jews) (1526)

Language:	German
Critical Text:	WA 20:569,25–570,12
English Translation:	LW 47:191, n. 63 {supplemented by Editors}

On November 18, 1526, the Twenty-Fifth Sunday after Trinity, Luther preached a sermon on Jer. 23:5-8.

> Behold, the days are coming, says the LORD, when I will raise up for David a righteous Branch, and he shall reign as king and deal wisely, and shall execute justice and righteousness in the land. In his days Judah will be saved, and Israel will dwell securely. And this is the name by which he will be called: "The LORD is our righteousness." Therefore, behold, the days are coming, says the LORD, when they shall no longer say, "As the LORD lives who brought up the people of Israel out of the land of Egypt," but "As the LORD lives who brought up and led the descendants of the house of Israel out of the north country and out of all the countries where he had driven them." Then they shall dwell in their own land.

For Luther, that the promised Branch/Messiah will be called "The LORD is our righteousness" means that the Tetragrammaton, the personal name of God, will be applied to the Messiah, that is, the Messiah will be called LORD. This in turn implies that the Messiah will be God. And because Jesus is the Messiah, this becomes a proof text for the divine nature of Jesus. This then leads Luther into recalling a debate he had had with some highly learned Jews (that is, at some point prior to November 1526) about this text and his Christian interpretation of it. The relevant excerpt from the sermon is as follows.

LW 47:191 [supplemented by editors]

> {Because Holy Scripture and the Jews themselves, as well as the holy fathers and all writers, agree that this name belongs alone and truly to the divine majesty and being, so we have here in the Prophet Jeremiah a powerful and strong strike

against the Jews and a splendid and great comfort for us Christians. For here this article of our faith—that Christ is true, natural God—is powerfully established.} I myself have discussed this with the Jews, indeed with the most learned of them, who knew the Bible so well that there wasn't a letter in it that they did not understand. I held up this text to them, and they could not think of anything to refute me. Finally they said that they believed their Talmud; this is their {interpretation}, and it says nothing about Christ. They had to follow this interpretation. Thus they do not stick to the text but seek to escape it. For if they held to this text alone, they would be vanquished. {For this statement leads strongly to the conclusion that this Seed of David is a true and natural God; for he will be called by the same name as the true, proper God is called.}

There are several later references in Luther to exegetical debates with three learned Jews, or Rabbis, about the proper christological interpretation of Old Testament texts. This has given rise to the belief that Luther was regularly in face-to-face debate with Jews. But according to the most recent study of the issue by Osten-Sacken, all of these references are likely refractions of a single encounter, that is, the one mentioned in this 1526 sermon.[1]

In this regard, it should be born in mind that Luther's personal encounters with Jews were almost exclusively limited to Jews who had converted. His encounters with Jews as Jews were likely extremely rare. Kaufmann has described the situation succinctly:

> For Luther the Jews were never at any point in his lifetime 'conversation-partners' in the sense that they had something to say that might have influenced either Christian theologians in their conversations with Jews or their theological judgments about them. There is no evidence Luther ever took the initiative to make contact with learned Jews to learn from them as some of his contemporaries did. . . . His own narrowly bounded world was located far even from the few remnants of formerly flourishing urban centers of Jewish life and Jewish learning in the Empire, and the few personal contacts which Luther had had with Jews during the course of his life occurred because others sought him out and asked for his support.[2]

Judging by the tone of the later references to the visit of the three Jews, Luther was clearly affected by Jewish resistance to his christological interpretation, and from 1526 on his comments about the Jews reek of bitterness, and ultimately become unrelentingly so. In *That Jesus Christ Was Born a Jew*,[3] he had sketched a two-stage proposal for dealing with the Jews: (1) treat them in a friendly manner, and (2) instruct them on how to read the Old Testament properly. It seems reasonable to conclude that as Luther came to realize that Jews were not exactly enamored with, or persuaded by, his christological exegesis, that this had a profoundly negative effect on him. And further, he came more and more to hold the Rabbis liable for this resistance. Just as Bernard the baptized Jew embodied to him the Jewish people in a positive sense (that is, the true remnant of Israel), so these learned visitors came to embody Jews and Jewish interpretation in the worst and threatening sense.

WATr 4:619,20—620,15 (#5026)

[A later refraction as described in a Table Talk from 1540.]

The Jews call Christ, "Thola,"[4] hanged man, and Mary, "Haria,"[5] latrine. Three Rabbis came to Luther to speak with him, Samaria, Solomon, and Leo. "What do you think about Mary," said the Doctor. "It is true that the prophet {Isa. 7:14} calls her 'Almah'[6]." Then one Jew said: "This word does not always mean 'virgin'; our Rabbis {can} teach you about this." But the Doctor said, "Whoever wants to debate must stick with the words {of the text} and not resort to human glosses." Thus the Doctor argued for the divinity of Christ on the basis of a passage from Jeremiah, which he quoted: "The LORD is our righteousness" {Jer. 23:6}. But the Jews invoked their Rabbis again. Finally Samaria said, "We are happy that you Christians are learning our language and reading our books, such as Genesis and others. There is hope that all of you will become Jews. "No way!" said Luther. "We hope that you will become Christians and turn to us. I believe that yet still more Jews will be converted. Christ is capable of much." When they left, Luther gave them letters {of safe conduct} with which they could travel without having to pay fees. But because Luther had added the words "for the sake of the name of Jesus Christ" {to the letters}, they said to Aurogallus,[7] "The letters are good, but this name offends us." Therefore they chose to pay travel fees rather than show the letters.

Text #13

Commentary on Psalm 109 (1526)

Language:	German
Critical Edition:	WA 19: (542), 595–615
English Translation:	LW 14: (14), 209, 257–77

On November 1, 1526, Luther dedicated and sent his commentary on the four traditional Christian "Psalms of Comfort" (37; 62; 94; 109) to the recently widowed young Mary (1505–1558), Queen Consort of Hungary and Bohemia. At the time when the evangelicals' fate was still in jeopardy, Luther hoped to find the sister of Emperor Charles V at least favorably inclined toward the Reformation, and offered from his part unsolicited words of comfort—assuming a pastoral role—and reinforcement in the battle against the common enemies, such as the Jews, as Luther wished to point out.[1]

The last of these "Psalms of Comfort" (Ps. 109) contains an extended imprecation or curse, commonly understood as being spoken by the Psalmist against his enemies. In this same vein, the New Testament book of Acts 1:20 understands the curse to be spoken against Judas. This New Testament reading of the Psalm then becomes in Luther's hands the curse of Christ himself against Judas and Judaism, and against all enemies of the gospel. The Jews of Luther's day continue to bear the ravages of this Christ-curse. Only three years removed from *That Jesus Christ Was Born a Jew*,[2] Luther here forcefully rejects any notion of a mass conversion of Jews, and emphasizes instead Judaism's Satan-induced hostility toward Christianity. Some— that is, a few—Jews will always convert but not Judaism. The Jews as a whole are portrayed as willfully stubborn and unconvertible. Contrary to the claim of the great Luther scholar, Martin Brecht, to the effect that Luther's words against the Jews here are "more descriptive than polemic,"[3] Luther's treatment of Psalm 109 stands as one of the most aggressively visceral things he ever wrote about the Jews, and this long before the fateful year of 1543. In light of his own words—"love does not curse or take vengeance, but faith does"—one can say that the issue Luther had with the Jews touched and shaped the core of his piety, the fundamentals of his faith. This was not a matter of politics but rather an occasion for Christians to gather the most powerful ammunition available to them: prayer.

In 1533 Luther composed brief summary statements for all 150 Psalms. His summary of Psalm 109 reads as follows: "Ps. 109 is a prayer-psalm, prayed in Christ's person against his betrayer, Judas, and [against] the Jews, his crucifiers. He complains fiercely about them and prophesies to them about how, being hardened by the wrath of God, they must perish and frightfully rot, just as we see all of this fulfilled before our very eyes."[4]

Psalm 109

{LW 14:257–58}

David composed this psalm about Christ, who speaks the entire psalm in the first person against Judas, His betrayer, and against Judaism as a whole, describing their ultimate fate. In Acts 1:20 St. Peter applied this psalm to Judas when they were selecting Matthias to replace him. He did not mean to say that the psalm speaks only about Judas; but, as he says there, Judas was the guide and ringleader in the capture and execution of Christ. Christ Himself testified before Pilate that Judas had committed the greatest sin by delivering Him (John 19:11).

The psalm is chiefly a denunciation of Judas, but also of all those who take Judas' part and continue to follow his lead. Christ Himself explains this here in the psalm when He says (v. 20): *"May this be the reward of My accusers."* The psalm begins with Judas and then extends to everyone of Judas' ilk, to all schismatics and persecutors of the Word of Christ; for they always slander the truth and persecute the genuine Christians. Against them this is a terrible psalm. It pronounces such curses and maledictions upon the enemies of Christ that some have made it a formula of imprecation for monks and nuns to pronounce against their enemies, and have said that if it is pronounced against anyone, he must die. But this is a falsehood and a fable.

Why does Christ pronounce such terrible curses when in Matt. 5{:44} He prohibits cursing and He Himself did not curse on the cross, as St. Peter says (1 Peter 2:23), but prayed for those who cursed and slandered Him (Luke 23:34)? I asked the same question earlier with regard to vengeance. In brief, the answer is: Love does not curse or take vengeance, but faith does. To understand this, you must distinguish between God and man, between persons and issues {*Sachen*}. Where God and issues are involved, there is neither patience nor blessing but only zeal, wrath, vengeance, and cursing. When the wicked persecute the Gospel, for example, this strikes at God and at His cause. We are not to bless them or wish them luck when they do this. Otherwise no one could preach or write even against heresy, because that is impossible without cursing. Anyone who preaches against heresy wishes that it be destroyed and tries as hard as possible to destroy it.

These I would call "curses of faith." Before faith would permit the Word of God to be destroyed and heresy to stand, it would prefer that all creatures be wiped out; for heresy deprives one of God Himself. The cursing of Christ in this psalm, then, is not on account of His person but on account of His office and His Word, because the error of the Jews is seeking to establish itself and to beat down the Gospel. He wishes that they be destroyed and have no success with their Judaizing {Jueden-thum}, just as Moses prays in Num. 16{:15} that God would not hear the prayer of Korah or respect their offering. Therefore it is necessary to curse, to wish evil, and to pray for vengeance against the persecution and perversion of the Gospel and against those who are guilty of it.

But the person should not avenge himself but should bear everything and even do good to his enemy, in accordance with the teaching of Christ and with the way of love. For here love is in charge, not faith; I am under attack, not faith. In the same way a Christian may act as a judge and sentence a murderer to death, yet not on his own behalf or for his own ends but on behalf of others and by virtue of his office. Then it is the same as if God had done it, for His ordinance is doing it. In short, it is permissible to curse on account of the Word of God; but it is wrong to curse on your own account for personal vengeance or some other personal end.

. . .

{LW 14:260–261}

{109:}6. *Appoint wicked men over him, let Satan stand at his right hand.* Nowhere in all the Scriptures have I read a more horrible curse or a more terrible misfortune than that described in these two verses, which are enough in themselves to bring terror and dread to all who persecute and attack the Word of God.

He says here: *"Appoint wicked men over them."* This "appoint" is פָּקַד in Hebrew, that is, "to install and ordain to an office," as bishops, pastors, and preachers, or secular lords and officials, are appointed. The meaning here is this: They simply refuse to tolerate Me and My teaching. If this is the way they want it, then so let it be. Let only false teachers, schismatics, and godless preachers come among them, teaching them lies, godless doctrine, and error, and leading them from one error into another. This is what they want!

In addition, *"let Satan stand at their right hand."* That is, let the devil so control them through his apostles that despite their desire to escape, their good intentions, and their efforts to do right and to know the truth the devil will be there disguising himself as an angel of light (2 Cor. 11:14) and restraining them. Let him so captivate them, so dazzle them and blind them with his fine appearance and lovely thoughts and words that they cannot escape, even though one were to present the truth to them so clearly and forthrightly that they could almost touch it.

We can see this punishment being visited nowadays on the Jews, who will not surrender their ideas even though they know that they have been refuted from the

Scriptures. What makes them that way? Not human reason or human blindness, for this could be budged; but, as this verse says, Satan is standing at their right hand. That has always been the attitude of heretics; it is the attitude of our schismatics toward the Sacrament, as well as that of the papacy.

But He is speaking about one person rather than about many, although previously He was complaining about many. For this concerns primarily Judas, the betrayer, who, as we have said, was the ringleader in guiding the mob against Christ; but it also concerns all others of his ilk. When he refused to listen to Christ, he had to listen to the wicked high priests; and although he was sorry afterwards and acted as though he wanted to do right, he did not return to the right path but fell into despair. For Satan was standing directly at his right hand and holding on to him. Paul speaks of such punishment in 2 Thess. 2{:11} when he says that God sends strong delusions upon those who did not accept the truth and insisted on believing lies. And Christ says in John 5{:43}: "I have come in My Father's name, and you do not receive Me; if another comes in his own name, him you will receive." This very thing is happening to us now in Germany, and it is going to get worse.

. . .

{LW 14:262–272}

{109:}8. *May his days be few; may another take his office!* St. Peter quotes this verse in Acts 1{:20} and says: *"Let another take his bishopric"*; he applies it to the replacement of Judas by Matthias. This application is correct, except that the Greek word ἐπισκοπή and the word "bishopric" sound strange to us because we think of a type of bishops and bishoprics unknown to Judas and St. Peter. For ἐπίσκοπος or "bishop," strictly speaking, means nothing more than an official, and "bishopric" means an office. The word means the same as was said earlier (v. 6): *"Appoint wicked men over them."* It refers to an office and to officials; for they are to be Christ's officials and to carry out His command, that is, to preach and support preaching. How well the bishops are doing this now is obvious! Therefore they have lost their office, and others have replaced them, as Matthias replaced Judas; for they have become Judases.

What He wants to say is this: Judas and his people, the Jews, are really entitled to hold the apostolic office and to preach the Gospel, but they do not want to. Therefore Matthias replaces Judas, and the Gentiles replace the Jews, preaching the Gospel which they were to preach and which had been promised to them. Similarly, because the bishops do not preach and because they follow the pope, their Judas, others who are not bishops will come to take over their office and to preach.

When He says: *"May his days be few,"* He means that he should not continue long. This was fulfilled even physically in the case of both Judas and the Jews; for Judas hanged himself soon after the betrayal, and the Jews were wiped out by the Romans soon thereafter. Now there follows a description of what will happen to the

Jews, Judas' people. For as we have said, He is speaking in particular about the Jews, although what He says applies in general to all wicked teachers.

{109:}9. *May his children be fatherless, and his wife a widow!* This is to happen to the women and children of the Jewish people, and it did when their men were killed by the Romans during the destruction of Jerusalem.

{109:}10. *May his children wander about and beg; may they seek, because their habitation is in ruins!* He pronounces every spiritual and physical plague upon the Jews. We can see that since the time of their destruction they have been wanderers, driven out here and there, and having no place to settle down. Everywhere they must beg, not for bread but for a place to live in a country. They must seek a place to live everywhere; for their own place to live in Palestine was destroyed, and they have no land, city, town, or government of their own anywhere. This verse ought to cause the Jews to think, for they can see that this has happened to them and to no other nation under the sun. Every nation except the Jews has its own villages, cities, and country. But the Jews are everywhere and have nothing of their own anywhere, no country, no city, no villages. They are always insecure guests and beggars.

{109:}11. *May the usurer seize all that he has; may strangers plunder the fruits of his toil!* It would seem that the opposite of what this verse says ought to happen, for the Jews are notorious usurers and bleed everyone white. But the psalm means to say that they will have no good fortune, but only misfortune, in body and soul, in children, property, and honor. Great usurers though they are, an even greater usurer is to come along and take it all away from them, as the second part of the verse says: *"May strangers plunder the fruits of his toil!"* This is what happens to the Jews. When they have saved for a long time, disaster strikes; they are hounded, robbed, punished, and deprived of what they have. They know that this will happen, and they bemoan it daily.

{109:}12. *Let there be none to extend kindness to him, nor any to pity his fatherless children!* My God, this is all too true! People regard the Jews as dogs, and anyone who can harm them or do them dirt supposes that he is doing a good deed. Because they and their children refuse to accept Christ, there is no mercy for these obdurate people. And yet they put up with it and cling to the vain hope for something better. So entrenched is Satan at their right hand!

{109:}13. *May his posterity be cut off; may their name be blotted out in the second generation!* Here He returns to a consideration of many; He says *"their name,"* not *"his name,"* to show us that He is talking about an entire nation. All this was fulfilled in the destruction of Jerusalem. Since that time there has never been a Jewish person who counted for much in Christendom and in the sight of God, except for the apostles. They were the last to have a name. Thus the memory and the name of the Jews have disappeared, although previously they had so many patriarchs and prophets whose names are not forgotten even today and whose teaching and life are praised throughout the world. But since that time they have had none such, and thus within one man's memory their name and honor have been blotted out.

If this verse were taken to mean that they would all be blotted out physically and have no memory of anyone even among themselves, it would conflict with the preceding verses, which say that their descendants are to beg and suffer want; if that is so, they must have some descendants. But it means that in the judgment of God and of God's people they no longer count for anything, as their forefathers and prophets do. They are indeed waiting for a prophet who will count for something, but they will be disappointed. This verse says that they have been done for since the time of the apostles.

{109:}14. *May the iniquity of his fathers be remembered before the Lord, and let not the sin of his mother be blotted out!* By "his" He means those of the Jewish nation. The verse means that everyone in the world will have to say what St. Stephen says to the Jews in Acts 7{:51}: "You have always resisted the Holy Spirit. As your fathers did, so do you." For it is evident that just as the fathers and mothers of the Jews, that is, their ancestors, always were disobedient to the prophets, so their children are today. They refuse to believe the same prophets their fathers refused to believe; the unbelief is identical. If their fathers had believed, they would not have persecuted the prophets. If the Jews today believed those same prophets, they would accept Christ. But they remain in the sin of their fathers. Therefore God does not forget them and continues to punish them as long as they go on sinning.

I would like to know what the Jews could say about this psalm. They have to admit that the Scriptures are talking about them, as St. Paul says in Rom. 3{:19}. All the verses of this psalm force one to the conclusion that they are describing a man, whether David or someone else, who is suffering this among the Jews and cursing them. History supports this text, because for the past fifteen hundred years no nation under the sun has been as cursed as the Jews. This did not happen to the enemies of David; but it is happening to the enemies of Jesus Christ, the Jews, just as these words describe it. This is incontestable. As I have said, reason could perhaps be persuaded; but Satan is standing at its right hand and refusing to let it understand.

{109:}15. *Let them be before the Lord continually; and may their memory be cut off from the earth!* That is, let the sin of their ancestors, which has been spoken of earlier, be before the Lord continually. For they refuse to give it up. Therefore God cannot hear their prayer or accept their works. This is why *"they remain before the Lord continually."* They always stir up their fathers' sin anew by the stubbornness of their hearts, and so they always remain accursed Jews, as He pictured them earlier.

In addition, *"their memory is cut off even on earth."* This does not mean that they will be unknown, but that they will not be referred to in sermons and narratives, as their patriarchs and prophets were. In this sense Ps. 16{:4} says: *"I will not remember them any more in My mouth."* For in the Scriptures "memory" does not mean that a person is only remembered—otherwise Judas, Pilate, and Herod would always be in our memory—but that he is lauded and praised, and has a good reputation. This does not happen to Judas and the Jews; they have been reviled continually ever since they were destroyed by the Romans. All this is spoken in particular about the Jews; for they committed their sin against Christ Himself, and they also have children and descendants. But the heretics, the schismatics, and the papacy, who do not have children, still have their punishment; for they will finally be destroyed, and their memory will be cut off forever. This is happening to the papacy now, as has been said often enough elsewhere.

. . .

{**109:**}**17.** *He loved to curse; let curses come on him! He did not like blessing; may it be far from him!* That is, he enjoyed cursing and malediction so much that he even cursed himself. Not that they overtly love cursing; but by these words the Holy Spirit indicates their horrible blindness and fearful obduracy, that they regard as a blessing what is the worst kind of curse and regard as a curse what is the most sublime blessing. Thus the Jews before Pilate cried out at Christ (Matt. 27:25): "His blood be on us and on our children!" I am of the opinion that this is a curse which is still bearing down hard on them. But they thought it was a wonderful blessing, saying to themselves: "Getting rid of this evildoer is a good deed in the sight of God. We are willing to take our chances with whatever threats may be involved, for we know that we shall obtain a blessing for it. So let His blood pour right over us!" . . .

{**109:**}**18.** *He clothed himself with cursing as his coat, may it soak into his body like water, like oil into his bones!* Here He shows that this stubbornness is so deeply seated and firmly established in their hearts that they simply cannot be converted. It does no good to preach to them or admonish them, to threaten them, sing to them, or speak to them. He describes their condition with three illustrations. The first is a "shirt" or article of clothing. Just as a man cannot be without a shirt or something next to his skin—for he should not go naked—and must have his clothes on every day, so the Jews must wear the stubbornness that makes them love their curse. There is no way out, because they cannot be without this stubbornness. It is part of their everyday business, just as one wears everyday clothes. In addition, they suppose that it becomes them and that they are doing the right thing by wearing it, just as clothes become a man and he does the right thing by wearing them and would do wrong if he walked around naked and unclothed. Thus the Jews suppose that they would be doing something shameful if they were to take off their stubbornness.

In the second place, when a man drinks water or something else—for by "water" Hebrew means any drink and by "bread" any food—and digests it to the point that it has become part of his flesh and blood, how can it ever be extracted from him? No bath, sweat, or medicine will do so; it has become part of his nature and, as the psalm says here, *"it has soaked into his body."* There it must remain, to go with him, and he with it, into the eternal fire of hell. This is what has happened to the Jews. Their stubbornness has soaked into them so far that it has become their very nature, and they can never change. Still they suppose that it is a good thing, a real elixir and a fine drink to refresh them, quench their thirst, and nourish them. They drink it in great quantities every day and use it to stay alive, just as a person satisfies and cools, refreshes and sustains himself every day by drinking. For they love and enjoy hearing and teaching such curses, just as a thirsty man enjoys drinking. This, I believe, is what "loving to curse" means.

In the third place, he speaks here of "oil," that is, of the good oil or balm with which one anoints oneself. For the oil from trees has the quality of being very beneficial to the body and making straight, strong, beautiful, and supple limbs. This is why boxers anoint their bodies with oil. Now when a man rubs off or salve on himself to the point that it penetrates into bone and marrow, as good salves are able to do, how can it ever be extracted from him? It is hard enough to extract it from clothing. Washing and rinsing, twisting and wringing, do no good. One would have to melt down the bones and marrow along with the salve, and even then one would not get it out! In the same way the curse and stubbornness of the Jews has so penetrated their heart, mind, and thought, their bones and marrow, that they are beyond help. They must be melted down in hell, and even then they will not be purged or cleansed of it. Still they suppose that it is a precious ointment, and that their teaching is as beneficial to them as oil is to the body. They imagine that it makes them strong, healthy, handsome, lovely, and shiny in the sight of God, as oil makes the body in the sight of men. And so they smear it on more and more all the time.

We see this in our daily contacts with Jews.[5] How stiff and stubborn they are from one generation to the next! They are incredibly venomous and spiteful in their language about Christ. What we believe and teach about Christ they regard as sheer poison and a curse. They suppose that Christ was nothing more than a criminal who, because of His crime, was crucified with other criminals. Whenever they mention Him, therefore, they refer to Him odiously as Thola,[6] "the hanged one." For since they believe that Jesus was a criminal, it is inevitable that they should regard us Christians as the most foolish and filthy people under the sun. Their reason must tell them that if a murderer were beheaded today and then tomorrow some people came along, worshiped him, and looked upon him as true God, this would be much more foolish than worshiping a log or a stone. It would be the most foolish thing imaginable.

What makes it worse is that we Christians are also bad and set a bad example. Thus they are so confirmed in their offense that this curse has penetrated into their bones and marrow and has poisoned them until they cannot escape and come to regard the crucified Jesus as Lord and God. It is always ridiculous to them that we Christians worship a condemned Jewish criminal, as though we worshiped Cain or

Absalom as gods. But there they are. The oil has soaked into their bones, and they go on soaking up the water. What a terrible judgment and illustration of divine wrath!

{109:}19. *May it be like a garment which he wraps round him, like a belt with which he daily girds himself!* That is, let it happen to him as he wishes. Let the curse for which he is asking cling to him. Let him regard the Gospel as a poison and a curse, and Christ as a criminal. Let him be and remain so obdurate that God withdraws His hand and refuses to send His Spirit and Word among them for their conversion, as He threatens in Is. 5{:6}: *"I will command the clouds that they rain no rain upon them."*

This does not mean that no Jew may ever come to faith again. Some crumbs must remain, and some individuals must be converted. But Judaism, as we call the Jewish nation, will not be converted. The Gospel, by which the Holy Spirit might find room among them, is not preached among them either. But where they gather in their synagogs, they keep their curse and poison; they curse Christ, regarding their poison as salvation and their curse as a blessing. Nevertheless, some will occasionally spring up individually from the group, so that God might still remain the God of the seed of Abraham and might not reject them altogether, as St. Paul says in Rom. 11{:1–2}.

You should note that He speaks here about the everyday "garment" and "belt," not the garment that lies in the chest or the belt that lies in the cupboard but the one he puts on and wears every day. This is to signify the obdurate mind which they never lose and the confirmed curse with which they deal every day and which they never give up, supposing that it becomes them very well.

{109:}20. *May this be the reward of My accusers from the Lord, of those who speak evil against My soul!* The prayer in this psalm is answered. This will happen to all the enemies of Christ, but especially to the Jews (whom He has particularly in mind), as the obvious course of events also shows. The real issue is their word or speaking, that they teach against Christ, curse, condemn, and blaspheme Him, and would like to see Him destroyed. This is meant by: *"They speak evil against My soul,"* that is, against My life. They would like to see Me dead and destroyed, so much do they hate Me. But the God of My praise is not silent. He praises and elevates Him even more when they curse and condemn Him . . .

That is what this psalm means when it says that all the enemies of Christ love to curse and do not like blessing, and that they do not change. Therefore St. Paul also says in Titus 3{:10–11} that one should have nothing to do with a factious man after admonishing him twice, for he is perverted. I have never read of false teachers and instigators of heresy being converted. They remain obdurate in their own opinions. The oil has soaked into their marrow and bone; the water has become flesh and blood, part of their nature. They will not listen or discuss. This is the sin against the Holy Spirit, which cannot be forgiven. It will not repent or be sorry, but will only defend and excuse itself, as though it were something holy and precious and as though the Gospel which opposes it were something demonic . . .

{LW 14:275–276}

{109:}26. *Help Me, O Lord My God! Save Me according to Thy steadfast love!* He closes the psalm with the petition that God be with Him and make the wickedness of the Jews and of all His enemies evident, together with His righteousness, so that they may come to naught and He may be vindicated. And God is to do all this *"according to His steadfast love."* Previously He has shown the curses and evil being directed against Him by their obdurate and insane hearts. Now He asks that through the judgment of God this may become evident before the whole world, so that they may be deprived also of the fine outward appearance which they still have, be put to shame before the whole world, and thus be caught in both their sin and their shame, as we see happening now to the poor Jews.

{109:}27. *Let them know that this is Thy hand; Thou, O Lord, hast done it!* Although they refuse to see that what Thou art doing to Me and to them is Thy work, let it become evident to the whole world, and let everyone say: "Of course, this is the work of God, that the Jews are defeated and on the decline, while Christ is soaring and increasing. Human powers could not have accomplished this."

{109:}28. *Let them curse, but do Thou bless! If they arise, let them be put to shame; but let Thy servant be glad!* "Do not let their curses on Me and Mine accomplish anything; but the more they curse, the more do Thou bless. And if they arise against Me, let that be put to shame soon." It seems to me that the Jews ought to be very familiar with this verse! My God, how often in various countries have they started something against Christ, only to be burned at the stake, killed, and hounded for it! It never fails. When they arise, they are put to shame, burned at the stake, or driven out. But Christ and His own remain joyous in God, for this confirms them in their faith.
. . .

Text #14

Lectures on Isaiah (1527–1530)

Language:	Latin
Critical Edition:	WA 31/2: (vii), 1–585. 2nd ed. (WA 25: (79), 87–401)
English Translation:	LW 16–17

In the late 1520's and as part of the ongoing project to translate the prophetic books into German, Luther lectured through the entire book of Isaiah. Begun in the summer of 1527 and interrupted twice, once by the plague (1527) and once by an extended trip to Marburg (1529), he was able to finish the book in February 1530 (published 1532). We are dependent on the work of two student scribes for the content of the lectures. A second expanded edition was published in 1534.

On thematic grounds, Luther regarded Isaiah as being two books in one, chapters 1–39 and 40–66. The first book deals with matters relating to the Assyrian period but also contains prophecies of Christ. He describes Isaiah as functioning here as a "historical prophet." But with regard to chapters 40–66 he states: "This second book is nothing but prophecy, first external, concerning King Cyrus, and then spiritual, concerning Christ. And here the prophet is the most joyful of all, fairly dancing with promises."[1] Throughout his treatment of Isaiah he is true to a lifelong conviction of his: "The chief and leading theme of all the prophets is their aim to keep the people in eager anticipation of the coming Christ."[2]

Excerpted below are selections from Luther's treatment of two judgment oracles, Isa. 63:1-6 and Isa. 65:8-16. Isaiah 63:1-6, a judgment oracle against Edom that portrays God as a blood-stained warrior, is one of the most repulsive oracles in the Bible. Luther reads the passage as the triumphant Christ taking vengeance on the synagogue, and in this context he utters the breathtaking statement: "Every calamity of the Jews is because of Christ."

Isaiah 65:8-16 reflects a bitter inner-community tension between "my servants" and an anonymous "you." Luther reads the passage as a prophecy of the bitter tension that will develop between Church and Synagogue. All of the judgment language in the passage is read as directed against the Synagogue, for the benefit of the Church, which, ironically, has its origin in the "remnant of the Jews."

{LW 17:352–354}

{Isa. 63:1-6}

{63:}1. *Who is this that comes from Edom, in crimsoned garments from Bozrah?* This text has received a variety of interpretations. Many think it refers to Christ's resurrection and His ascension into heaven. This is our opinion: The prophet adds some threats for those who despise the Word, so that those who did not want to obey the promises must hear threats, for such is the custom of the prophets after they have taught, instructed, and exhorted. Thus this chapter is nothing but a very harsh threat, in which the prophet by means of personification sets the angry person of God before them. Christ says, *"He who believes will be saved"* (Mark 16:16). Then follows the threat, *"he who does not believe will be condemned."* So here, following the promises, he sets forth an angry Christ and rebukes their stubbornness by means of threats, as if to say, "If you will not accept the promise, God will grind you down and break you in pieces. If you do not want grace, then receive wrath. Therefore grasp the word *Edom*. In a passage above (34:6) Edom is the slaughter. Edom denotes the ungodly synagog, which lies in wait for Esau when the name of God is lost and it has divested itself of the Spirit of God. Summary: This has to do with the devastation of the synagog.

Who is this that comes from Edom? Jeremiah speaks of Bozrah (Jer. 48:24). There were two cities called Bozrah. One was in the kingdom of Israel. The other was in the region of Moab, which is called the city of Arabia, where the Arabs are and where the Bozrah episcopate was. Nothing is said about these two Bozrahs. But the prophet is speaking about Idumea, about which Jeremiah speaks. Edom is a part of Arabia Petraea. The Edomites, Ishmaelites, and Moabites live in this Arabia. This is what the prophet wants to indicate, that he does not mean the chief city of Petraea, but *Bozrah*. He calls them *Edom*, red Jews,[3] bloodthirsty and murderous. Esau was bloodthirsty and ungodly. He wanted to kill his brother. Because they are most violent in wrath, they are called Edomites, the red Jews. He calls him *Bozrah*, that is "armed," "a fortress," for the Jews were armed with promises, testament, and covenants, in which they gloried as if they were thoroughly armed. *Who is this?* The prophet begins to terrify the Jews. "Good God, what a frightful thing this is to see! I see someone coming up from Edom with red garments." So today someone might in a frightful vision terrify Germany with some star of a comet. Thus here: "We thought God was a Savior. Now He comes as an enemy and an avenger. What a terrible thing I see." It is a personification and a figure depicting an angry Christ and a great slaughter and vengeance coming upon Edom. Summary: This is a dreadful personification taken from a dreadful giant who will take revenge on his enemies and kill them.

He that is glorious in His apparel. First He was crucified and lowly, a person they did not want to accept by faith. Now He walks *glorious in His apparel*, that is, He has received a kingdom, and He is Lord of kings and rulers. Who are you?

It is I, announcing vindication. He frightens, but He says, "Fear not, I am the Savior of the godly, *I announce vindication* to them, and I am *mighty to save* them." This is a description of the reign of Christ: to speak to men, to proclaim salvation, and not to condemn the sinners but receive them, and "I fight for them and protect them."

{63:}2. *Why is Thy apparel red?* There you have the land abounding with grapes. He washed His garments in the blood of grapes, because this area abounds in red grapes. Those who tread such grapes bespatter themselves with red. He repeats this personification against the hardened. "Oh, I have seen His strength, that He crushes His enemies, just as some winepress crushes the grapes."

{63:}3. *I have trodden the winepress alone.* Some have twisted this text to refer to the Passion, and they have pictured Christ with a winepress, where a lamb stood by, but this is absurd. Here winepresses denote the punishment itself, slaughter and calamity, where the people are burned and slain. So it is in the Apocalypse (cf. Rev. 9:15). So here: "The reason why I am spattered with red is that I have trodden the winepresses. I am alone, and there is no one with Me. The Jews had sinned against Me, and by that one sin alone of refusing to believe Me they should perish, if for no other sin than that they sinned against Me." By this word he wants to admonish the Jews not to lay hands on this Christ, as if to say, "Sin as you like, but do not sin against this Christ." Hence the personification here describes Christ, who alone should crush the Jews because of this one sin "of not believing in Me." He crushed all the Jews, and therefore they suffered and were scattered "for My sake alone." Otherwise they would have sinned as they wished.

In anger and wrath, that is, there is no mercy for them.

Their blood is sprinkled, that is, every calamity of the Jews is for the sake of Christ. "I am the cause of the destruction of this people. I had to do it because they refused to believe." Thus at the last advent we shall see all our kings perish because of this one sin. They will be sprinkled.

{63:}4. *For the day of vengeance was in My heart.* "They have persecuted Me, they have killed the apostles and prophets, who were offering the grace which they did not want. Therefore they shall have wrath and vengeance. He who does not want to have life, let him have death. Then, when the vengeance comes, they will not blame it on the ungodliness of Christ crucified." This shows how blind they are.

{63:}5. *I looked, but there was no one to help.* This is said concerning His passion. "In that time when I was their servant, still mortal. They imagine that I am now still mortal and dead. But I suffered in order to be exalted."

I was appalled. "I sought," that is, "I was terrified," that is, "I was dead in order to make alive; I was oppressed in order to exalt; I was disgraced in order to bring honor."

So My own arm brought Me victory, and My righteousness preserved Me. "Even though they refused to help Me, I am saved, and this because of My arm, My righteousness and strength."

{63:}6. *I trod down the peoples in My anger.* He describes the manner in which the Jews perished. The weak Christ comes "to save and justify them, but they killed Me. Therefore, since they did not want Me, they have perished by My vengeance." Thus we can say today: "What a dreadful thing will come upon the priests." This is the meaning of this little chapter, that at the close of the promises it brings terror, as if to say, "If you do not want to have salvation and Christ, receive Him from Edom with stained garments."

And I pulled down, that is, "they are powerful in armaments, in the glory and pride of promises, but I will deprive them of these things."

{LW 17:381–385}
{Isa. 65:8-16}

{65:}8. *Thus says the Lord: As the wine is found in the cluster.* An objection precedes the question, as Abraham says (Gen. 18:23), "Wilt Thou indeed destroy the righteous with the wicked?" To this objection God answers, "I will not do it." For God knows how to save the godly and confound the ungodly. The ungodly are flint, iron, and steel. The more you preach to them, the more they are hardened. The godly, however, are soon plunged into despair by the appearance of those words. Those for whom the message is intended give it no heed, while those whom it does not concern pay too much attention to it. For that reason they are consoled. *As the wine is found in the cluster.* He draws a comparison from one who destroys a vineyard. It is like the father of a family who at great cost acquires a vineyard and yet gets nothing and for that reason wants to uproot the vineyard. And yet he can be concerned about one or two vines, and for their sake he spares the vineyard. It is as if one or two grapes were interceding. "Therefore some upright people should plead with Me, lest the whole synagog be destroyed, although the synagog has been totally dispersed."

Do not destroy it, for there is a blessing in it. Do not tear it up altogether. There must be something good left in it. There will still be some saint who is blessed.

So I will do for My servants' sake. "These, I say, are good grapes. Have no fear. No harm shall come to you, because you are the clusters and grapes and the source of blessing, and through you the vineyard shall rise again." Even so the church arose from the remnant of the Jews.

{65:}9. *I will bring forth descendants from Jacob.* "I will not destroy in such a way that there will be no seed left from which a new people may grow. Thus *I will bring forth,* I will produce, I will let it sprout and germinate. I will bring forth bread from the earth. So *I will bring forth descendants from Jacob and from Judah,* from whom My new holy people shall arise."

Mountains, princes, rulers, parish pastor, church, congregation. In Hebrew they are called mountains. So God here promises that the Word, the church, and the synagog shall remain.

My chosen shall inherit it, the mountain. *My chosen.* This is a promise that the church will endure. Where the Word of God is, there is a proper knowledge of ourselves and of God, there will be a threat to the world and Satan, and so the church will endure ...

{65:}13. *Therefore.* Here He threatens retribution. *Behold, My servants, etc.* He speaks of the abundance of Esau, because He is at pains to terrify the people. For that reason He makes so many threats.

This is a very severe statement, that we always rage against God with a stiff neck, that we always prefer to choose what we like rather than what God has ordained. *Therefore ... behold, My servants.* These are promises which God shifts from the Jewish people to the remnant and to the Gentiles. It is a complete repudiation by which He rejects the synagog because its iniquities are unyielding. It is stiff-necked, and because of its obstinacy everything is taken away from it and everything is changed. Here I do not make a distinction between the spiritual and the physical abundance of God's people, but I say that they should be prodigal both in body and in spirit. They shall eat and drink and be happy with all their heart. The godly are always rich, even though they are poor. Honor and riches are in his house (cf. Prov. 3:16). A pious Christian has more in one biscuit than the ungodly has in the whole bag. "Better is a little that the righteous has than the abundance of many wicked" (Ps. 37:16). This "little" is much because of the blessing. He says here that He will take this blessing from the Jews and give it to the Christians, who are to live well and safely. Christians are described "as having nothing, and yet possessing everything" in 2 Cor. 6{:10}. In extreme poverty they have riches in blessing, while the ungodly hunger in the midst of great wealth. "Better is a handful of quietness than two hands full of toil and a striving after wind" (Eccl. 4:6).

{65:}14. *Behold, My servants shall sing for gladness of heart.* "They shall shout and praise and give thanks, but through our preaching you shall howl." *You shall wail for anguish of spirit.*

{65:}15. *You shall leave your name, etc.* This is a Hebraism used by the prophets, as if to say, "I will set you for a hiss and for gossip. *For a curse*, that is, *your name* will be *a curse*, that is, will be used for cursing and swearing." So we say, "May St. Valentine's disease get me!" So we swear, "If I do this, may God let me become a Jew." Thus the name of the Jews is so completely disastrous that people use it to curse and swear by. There is no name under heaven that is more accursed than the name of the Jews. "Pew! May I become a Jew!" Summary: The Jewish name was once a most glorious name. It has now become the most accursed among Christians.

The Lord God will slay you. They shall no longer be called Jews. The synagog will be utterly destroyed, and kingdom, priesthood, government, and every kind of ruler has come to an end.

But His servants He will call by a different name. This is a blessed name that is to be given to the Christians.

. . .

Text #15

Preface to Daniel (1530)

Language: German
Critical Edition: WA DB 11/2:2–130 (even)
English Translation: LW 35:294–316

Luther composed prefaces to the books of the Bible (including the Apocrypha) as part of the masssive project of translating the Bible into German, and these prefaces were then printed as part of the *Luther Bibel*, which first appeared in complete form in 1534 and then subsequently revised between 1541 and 1545. The German New Testament, which Luther had translated over a three-month period while on the Wartburg, had appeared already in 1522, but it took twelve years for him and his translation team to complete the work on the Old Testament. Though the prefaces were intended to aid the general reader, they are of high value toward understanding the basic principles of Luther's approach to the biblical text.

The translation of Daniel was first issued as a separate publication in 1530, and the preface for it was composed at that time. In that same year Luther also wrote a new Preface to Revelation, but unlike this one it is strikingly lacking in anti-Jewish polemic. Luther had a supremely high estimate of the prophetic qualities of Daniel, and he was convinced that the book contained the blueprint for the time of the coming of the Messiah as well as the progression of subsequent human history. Over the course of his career, Luther came more and more to believe that the end of the world was imminent. His reading of Genesis, Daniel, Ezekiel, and Revelation, coupled with his "reading" of contemporary world events and figures played the central role in this developing conviction of his.[1]

This period was a particularly stressful time for the Evangelicals. At the Diet of Speyer (1529), the notorious edict of Worms (1521) was revived with an agenda to destroy Evangelical presence in Germany and so return all of Germany to the Catholic faith. Then the Diet of Augsburg (1530) similarly seemed to bring an end to hopes for the legitimizing of Evangelical faith practices, not to mention the reformation of Christendom. In many ways, this did in fact seem like the end. It would not be until 1555 and the Peace of Augsburg that the existence of Lutheran churches would be authorized.

Excerpted below are selections of Luther's 1530 treatment of Daniel 9 as well as his concluding summary to the book. Daniel 9 contains the reinterpretation of Jeremiah's prophecy of a seventy-year exile (see Jer. 25 and 29) as seventy "weeks of years," that is, 490 years. This passage was one of Luther's most important proof texts, for it, he argues, contains the exact prediction of when the Messiah would come, that is, in the seventieth week, which corresponds precisely with the life and ministry of Jesus. Luther points out as well that a strict corollary of the death of the Messiah is the end of Judaism. Throughout his treatment of the passage, Luther is confused on both the names of Persian rulers as well as the dates of their reigns, and this is attributable to the inadequacy of the historical sources on which he was dependent. In his concluding summary to the book as a whole, he states that the chronology of the coming of the Messiah is so clear and certain that the only way to miss it is via willful resistance. This is directed straight at the Jews.

In 1541 Luther added an expanded commentary on Daniel 12 in the direction of the Pope as Anti-Christ and also adjusted the commentary on Daniel 9. The primary difference in the Daniel 9 section is in his adjusting the ministry of Jesus from the middle of the seventieth week to the beginning. The 1530 and 1541 Prefaces to Daniel are by far the longest he would write for any biblical book.

{Daniel 9}
{LW 35:303–305}

The ninth chapter opens with a splendid prayer in which Daniel prays for his people who are held captive in Babylon, and for the city of Jerusalem and the temple. He prays that the Jews might return to Jerusalem and there resume their worship of God. The prayer is answered, and to Daniel is revealed the number of years until Christ should come and begin his eternal kingdom. Now this is a remarkable and great revelation of Christ which sets the time so surely and accurately.

These seventy weeks, as decreed by the angel, are unanimously regarded by all teachers as weeks of years and not as weeks of days; that is, one week denotes seven years and not seven days. Experience also demands this interpretation, for seventy weeks of days add up to less than two years, and this would be no remarkable [span of] time for such a glorious revelation. But seventy weeks of years total four hundred and ninety years. This is how long men were still supposed to wait for Christ, and then his kingdom was to begin.

Here, of course, we must inquire as to where and when these seventy weeks begin. The angel explains them; he begins in the year that a command goes out for the rebuilding of Jerusalem. For he speaks thus, "From the going forth of the word to restore and build Jerusalem," etc. [9:25], which some have badly stretched and twisted. But in order that we may proceed correctly in this matter we must begin these seventy weeks with the second year of King Darius, who was called Longimanus. For in that same year the Word of God came through the prophets Haggai [1:1–15] and Zechariah [1:1–17], and Zerubbabel gave orders to build the temple; as we read in the first chapter of both of these prophets. This same Darius commanded the very same thing, and his commandment was executed accordingly, Ezra 6[:6–15].

★Now the calculation [of the years] agrees with this. From the commandment or word spoken through Haggai, up to the baptism of Christ when he took up his office and when his kingdom or the New Testament began—the angel here speaks of him as a "prince"—is incidentally 483 years. This makes sixty-nine of these weeks, of which the angel says, *"Unto Christ, the prince, there shall be seven weeks, and threescore and two weeks,"* that is, sixty-nine weeks. The calculation is as follows: from the second year of Darius to Alexander the Great are 145 years, according to Metasthenes; from Alexander to the birth of Christ are 311 years, as the histories attest; and from the birth of Christ to his baptism are thirty years, according to Luke 3[:23]. That makes a total of 486 years; these are the sixty-nine weeks. There is a remainder of three years. These we must ignore in our calculations because it often happens in such calculations and histories that a half-year is called a whole year. It is impossible to account for every day and hour when writing history. It is good enough for us to come this close, especially since we have such specific scriptural information concerning the main items.

This opinion approximates that of those who begin the seventy weeks with the twentieth and last year of Cambyses, the father of Darius, who gave permission to Nehemiah to return and restore Jerusalem, Nehemiah 2, for the twentieth year of Cambyses is actually two years before the second year of Darius. Now when a great event happens within [a matter of] three years, one must really understand it as comprising one year, that is, a single period of time, and say: it happened about such and such a time. So here one must say: The word of God—that Jerusalem should be restored and built—went forth in the second year of Darius, about the time that Nehemiah came from Cambyses and began to rebuild Jerusalem, etc. For this was a great event, begun by many—and even promoted by angels, as Zech 1[:7–17] declares—yet not by everybody at once on the same day or at the same hour [Ezra 1–6].★[2]

Now the angel further divides these seventy weeks into three parts. In the first seven weeks—that is, in forty-nine years—(he says) the wall and streets shall be rebuilt, in troublous times. And he really had trouble too, because of the intense opposition in the neighboring countries [Neh. 2:10; 4; 6]. ★This agrees with the statement of the Jews to Christ in John 2[:20], *"It has taken forty-six years to build this temple, and will you raise it up in three days?"* Then after sixty-two weeks (he says) Christ shall be put to death.

Here he shows what is to happen when these sixty-nine weeks are up, and Christ has begun [his ministry], namely, that Christ shall be crucified (which happened in the fourth year after the sixty-nine weeks and after the beginning [of his ministry]), and that the city of Jerusalem shall therefore finally be destroyed, and Judaism come to an end (which afterward happened at the hands of the Romans). The one last week—that is, seven years—is the time which follows the sixty-nine weeks, during which (as has been said) Christ was supposed to be put to death. And that took place in this way (as the angel states [9:27]): He shall make a covenant with many for one week. For the preaching of Christ spread mightily during those seven years, both through Christ himself up into the fourth year, and thereafter through the apostles, proclaiming to the people the promised grace. In the midst of that same week—that is, during the fourth year after his baptism—Christ was put to death. And then the sacrifice ceased; that is, through Christ's death, which is the true sacrifice, the Jewish sacrifice and worship were abolished. Then the Romans under Emperor Caius Caligula placed an idol in the temple (as the angel says here [9:27]) as a sign that the temple and Judaism were to be at an end.★³

{Concluding Summary of Daniel}
{LW 35:313–314}

From this book we see what a splendid, great man Daniel was in the sight of both God and the world. First in the sight of God, he above all other prophets had this special prophecy to give. That is, he not only prophesies of Christ, like the others, but also reckons, determines, and fixes with certainty the times and years. Moreover he arranges the kingdoms with their doings so precisely and well, in the right succession down to the fixed time of Christ, that one cannot miss the coming of Christ unless one does it wilfully, as do the Jews. In addition, from that point on until the Last Day, Daniel also depicts the condition and state of the Roman Empire and the affairs of the world in such an ordered way that one cannot miss the Last Day or have it come upon him unawares, unless one does this too wilfully, as our Epicureans are doing just now.

Therefore it seems to me that St. Peter had Daniel especially in mind when he says in 1 Peter 1[:11], *"The prophets searched what, and what manner of time the Spirit of Christ did signify,"* etc. The "what" means that he definitely reckons and determines the time, how long and how many years it was to be until then. The "what manner" means that he depicts well how things are to be in the world at that time, who is to exercise supreme rule, or where the empire is to be. Thus Daniel proclaims not only the time but also the activity, shape, and nature of that time. And this strengthens our Christian faith immeasurably and makes us sure and firm in our consciences. For we see in operation before our very eyes that which he described and depicted for us so plainly and correctly in his book so long ago.

For Daniel freely prophesies and plainly declares that the coming of Christ and the beginning of his kingdom (that is, Christ's baptism and preaching ministry) is to happen five hundred and ten years after King Cyrus (Daniel 9),—when the empire of the Persians and of the Greeks is at an end, and the Roman Empire in force (Daniel 7 and 9)—and that therefore Christ assuredly had to come at the time of the Roman Empire, when it was at its height, the empire which was also to destroy Jerusalem and the Temple, since after Rome there is to be no other empire but only the end of the world as Daniel 2 and 7 clearly state.

. . .

Text #16

Letter to Josel of Rosheim (1537)

Table Talk, no. 3597		Letter to Josel of Rosheim	
Language:	Latin	Language:	German
Critical Edition:	WA TR 3:441 (no. 3597)	Critical Edition:	WA Br 8:89–91 (no. 3157)
English Translation:	LW 54:239 (#3597)	English Translation:	Editors[1]

In August 1536, Elector John Frederick issued an edict making Electoral Saxony off limits for Jews; they were not to live there, do business there, or even pass through the territory. Permanent residence in Electoral Saxony had been denied Jews since 1432, but obviously at least in small numbers Jews had continued to function there, as well as in other Evangelical territories, such as neighboring Hesse. That the 1530's again brought tightened regulations for Jews, especially in strongholds of evangelical faith, raises the question of the reformers' impact.[2] In Saxony the most powerful theologian remained oddly quiet in regard to his prince's anti-Jewish legislation. Given the influence Luther had on the Elector, with whom he had recently met in late July,[3] and in light of what we know of Luther's anti-Jewish theological arguments, his silent approval is apparent. If his silence was misinterpreted by those seeking in him a possible ally of the Jews in these volatile times, Luther would make his position clear in a private letter to a famous Jewish man he should have met.

As soon as this new edict in Saxony came to the attention of Rabbi Joseph (Josel) of Rosheim (1478?–1554), the appointed spokesman for the Jews of Germany looked immediately in Luther's direction.[4] Josel had tirelessly and often successfully intervened on behalf of Jewish individuals accused of faith crimes and Jewish communities facing expulsions. Finding his way before different governing authorities, from private audiences to imperial diets and princely gatherings (Frankfurt 1539), he debated with those slandering the Jews (such as Antonius Margaritha, Diet of Augsburg 1530) and actively participated in seeking reasonable regulations for business affairs involving Jews as well as rights and protection for travel, dwelling, and business in the empire.[5] Josel was able to persuade the Strasbourg reformer, Wolfgang Capito, to write a letter to Luther on his behalf requesting an "audience," in hopes that he could persuade Luther to intercede with the Elector and have the edict rescinded.[6] This meeting never took place.

Capito's letter, which stressed Josel's good character to counter rumors of recent incidents of Jewish financial malpractice, was received by Luther in April 1537.[7] He then responded directly to Josel shortly thereafter. In his letter, which is riddled with condescension and foreshadows the "roar" in the soon to be written *Against the Sabbatarians*,[8] Luther makes clear that he will do nothing to help Josel—or the Jews of Saxony—because the Jews have misused his *That Jesus Christ Was Born a Jew*[9] as licence to remain Jews, that is, not convert.

In addition to a translation of Luther's letter to Josel, presented below is also a relevant Table Talk in which Luther alludes to the Josel situation and also expresses his belief that Jews are actively proselytizing Christians.

Table Talk: The Petition of a Jew Is Refused
Between May 27 and June 18, 1537
{LW 54:239}

A letter was delivered to Dr. Martin from a certain Jew who requested and pleaded (as he had often written to the doctor before) that permission be obtained from the elector[10] to grant him safe entrance into and passage through the elector's principality. Dr. Martin responded, "Why should these rascals, who injure people in body and property and who withdraw many Christians to their superstitions, be given permission? In Moravia they have circumcised many Christians and call them by the new name of Sabbatarians. This is what happens in those regions from which preachers of the gospel are expelled; there people are compelled to tolerate the Jews. It is said that Duke George[11] declared with an oath that before he would tolerate the Lutherans he would lay waste all churches, baptism, and sacraments. As if we didn't preach the same service of Christ and the same sacraments! In short, the world wants to be deceived. However, I'll write this Jew not to return."

Letter to Josel of Rosheim (June 11, 1537)

To the cautious Jesel, Jew of Rosheim, my good friend. My dear Jesel! I would gladly have appealed to my most gracious lord on your behalf, both orally and in writing, for my [previous] publication[12] has served all of Jewry so well; but because your people so shamefully misuse my service and undertake such things, which we Christians cannot accept from them, they themselves have thereby taken from me any influence that I otherwise might have had with dukes and lords.

For my heart has been, and still is, that one should treat the Jews kindly, out of the conviction that God might now graciously consider them and bring them to their Messiah; but [certainly] not out of the conviction that through my benevolence and influence they should be strengthened in their error and become worse.

If God gives me the space and time, I will write a booklet about this, that I might win several from your paternal stock of the holy patriarchs and prophets, and bring [them] to your promised Messiah. Although, it is quite odd that we should have to entice and lure you to your natural Lord and King, in the same way as formerly your ancestors, when Jerusalem was still standing, enticed and lured the Gentiles to the true God.

Therefore, shouldn't you think that we Gentiles would be so arrogant and despicable—for apart from this Gentiles and Jews have at all times been deadly enemies—that we wouldn't worship even your best King, much less such a damned crucified Jew, unless the power and might of the true God would forcefully bring it into the hearts of us arrogant Gentiles, your enemies? For you Jews would never worship as Lord a hanged or tortured Gentile after his death; this you know.

Therefore, you shouldn't consider us Christians to be fools or [dumb] geese. Instead, you should reflect on whether God will release you from the present misery, which by now has lasted more than 1500 years. This will not happen, unless you accept with us Gentiles your cousin and Lord, the dear crucified Jesus.

For I have also read your Rabbis, and if their writings contained this, I would not be so stubborn and stone-hearted, and it might have convinced me as well. But they can do nothing more than scream that he is a crucified, damned Jew, even though all your ancestors were incapable of leaving the saints and prophets undamned, unstoned and untortured. In fact, they would have to be damned if your opinion is correct, namely, that Jesus of Nazareth was crucified and damned by you Jews. For you have done such things in the past and always.

Just read what you did with your king David and with all pious kings, indeed, with all holy prophets and people, and then you won't consider us Gentiles such dogs. For you see that your imprisonment lasts too long, and [yet] you find us Gentiles, whom you consider your greatest enemies, favorable and willing to advise and help you, even though we can't tolerate the fact that you curse and blaspheme your own flesh and blood, Jesus of Nazareth, who has done you no harm, and that if you could you would rob his followers of everything they are and have.

Now, let me be a prophet, although I am a Gentile like Balaam[13] was. What you hope for will not happen, because the point in time determined by Daniel has long passed. And even if you craftily twist and change the text so that it suits you, the fact remains.

Take this from me as friendly advice, as an admonition to you. Because I would happily do the best for you Jews for the sake of the crucified Jew—whom no one will take from me—unless you use my favor [as an excuse] for your obstinacy. You know exactly what I mean. Therefore, perhaps you ought to have your letters to the Elector delivered through others. God bless! Dated in Wittenberg on the Monday after St. Barnabas Day, 1537.

Mart. Luther

Text #17

Lectures on Genesis 12 (1537)

Language: Latin
Critical Edition: WA 42–44 (here WA 42:446–51)
English Translation: LW 1–8 (here LW 2:259–66)

Luther's career as a professor of Bible at the University of Wittenberg began with lectures on the Psalter, which he delivered over the years 1513–1515. These first lectures by the young professor are saturated with anti-Jewish references and allusions. At the opposite end of his career stand the lectures on Genesis (1535–1545), a work rightly called his *magnum opus*. Here Luther in many ways concludes on the most essential theological topics of his time, such as creation, the fall, the origins of sin, the issue of free will, God's omnipotence and omniscience, the limits of human knowledge of God manifest in three persons, and, above all, the work of the Word. The chronology of these lectures is not precise, and in addition it is known that they were interrupted on numerous occasions, not least of which was the plague.

It is noteworthy that Luther's rigorous exegetical engagement with Genesis coincides with the period of time when his most infamous anti-Jewish treatises were written and published. When these two corpora are compared, one finds a high degree of coherence in terms of what Luther says about the Jews in general and about Rabbinic interpretation in particular, with the important difference that the Genesis lectures lack any reference to the medieval atrocity stories about the Jews that become commonplace in the 1543 treatises.

Luther's *Genesis* is polemical, and the usual suspects, Jews—Heretics—Pope—Turks—*Schwärmer* ("Enthusiasts"), are attacked with regularity. A prominent characteristic of his anti-Jewish invectives (which appear throughout the lectures) is the overt hostility he expresses toward Rabbinic interpretation of the Bible in general and of Genesis in particular. Over the course of his career Luther developed a visceral antipathy toward the Rabbis, and he came to hold them liable for Jewish resistance to the message of the gospel. In the Genesis lectures in particular, one encounters denigration after denigration. At best the Rabbis are arbitrary, at worst nonsensical. At best they know grammar, at worst they are devoid of theological understanding. He reacted vehemently against Rabbinic ambiguity/plurality of meaning, and he called their readings "*gemachte Grammatica*" (artificial grammar). By way of example we quote here an extended diatribe, which captures in one place the level of antagonism that one encounters throughout the Genesis lectures, and illustrating as well the overall attitude with which Luther pursues his interpretation of Genesis over against Judaism. It occurs in his treatment of Gen. 25:21, the story of Rebecca's conception of Esau and Jacob:

> For the sake of those who at some time or other will read the commentaries of the rabbis let us next add something of the Jewish nonsense. At this point they raise the question why Isaac did not marry another wife after he had discovered in the course of almost twenty years that his wife was barren, while in the example of Sarah they conclude that ten years should be allowed for discovering barrenness or fecundity. Their answer is that in Isaac's case the situation is different from what it is in the case of Abraham. They say that because Isaac was sacrificed to God and became a burnt offering by the direction of God, he was not permitted to marry another wife.... Everybody sees how absurd and worthless these ideas are. Nevertheless, they must be touched on at times, in order to advise those who are students of the Hebrew language to read the sayings and writings of the Jews with discretion. We acknowledge, of course, that it is a great benefit that we have received the language from them; but we must beware of the dung of the rabbis, who have made of Holy Scripture a sort of privy in which they deposited their foulness and their exceedingly foolish opinions. I am advising this because even among our own theologians many give too much credit to the rabbis in explaining the meaning of Scripture. In the matter of grammar I readily bear with them; but they lack the true sense and understanding, in accordance with the well-known words in Is. 29{:14}: *"The wisdom of their wise men shall perish, and the discernment of their discerning men shall be hid."* This statement declares that there will be no understanding of Scripture among the Jews. No, this book of Holy Scripture has been closed for them and sealed. *"With an alien tongue the Lord will speak to this people"* (Is. 28:11). And they know nothing else than sheer blasphemies against the Christian religion.[1]

Excerpted below is a portion of Luther's treatment of Gen. 12:3, the call and blessing of Abraham, which most likely derives from the summer or fall of 1537. Luther stresses the blessing of the Gentiles that comes via Abraham and then argues at length that the Jews have lost everything promised to Abraham. The text in question, Luther states, is one of the key texts for "refuting the perfidious [that is, treacherous] Jews," who are most definitely not the true seed of Abraham.

Genesis 12

{LW 2:259–266}

12:3. *I will bless those who bless you, and him who curses you I will curse.... And in you all the families of the earth will be blessed.*

So far the Lord has promised material blessings. For even though these are properly called spiritual blessings—that the Lord dwelt among this people, and that He revealed Himself through signs, miracles, and His Word in the holy prophets—these were nevertheless blessings that belonged to this earthly life.

But now there follows that promise which should be written in golden letters and should be extolled in the languages of all people, for it offers eternal treasures. For it cannot be understood in a material sense, namely, that it would be confined to this people only, as the previous blessings were. But if, as the words clearly indicate, this promise is to be extended to all nations, or families of the earth, who else, shall we say, has dispensed this blessing among all nations except the Son of God, our Lord Jesus Christ?

Therefore the simple, true, and incontrovertible meaning is this: "Listen, Abraham, I have given you and your descendants grand promises; but this is not yet enough. I shall distinguish you also with a blessing that will overflow to all the families of the earth." Abraham understood this promise well. For he reasoned thus: "If all the families of the earth are to be blessed through me, then of necessity this blessing must not depend on my person. For I shall not live till then. Furthermore, I am not blessed through myself, but through the mercy of God the blessing has come to me too. Therefore all nations will not be blessed because of my person or through my power. But from my posterity will be born One who is blessed in His own person and who will bring a blessing so long and wide that it will reach all the families of the earth. He must necessarily be God and not a human being, although He will be a human being and will take on our flesh so that He is truly my seed."

No doubt Christ referred to these thoughts of the holy patriarch when He said (John 8:56): *"Your father Abraham rejoiced that he was to see My day; he saw it and was glad."* The statement of the text, *"all the families of the earth,"* is not to be understood of extent only, of the families of one time, but of duration, as long as the world will stand. It is altogether in accord with the statement of Christ (Mark 16:15–16): *"Go, preach the Gospel to the whole creation. He who believes and is baptized will be saved; but he who does not believe will be condemned."* This blessing has now endured for 1,500 years, and it will endure until the end of the world, since the gates of hell (Matt. 16:18), tyrants, and ungodly men will oppose it and rage against it in vain.

But above all it must be noted that the text does not say that all the nations will flow together to the Jews and will become Jews; but it declares that the blessing this people is to possess will be transferred from this people to the heathen, that is, to those who are not circumcised and who know nothing of Moses and of his statutes.

Therefore it is proper for us to contrast the blessing in this passage with the curse under which all human beings are because of sin. The curse has been taken away by Christ, and a blessing will be bestowed on all who receive Him and believe in His name. The remarkable blessing is this, that after being freed from sin, from death, and from the tyranny of the devil, we are in the company of the angels of God and have become partakers of eternal life.

Out of this promise flowed the sermons of the prophets concerning Christ and His kingdom, about the forgiveness of sins, about the gift of the Holy Spirit, about the preservation and the government of the church, about the punishments of the unbelievers, etc. They saw that these conclusions were definitely implied: If the Seed of Abraham does this, He must necessarily be a true human being by nature; on the other hand, if He blesses others, even all the families of the earth, He must necessarily be something greater than the seed of Abraham, because the seed of Abraham itself stands in need of this blessing on account of its sin.

In these few simple words the Holy Spirit has thus encompassed the mystery of the incarnation of the Son of God. The holy patriarchs and prophets explained this more fully later on in their sermons, namely, that through the Son of God the entire world would be made free, hell and death would be destroyed, the Law would be abrogated, sins would be forgiven, and eternal salvation and life would be given freely to those who believe in Him. This is the day of Christ about which He discourses in John (8:56), the day which Abraham did not see with his bodily eyes but did see in the spirit, and was glad. To the flesh these things were invisible, impossible, and for this reason incredible.

This passage is profitable not only for instruction and encouragement but also for refuting the perfidious Jews. Because God promises Abraham the material blessing that his descendants will be a great nation, let them declare about themselves whether they are a blessed and great nation today! But if their very situation compels them to declare that they are both an afflicted and a small band, what else can be concluded from this passage except that God is a liar in His promises or that they themselves are in error and are not the true seed of Abraham? But to maintain the former is wicked; therefore the latter necessarily follows. For what the blessing consists of is familiar.

Furthermore, a people is called a nation when it has a government, a body politic, laws, and liberty. But what of this do the Jews have today? They are a people scattered here and there, oppressed in various ways, and all but held in captivity wherever they live. They fancy that they have great power and prestige and wealth in some Babel, of which I know nothing, and among the Turks. And it is true that the Turks favor them because of their traitorous activities. For whatever secret plans the Jews are able to fish out from all the courts of Christian princes, they immediately betray to the Turk. Great is not only the folly but also the ungodliness of some princes, that they have Jews as such close friends. But if you consider the actual situation, the Jews are prey for the Turks themselves, as I know for sure from those who lived not only at Constantinople but in Damascus itself, where the number of the Jews is very great.

Therefore let the miserable Jews confess that they are not the true seed of Abraham, that is, that they are in error and are under God's wrath because they oppose the true religion; or we ourselves shall drive them to the blasphemy of maintaining that God is a liar. For what middle ground can there be?

The statement we have made about the blessing and about the great nation, however, we also make about the great name that God promises to make for Abraham. What sort of name have the Jews today? Are they not the reproach of all human beings? Nothing is more despised than the Jews, as the discourses of the prophets threaten that they will be a reproach and laughingstock for all nations. Where, then, is their great name? Must they not declare by their own witness that they have lost it? And yet the seed of Abraham must have a great name, for God does not lie.

But consider this too: whether those who bless the Jews and intimately associate with them are blessed. There are obvious examples, not only of private individuals but also of great princes, who can bear witness concerning this blessing that they experience because of their intimacy with Jews, namely, that they are being ruined with respect to fortune, body, and soul.

But perhaps the Jews will object that the psalm (109.11) says. "May the creditor seize all that he has; may strangers plunder the fruits of his toil!" They will say that the Jews do not experience this from Christians, but the Christians from the Jews; for it is well known how much harm they cause the state with their excessive interest.

My answer is this: In the first place, reason itself teaches that interest or usury is contrary to nature and for this reason is actually a sin. Therefore Christians have the rule (Luke 6:35): *"Lend, expecting nothing in return."* Those who are disciples of Christ observe this rule and beware of interest as of a real sin. Moreover, experience also shows that riches gained in this manner are cursed by the Lord and do not last. Therefore if the Jews consider interest or usury a blessing, let them enjoy it. For it is certain that it is a sin; and a sure penalty is attached to this sin, as Scripture teaches again and again, and as the Jews themselves prove by their own example.

Consider whether they are not being drained of their possessions. While they are scraping together their wealth by pennies, they pay a large number of tolls, levies, and real estate taxes. And yet they are being treated considerately by Christian governments in comparison with what they suffer from the Turks. These would not even spare their bodies and life if they did not recall the great advantages of the treason for which the Jews are very well trained by their hate of the Christians.

However this may be, let them boast of their wealth for all I care; let them glory that they do not pay interest but collect it. What a small matter this is in comparison with what they are compelled to admit that they have lost! They were driven out of the land that God had given them and had blessed; they lost the kingdom; they lost their worship; they live in deepest darkness and have no understanding of the sacred prophecies. In short, they have no hope for salvation except to invent some idea about God's mercy and goodness. If all this does not compel those unhappy people to confess that they are thrice wretched, let them be happy with this blessing, that they lend money to others at interest and do not borrow money.

But how much better it is to seek alms from street to street than to use this sinful means to gain riches, out of which others, in turn, cheat them later! And to this supposedly extraordinary blessing, of which they boast so much, there are attached many great liabilities. Nowhere do they have a continuing abode; they are hated and despised by all men; they live most wretchedly in dirt and filth; they are not permitted to engage in the more honorable occupations—and who could enumerate all the hardships of the enemies of Christ?

Hence this is a most powerful argument to support our religion and faith and to refute the deceitful Jews, namely, that they have lost everything promised here to Abraham, and especially what is promised last, that the blessing will spread from the seed of Abraham to all the families of the earth.

They are hard pressed by this reasoning. Therefore they prate that this statement was fulfilled in Solomon, the son of David, and that he was blessed by the nations, that is, was renowned and was praised by everybody. But what has it to do with the text if he was blessed or praised by others? What the words mean is this, that this seed will bring a blessing to all nations. Now what did Solomon bring to the nations?

Therefore this text clearly compels us to confess that the Messiah or Christ has long since come and was revealed, and that He brought a spiritual and eternal blessing with Him into the world. When the unbelieving Jews rejected this and would not have it, it was brought to the heathen. But the wretched Jews were deprived of both their material and their spiritual blessing, as experience demonstrates. They have now been living for almost 1,500 years under great hardships and in uninterrupted captivity, and they have nothing of the promises of which the Lord is speaking here. If God is truthful in His promises, then they must be liars; and through their unbelief they have forfeited these promises and are no longer the seed of Abraham to which these promises were given.

The error under which all Jews labor today is well known: they are waiting for a Messiah to beat down all the heathen and restore to them an earthly kingdom over all nations, just as under Ahasuerus (Esther 8:10).[2] For then the power and the prestige of the Jews was great.

The passage before us clearly gives the lie to this vain hope. It does not state that the heathen will be oppressed by the seed of Abraham or will be reduced to servitude, but that they will be "blessed," that is, that they will be given aid against death and sin. But for all I care, let the gloss of the Jews stand that "to bless" has this meaning; for then it will become apparent that they have the greatest blessing, that is, that they are most severely oppressed by the heathen. To call this a blessing is the devil's language.

Because God is good, He uses "blessing" to mean deliverance from the curse and wrath of God, and He promises that this will occur through the seed of Abraham, not only for the descendants of Abraham but for all the families of the earth. This blessing the Son of God, Jesus Christ, brought us. He was born from the seed of Abraham by the Virgin Mary. But because the unbelieving synagog did not want this blessing, it was withdrawn; and it lost not only this eternal blessing but also those earlier material ones. Therefore it is manifest to all that this is a nation that is cursed and subjected to God's wrath.

Hence this passage is profitable for us in various ways, and therefore it deserves to be noted by students of the Holy Scriptures. Not only does it emphatically refute the stubborn Jews and portray the person of Abraham, whom all godly people ought to contemplate in order that they may learn to believe from his example; but, together with Abraham, it also describes the progress and the good fortune of this entire people, indeed of the entire church to the end of the world. Whatever will be achieved in the church until the end of the world and whatever has been achieved in it until now, has been achieved and will be achieved by virtue of this promise, which endures and is in force to this day.

If you desire to reduce to a few words the history of the church from the time of Abraham until today, carefully consider these four verses. You will see the blessing, and you will also see some who curse; but these, in turn, God has cursed so that they utterly perished, while the eternal blessing of the church has remained unshaken. Hence this passage is in agreement with the first sermon about the Seed who crushes the head of the serpent (Gen. 3:15). The church does not lack enemies; it is troubled, and it sighs; and yet it overcomes through the Seed and finally triumphs forever over all its enemies.

But just as the Lord gave a warning above about the bite of the serpent, so here He warns that the seed of Abraham will encounter some who will curse it. But if we are hurt by the world and the devil, the damage is slight, since we have the angels, yes, even God Himself to bless us and annihilate our adversaries. But such an explanation of this passage must be looked for in the prophets. This is the source from which they drew both their consolations and their threats. Hence the divine wisdom is truly admirable, that such important matters and the history of all ages, so far as it concerns the church, have been reduced to a few words in this passage.

. . .

Text #18

The Three Symbols of the Christian Faith (1538)

Language:	German
Critical Edition:	WA 50: (255), 262–83
English Translation:	LW 34: (197), 201–29

This treatise on the Christian Creeds was written as a defense of Luther's christological and trinitarian orthodoxy. He was at work on this treatise already in
late April 1537, but publication was delayed until January 1538. We excerpt the
concluding portion, where he assembles a series of Old Testament proof texts for
the doctrine of the Trinity (Gen. 1:1, 26; 3:22; 18:1-4; 19:24; Deut. 6:4; Josh. 24:19;
2 Sam. 7:23; Zech. 3:2; Ps. 2:7; 110:1) and argues directly against Jewish readings of
these same texts. All of this is intended to demonstrate against Jews (and Muslims!)
that the Christian doctrine of the Trinity is not polytheistic. By stressing the biblical
basis of the doctrine of the Trinity, Luther seeks to highlight the Trinity as something
already known to the prophets, which they taught—in vain—to the stiff-necked
Jews. Luther's bottom line is that Jews believe and teach unbiblically, whereas Christians do just the opposite. The doctrine of the Trinity serves as proof of that.

In connection with this Luther also announces his growing intention to launch
a full-fledged assault on the Jews in defense of the Christian faith, in order perhaps
to convert some of them. This stated goal is revelatory, in that it shows that—at least
from Luther's own perspective—his vigorous, polemical, and increasingly belligerent
defense of Christian beliefs over against Judaism was launched with the intention of
persuading "some" Jews to the truth of Christianity.

The Three Symbols of the Christian Faith
{LW 34:222–229}
... {The passage under discussion is Heb. 1:3, *"He is the brilliance of his glory and the
image of his substance."*}
So, now, the final conclusion and real sense of this is that Jesus Christ is real, eternal
God by nature, not made, uncreated, having been from eternity onward, arisen, born
(or however one may call it) a different Person from the Father, but not a different

God from the Father, rather, equal to him in one single, eternal substance. That is the faith, so the faith teaches, and with that the faith remains—I mean the Christian faith, which is based on Holy Scriptures. If anyone does not want to believe the Scriptures, but instead wants to follow reason, then let him do so. If he will take my advice, however, he will leave his servants and his ass at the foot of the mountain, as Abraham did [Gen. 22:5], and not climb this mountain. For Moses says, *"Whoever touches the mountain shall be put to death"* [Exod. 19:12]. This means believe, or be lost. Adam was the first to learn that, and all of us after him.

The prophets in the Old Testament also believed and well understood this article of faith, without, however, bringing it out into the open, as the New Testament does, on account of the stiff-necked, unbelieving, wicked people. Nevertheless, they powerfully indicated their belief. For Moses begins his first book thus: *"In the beginning Elohim created the heavens and the earth"* [Gen. 1:1]. It is indeed self-evident that *Elohim* is plural number and does not signify one, but many, so that to be grammatically correct one must translate, "In the beginning the Gods created the heavens and the earth." That Moses does not say, "In the beginning created," *plural number* (corresponding to the plural subject), but: "created," *singular number* (as if corresponding to a singular subject), shows clearly that there is not more than one single God and Creator. But that he says "the Gods" shows that in the same single divine substance there is nevertheless the number known as plural or more than one. Therewith our faith is preserved: we believe in no other god than the single eternal God, and yet we learn that the same single Godhead is more than one Person. From then onward throughout the entire Scriptures God is called *Elohim*, that is, "Gods." And after that the same name is also given to the creatures which sit in God's place, as in Exodus 22[:20], and in Psalm 82[:1, 6], where it says, *"God stands among the gods and judges the gods,"* and, *"I say, 'You are Gods.'"*

Again, Moses writes in his first book, in the first chapter [Gen. 1:26], *"Then God said, 'Let us (or we will) make man after our image and likeness.'"* Here God himself refers to himself as "we" and "us" and does not say "I will," *singular number*, as he does, to be sure, everywhere else, saying soon afterward in chapter 2[:18], *"I will make a helper for the man,"* not "We will make him a helper," also, *"So God[1] caused a deep sleep to fall upon the man,"* etc. [Gen. 2:21]. Here the Scriptures speak of God as one, who is there creating, making, and doing everything alone; and yet in close proximity to that God is spoken of as many, saying "us" and "our," who create the man, etc. This is to indicate to us believers that God is only one single God, but that the Godhead is more than one person. Furthermore, in the third chapter [:22], after Adam's Fall, God the {LORD}[2] said (said as one alone), *"Behold, the man has become like one of us"* (of us, as more than one, etc.).

When the Jews argue at this point, foaming at the mouth with anger, that God was talking to the angels when he says, *"Let us make man after our image,"* etc., they are not correct and their argument does not hold, for the Scriptures do not support any contention that the angels created us and are our gods or that we are made in their image, so that we should honor them as gods, worship them, or be called their creatures. There is only one single God and single Creator. It makes even less sense when they torment themselves and fairly sweat to produce the interpretation that God said this to the earth, namely, *"Let us make man,"* because we are made by the earth. No, blind Jew, the earth did not make us (the passage reads, after all, *"We* will make man"), and we are not the earth's image, but instead the earth is subject to man and in servitude to him.

The following is much fouler still: since they can find no foothold anywhere in the face of such texts, they allege that God is speaking of himself, that he is using the plural form to do himself honor, as kings and princes nowadays call themselves "we" and "us." No, that is a modern, human fashion and is never used once in the Scriptures by any king, not even by the heathen kings. Moreover, God also indeed uses the singular form in regard to himself in the Scriptures generally, and not always the plural form. And even though such fraud and evasion may make some impression on human beings, ought I or must I therefore believe the Jews when they simply state that the Scriptures are to be understood thus, while I have before my eyes powerful texts and dear, plain words which have so captured my conscience that I could not yield my conviction even to an angel? Yes, truly, that would mean abandoning the powerful text and using mere Jewish chatter as the foundation stone of my heart and conscience. Moses himself says, however, that the Jews have been from the beginning and ever onward a disobedient, stiff-necked, wicked people which has never yet been able to tolerate or listen to any prophet who taught correctly. And now they should be the ones to teach, twist, and interpret the Scriptures and the prophets for me, according to the foolish notions of their own heads! But more about this at another time. For indeed I do intend (if it should be God's will) to make a formal defense of our faith against the foolishness of the Jews, with the hope that some of them might be won for Christ. Now I must break off in order to turn to the council, about which the pope and his men have lied and perhaps they have never seriously intended to hold it at all. For the present I only have intended to broach and sketch these matters, so that I do not forget them.

In Genesis 18[:1–4] Moses writes, *"And the {LORD} appeared to Abraham by the oaks of Mamre, as he sat at the door. . . . He lifted up his eyes and looked, and behold, three men stood in front of him . . . he ran . . . to meet them, and bowed himself to the earth, and said, '{LORD}, if I have found favor in your sight, do not pass by your servant. Let a little water be brought,'"* etc. Here God talks with Abraham, and Abraham with God, in both ways, with a "you" singular and a "you" plural, or as with one and with many; yet the text says clearly that this vision or manifestation was God himself, appearing to Abraham before his door. For the two angels who afterward, in chapter 19[:1], go toward Sodom are something quite different from these first three who talk and eat with Abraham as one single God; and the whole chapter bears witness to this fact.

Here again it makes no difference what juggler's tricks the Jews try to play, the text stands there. It is the {LORD} who appeared to Abraham in three Persons, and he also worshiped all three of them as one. Therefore, Abraham here well recognized the Holy Trinity, as Christ says, John 8[:56], *"Abraham saw my day."*

Likewise, in Deuteronomy 6[:4], Moses writes thus: *"Hear, O Israel: The {LORD} our God{s}³ is one {LORD}."* Here it is written that the one {LORD} (a name which is given to no one in the Scriptures except to the real, single God, as the Jews are well aware) is our *Elohim* or "Gods," to indicate that God is single in substance and yet three Persons are distinguishable, as has been said.

And Joshua in chapter 24[:19] spoke to the people thus: "You cannot serve the {LORD}; for he is holy Gods." Here is written not only *Elohim*, "Gods," but "holy" also is in the plural, as for many or more than one; and nevertheless it is stated that this is the {LORD}, the one God.

Again, in 2 Samuel 7[:23], David says in his prayer to God, *"What other nation on earth is like thy people Israel, whom Gods went to redeem to be his people?"* etc. Here David, too, calls God "Gods" and says "they went" (as more than one), but immediately afterward, "to redeem to be his people," as though speaking of *one*, who went forth to redeem for himself a people out of Egypt.

Again, in Genesis 19[:24], *"The {LORD} caused it to rain brimstone from the {LORD}."* And in Zechariah 3[:2], *"And the {LORD} said to Satan, 'The {LORD} rebuke you . . .'"* Here the {LORD} speaks of the {LORD}, and the {LORD} rains brimstone from the {LORD}, always as one and yet as many. Therefore now in the Psalter David says openly as a prophet, *"The {LORD} says to my {L}ord: 'Sit at my right hand.'"* [Ps. 110:1]. And in Psalm 2[:7], *"You are my son, today I have begotten you."* Not, "Today I have created you." And there are also many passages in Isaiah and other prophets wherein Christ's kingdom is described as equal to and the very same as God's kingdom. If, now, the Jews want to be so wondrously, wondrously malicious as to pervert these texts and to pay no heed to them, that is without significance. Their contradiction is nothing more than {their own darkness},⁴ without any basis whatever in Scriptures, and is only invented as a subterfuge. But here stand text and Scriptures; they cannot be overturned thus by human {darkness}.

When they want to prove how profoundly wise they are, then they teach us that there is only one God, as the Turks do also. This, however, we too confess and indeed teach with as much staunchness and firmness as they, and there is not a Christian who would confess or recognize more or other than one God, the only Creator of heaven and earth. What can they teach that would be more sublime than that, or what more can they demand of us? There stands our Christian faith, saying that there is no more than one God, beside whom there is no other god, and all the rest are creatures, not gods. What can be the meaning of this, then, that both Jews and Turks, either out of great maliciousness or great ignorance, presume to reprove us Christians, as though we had more than one God? Actually they should know that they are openly and shamefully lying about this. They traitorously and viciously slander us before their hearers, so as to lend support to their own error and to defame our truth. God's wrath has blinded them and they are impenitent sinners.

Let them look at the Scriptures with us, to see further that we acknowledge and believe in one God who, within his Godhead, is three distinct Persons. For we did not think this up ourselves, nor could we have thought it up, if the Scriptures did not persuade us of it, especially our New Testament, which, although they do not believe in it, is based on and proclaimed in the Old, as I do not have time to prove here. And our belief that the three Persons are one God takes nothing whatever away from the true single Godhead. Indeed, he remains one God and one Godhead. If we, however, were so arrogant and rash as to judge according to our reason, as seems right to us, that God must be one Person within his Godhead (we who have never seen anything of all this which no man can see, in any case); and yet we have indications in Scripture that there are three Persons in the divine substance, why then we would be really crude fellows, esteeming our poor blind reason more highly in such sublime matters than the very indications of Scripture! The Scriptures are God's testimony of himself, while reason can know nothing at all about the divine substance. Shall then reason try to judge concerning that of which it knows nothing? That is really what might be called a blind man's attempt to judge colors!

If they now rap on the Scriptures saying there is one God, so let us rap thereon in turn, since the Scriptures indicate just as strongly that in this one God there are more than one. Our scriptural texts are as valid as theirs, because there is not a superfluous letter in the Scriptures. But we will not submit to their attempts to interpret our Scriptures, because they have neither the right nor the might to do it. They are God's Scriptures and God's Word, which no man is supposed to or can interpret. If they say, "The Scriptures teach one God," well, we simply confess this and by no means "interpret" it. When we, however, say, "The Scriptures teach (as we have cited them above) that there is more than one in the single Godhead," at this point they want to interpret the Scriptures and not simply confess them. Yes, what devil has commanded them to start interpreting here, inasmuch as it is no less God's Scriptures here than where it teaches of the one God? They want to interpret our scriptural texts and we are not to interpret their scriptural texts? Rather let them leave the Scriptures uninterpreted on both sides, as we do, and simply confess that there is one God and yet more than one Person in the Godhead, because the Scriptures obviously teach both things. But enough for now . . .

. . .

I shall at this time cite nothing from the New Testament, for in it everything about the holy divine Trinity or Threefoldness is clearly and powerfully attested to. In the Old Testament this is not so clearly underlined, but is nevertheless powerfully indicated.

Text #19

Lectures on Genesis 17 (1538)

Language: Latin
Critical Edition: WA 42–44 (here WA 42:651–57)
English Translation: LW 1–8 (here LW 3:144–52)

For general introductory material on the Genesis lectures, see Text #17. Genesis 17 describes the institution of circumcision as the sign of the covenant between God and Abraham and Abraham's descendents. Over the centuries, circumcision, Sabbath observance, and the dietary regulations known as *kashrut* would come to be the defining characteristics of Jewishness. Within Gentile Christianity, attempts to introduce such practices came to be called "Judaizing."[1] Early in his lecture on Genesis 17, Luther states: "I hear that in Austria and Moravia some Judaizers are today advocating both the Sabbath and circumcision."[2] Luther had indicated knowledge of such a movement as early as 1532,[3] but his formal treatment of the issues at stake derives from 1538. His major treatise *Against the Sabbatarians* would be written immediately after his extended exegetical engagement with Genesis 17. For more on Sabbatarianism, see the introduction to Text #20.

In the section excerpted below, Luther argues that circumcision was a temporal covenant and that it was never intended for anyone but the Jews alone. With the coming of Christ, the covenant of circumsion has ceased, along with the Mosaic law as a whole. This claim, though not explicitly stated, derives directly from Luther's understanding of Rom. 10:4a—*"For Christ is the end of the Law."* Just as the physical promise must now give way to the spiritual promise and Sarah's child must now give way to Mary's child, so the Law of Moses must now give way to God's promise, which is accessed only via faith. He further argues that since the Jews rejected the promised Christ, God has now rejected them. The Jews are no longer the people of God, and their 1,500-year exile proves this. Most striking in this entire section is Luther's comparison of post-biblical Judaism to a cadaver. All of this anticipates the further elaboration of these same arguments in *Against the Sabbatarians*.

Genesis 17
{LW 3:144–145, 148–152}

17:15. *And God said to Abraham: As for Sarai your wife, you shall not call her name Sarai, but Sarah shall be her name.* 17:16. *I will bless her, and moreover I will give you a son by her; I will bless her, and she shall be a mother of nations; kings of peoples shall come from her.*

We have finished with the command concerning circumcision, which God so surrounded with His own bounds that He excluded not only the Gentiles but also the entire female sex and likewise the males who died before the eighth day. Hence the Jews, who want circumcision to be universal, clamor in vain. The part of the body which is to be circumcised was also designated. Hence the priests of Baal cut and slashed their bodies in vain (1 Kgs. 18:28).

When Christ came, this law was abolished; for circumcision was not given as an everlasting law but for the preservation of the seed of Abraham until Christ should be born from it. At His birth not only circumcision but the entire law, with its ceremonies and forms of worship, came to an end.

What now follows unfolds the promise concerning Christ, for it gradually began to become clearer and more distinct. First Abraham had doubts concerning an heir, and he came to suspect that if he should die without an heir, his Damascene servant would get possession of the blessing. But later on he is assured by a word of God that an heir shall be born to him from his own body. When he has this explanation and assurance about the promise, there follows another uncertainty—about Sarah, who was advancing in years and was barren. Therefore he acquiesces in her plan and lies with the maid Hagar. From her he begets Ishmael, whom he fully expects to become the heir of the blessing. But now at last the saintly couple is delivered even from this error, for Abraham is promised an offspring from the aged and barren Sarah herself.

In the course of time the promise is transmitted to Jacob, not to Esau; and when Jacob had twelve heirs, the promise falls to Judah alone. Eventually David is designated as the heir of the promise. From his house came the Blessed Virgin Mary, the mother of Christ, who was the end of the Law and of circumcision.

Therefore the Jews achieve nothing when they contend both for the eternal duration of circumcision, as though it had to continue in existence forever, and for its unlimited practice, if I may say so, as though it had to be extended to all nations.

There was need of circumcision for a fixed time as a visible sign to which the children of God might look and to which they might come when they were about to hear and worship God, just as there had previously been the sacrifices of the fathers instead of a sign at which the Gentiles might gather.

These marks, by which God has manifested Himself to the world, must be regarded more highly than any miracles. For there even the Gentiles heard God speaking through His instruments, and they were saved if they believed the Word. Therefore it is great praise of God's mercy that He did not let the human race walk and go astray in its own thoughts but set up for those who feared Him public signs at which they might gather.

Abraham and all his descendants were circumcised in order that the heathen might be attracted and also obtain salvation themselves. Therefore we justly give thanks to so merciful a God, who manifested Himself in this way at all times and gathered a church for Himself.

. . .

Accordingly, what this story sets forth is analogous to the resurrection of the dead, inasmuch as from a dead womb there is born not only an offspring but a male who is appointed to be the father of many nations and of many kings and peoples.

Therefore it is a most extraordinary account. In it we must direct our attention chiefly to the Word of God. Here God speaks with Abraham at such length and so intimately that the reader is compelled to forget the Divine Majesty and to think of a guest or an intimate friend.

Moreover, it must be noted especially that these promises include Christ Himself, yes, eternal life, even though they appear to be speaking, not of Christ but of Isaac. For this reason Paul adds (Rom. 4:23–24) that this was written, not for Abraham's sake but for the sake of us, who would believe after the example of Abraham; for the promise is temporal, like a nut which covers the kernel, namely, Christ and eternal life. When Christ comes, the shell or hull in which the kernel is enclosed is broken; that is, the temporal blessing comes to an end, and the spiritual blessing takes its place.

Abraham did not see these promises fulfilled. He saw his son Isaac and his little grandsons Esau and Jacob, the sons of Isaac. But Sarah was called out of this life before these men were born. You will say: "What is this in comparison with such grand promises? They did not benefit Abraham and Sarah; they benefited the descendants of Abraham and Sarah."

Such is commonly our thought, and this is an offense especially to the Jews, who see only the shell but do not see the kernel—Christ and eternal life—which is enclosed in this shell or hull, as it were, of the material blessing concerning the land of Canaan and the descendants of Abraham.

But Sacred Scripture points out very clearly that eternal and spiritual blessings are included in the material blessings. For we were not created like oxen and asses; we were created for eternity. Therefore when God speaks with us to give a promise, He is not speaking with us for the sake of temporal things only; nor does He concern Himself with the belly only. No, He wants to preserve our soul from destruction and to grant us eternal life.

. . .

Even though Abraham did not see those promises during his lifetime, he nevertheless believed God. Therefore he had eternal life and could not die but still lives. For he believed God when He promised kings, peoples, and a son as the heir of the blessing. Therefore he closed his eyes and withdrew into the darkness of faith. There he found eternal light.

. . .

But at this point, too, we shall argue with the Jews for a while. They cannot deny that this temporal blessing is now at an end. For the shell has been opened and broken, and the chaff or hull has been removed from the kernels and the grain, just as John the Baptist prophesies in his sermon that it would happen (Matt. 3:12). The nut had to be broken when the kernel was revealed, and 1,500 years have now elapsed. Meanwhile they have had no king and no definite place. Moreover, with the destruction of the temple their worship ceased completely.

Therefore I ask what vestiges or what signs they retain of the promise made to Sarah and Abraham. The fact that the Jewish nation was completely destroyed and was scattered throughout the entire earth—this does nothing for them, for Abraham is promised a kingdom.

But we do not understand kingdom in a material sense; we understand it in a formal sense, namely, a state established by laws in a definite place, together with everything that pertains to a people or to the government and administration of the people. A band of brigands certainly cannot be called a kingdom, even though they choose a head for themselves and occupy a definite place. In a kingdom, as in the human body, there are various functions and various duties. Nevertheless, all these functions and duties have been provided to the end that the body may remain healthy and have its proper strength. But a body that is torn in pieces—where no hands, no eyes, and no feet perform their duty—is more properly called a cadaver than a body. Thus the descendants of the Jews are like a cadaver and not like a kingdom, as even they themselves bear witness. For what similarity is there to that people which was in existence before and after the captivity up to the coming of Christ?

What, then, shall we say? God does not lie. His promises are true and firm. They do not promise that some dregs of a people will come from Abraham; they promise kings and peoples. Where, then, has the kingdom remained during these 1,500 years? Where have their laws remained, the institutions of the fathers, and their worship? What else are the Jews today than a body miserably torn to pieces and scattered throughout the entire world? They have no definite place and no offices that are necessary for the establishment of a state; they are servants, and they seek their livelihood solely through sins. Hence God is either lying in His promise, or the Jews are no longer the people of God but have been rejected by God and put out of the church.

Therefore this promise helps to strengthen our faith. Consequently we are sure that since the Jews are without a kingdom and the hull of the nut has been broken, Christ must necessarily have been revealed and that the multitude of the Gentiles has taken the place of the Jews.

For the promise made to Sarah cannot lie. *"Kings and nations shall come from you,"* it states. But mention to me one king or prince the Jews have now had during 1,500 years.

History itself will indeed compel one to admit that the restoration of the people and of the kingdom was repeatedly attempted, but most unsuccessfully. Moreover, they were especially to keep possession of the land of Canaan. But because they were deprived of it and have been scattered throughout the entire world in most wretched bondage, history declares that they are no longer the people of God or the seed of Abraham to which God promised and also gave kingdoms up to the time of Christ.

It is altogether absurd for the Jews to continue to hope so tenaciously for a kingdom and for a restoration of the land of Canaan, nor is there anything to encourage them. In the first place, they have no promise. Therefore they hope in vain. In the second place, how is it possible for them to hope for a return to the land of Canaan from which they have now been exiles for a longer time than they dwelt in it? Moreover, what kind of promise is this which is unfulfilled for a longer time than it is fulfilled?

But their retention of circumcision and their use of the Law even though they are outside the land of Canaan—it is not right for them to do this. For it is only in the land of Canaan that they are obliged to use the Law. Circumcision, like the whole Law, must continue as long as the people continues, as long as their descendants continue, as long as the possession of the land of Canaan continues.

Hence this promise itself serves to strengthen our own faith and to weaken the obstinacy of the Jews. For we maintain that long ago, while their state was still in existence, the promise both of the shell and of the kernel was fulfilled, that is, the physical promise. The spiritual promise, which, as we have said, is included in the physical promise, was also fulfilled.

From the womb of Sarah there came not only kings—David, Solomon, etc.— but also peoples, the Edomites and others, who are reckoned among the descendants of Esau. This is the physical promise. When Christ was born of the Virgin Mary, the spiritual promise was also fulfilled.

That was the real time of blessing. Then there were valiant kings: the apostles and their successors. Next came Gentiles who, because of faith in the Blessed Seed, are also descendants of Abraham, not according to the flesh or by nature but "engrafted," as Paul calls them in Rom. 11{:17}.

Of course, the promise concerns the spiritual seed, that is, the believers, more than it does the physical descendants. And although Isaac himself was born from the flesh of Abraham, he was nevertheless a son of the promise; for he was not born according to the flesh, inasmuch as the bodies of Sarah and Abraham were dead, as it were, so far as procreation was concerned.

Just as we correctly call Isaac a son of faith and not of the flesh—for if you consider the flesh, Abraham and Sarah are like two corpses which procreate in spite of this, not by virtue of the corpse but by virtue of faith—so all who believe according to the example of Abraham are descendants of Abraham and partakers of the blessing, whether they are Gentiles or Jews, whether they are circumcised or uncircumcised. This is the apostolic argument, which abounded in ill will and hatred when the Jewish nation was still in existence; for it put the Gentiles on the same level with the Jews. Paul calls them fellow citizens of the prophets and the apostles.

But today, after the Jews have ceased to be a people and are miserably scattered throughout the world, this discussion does not seem to be of such great importance. Therefore we know that the promise has been fulfilled. For wherever Christ, the Blessed Seed, rules, there the church is, and there are kings and peoples born of the faith of corpselike Abraham who have the promise and believe. But because the physical descendants of Abraham refused to accept the promised Christ, they were rejected according to the prophecies of Moses and other prophets, like Hos. 2{:23}: *"I will say to Not My People, 'You are My people,'"* Moses (cf. Deut. 32:21): *"I shall vex you among a foreign nation,"* and Christ [Matt. 21:43]: *"The kingdom will be taken from you and given to a nation producing the fruits of it."*

. . .

Text #20

Against the Sabbatarians (1538)

Language:	German
Critical Edition:	WA 50: (309), 312–37
English Translation:	LW 47: (58), 65–98

This is the first of Luther's "Big Four" treatises against the Jews.[1] Having received a report from a "good friend," Count Wolfgang Schlick of Falkenau, about "Judaizing" activities among Christians in Moravia, Luther proceeds to mount an argument from Scripture against any Jewish claims upon Christian faith and practice.[2] Behind Luther's fury, it is important to distinguish here between what may have been happening in Moravia and what Luther thought was happening. Luther's opening remarks paint a confusing picture, because what he says does not square with what is known about sixteenth-century seventh-day-Sabbath Christian groups, that is, "Sabbatarians.[3] His description rather portrays a successful proselytizing effort on the part of Jews directed at Christians. Here Luther is speaking out of fear rather than reality: While individual Christian conversions to Judaism were not unheard of, they were rare at a time when Jewish proselytizing was punishable by law.[4] Thus Kaufmann has argued that Luther's "Sabbatarians" are best understood as "a bogey man that grew out of the Christian fear that Jews would make proselytes of Christians."[5] In this treatise, written at a time of fluctuating political policy toward the Jews (1536–1543), whose rights were revisited in both Electoral Saxony and Electoral Hesse, Luther begins to promote his conviction that Protestant territories would be better off not tolerating Jews at all. Luther's polemic here against Jewish influence on Christian faith and practice as well as against Jewish attempts to convert Christians has a political goal in mind: the expulsion of Jews from Protestant territories.

This letter/treatise is divided into two parts: (1) How to account for the 1,500 year Roman exile of the Jews? (2) What is the status of Mosaic Law? Throughout both parts, Luther's polemical mantra is "1,500 years," which is repeated some twenty-six times and which rightly ought to be the title of the treatise. Luther uses it as his most definitive proof that God has rejected the "stiff-necked" and disobedient Jewish people, viz., the Jews have been and are forsaken by God and can no longer claim to be the people of God. Overall, the treatise constitutes Luther's advice on how to argue with a Jew, and it anticipates much of *On the Jews and Their Lies* (1543),[6] especially in regard to the accusation of lying. As Brecht points out, *Against the Sabbatarians* was intended to be used by Christians as a theological and apologetic argument against Judaism."[7] Presented here are extended portions of Part One, together with the conclusion to the whole.

─────────────────

Against the Sabbatarians: Letter to a Good Friend
{LW 47:65–70, 73–75, 77–78}

Grace and peace in Christ! I received your letter and the oral request of your messenger. However, I was kept from answering as promptly as I should have liked, and as I promised to do, by many unavoidable obstacles. Please excuse me for this.

You informed me that the Jews are making inroads at various places throughout the country with their venom and their doctrine, and that they have already induced some Christians to let themselves be circumcised and to believe that the Messiah or Christ has not yet appeared, that the law of the Jews must prevail forever, that it must also be adopted by all the Gentiles, etc. Then you inquired of me how these allegations are to be refuted with Holy Scripture. For the time being and until I am at greater leisure, I will convey my advice and opinion briefly in this matter.

In the first place, the Jewish people have become very stubborn because of their rabbis. As a result they are difficult to win over. Even when one persuades them out of Scripture, they retreat from the Scripture to their rabbis and declare that they must believe them, just as you Christians (they say) believe your pope and your decretals. That is the answer they gave me at one time when I disputed with them and adduced Scripture against them.[8] Therefore, to fortify the Christians, you must enlist the old argument which Lyra and many others have employed and which the Jews have not been able to refute down to the present day, even though they have shamefully perverted many Scripture passages while trying to do so, in contradiction of their own most venerable teachers. However, time and space are lacking for a discussion of that now.

This is the argument: The Jews have been living away from Jerusalem, in exile, for fifteen hundred years, bereft of temple, divine service, priesthood, and kingdom. Thus their law has been lying in the ashes with Jerusalem and the entire Jewish kingdom all this time. They cannot deny this, for it is proven clearly and emphatically by their wretched situation and experiences and by the place itself, which is even today called Jerusalem and which lies desolate and devoid of Jewry before the eyes of all the world. However, they cannot observe Moses' law anywhere but in Jerusalem—this they themselves know and are forced to admit. Outside of Jerusalem they cannot have or hope to have their priesthood, kingdom, temple, sacrifices, and whatever Moses instituted for them by divine command. That is one point, and it is absolutely certain.

Now you must ask them the nature and name of the sin that caused God to punish them so cruelly, obliging them to live in exile so long, without priestly and princely, that is, Mosaic, office and government, without the sacrifices and the other regulations of the law, and particularly without Jerusalem. For God's promise—of which they also boast—is that the law will endure forever, that Jerusalem shall be God's own residence, and that both the princes of the house of David and the priests of the tribe of Levi will forever remain before God. The prophets and the Scriptures are filled with such promises, as they know and (as said) of which they boast. Yet these glorious, great, and numerous promises have failed of fulfillment all these fifteen hundred years. Of this they are woefully aware.

Since it is nonsense to accuse God of not keeping his promise and of having lied for fifteen hundred years, you must ask what is wrong, for God cannot lie or deceive. They will and must reply that this is due to their sins. As soon as these are atoned for, then God will keep his promise and send the Messiah. Here again you must be persistent and ask them to name these sins. For such a terrible, long, and gruesome punishment indicates that they must have committed gruesome and terrible sins previously unheard of on earth. For God never tormented even the heathen for that long a time, but destroyed them quickly. Why, then, should God torture his own people so long and in such a way that they foresee and can foresee no end of it?

Of course, it is meaningless if they declare that this is because of their sin and yet they cannot name this sin. They might as well say that they had committed no sin—since they are not aware of any sin that they can name—and therefore that they were being punished unjustly by God. Therefore you must press them hard to name the sin. If they do not do it, you have made the point that they are employing lies and are no longer to be believed.

If they do name the sin, well and good, note it carefully. For this argument hurts them; and even if I were a Jew and had been born from the body of Abraham and taught most diligently by Moses, I surely would not know how to answer this question. I should have to forsake Mosaic Jewry and become what I became.

Some of their rabbis, to comfort and to blind their poor people, answer this question by saying that this sin was their fathers' worship of the calf in the wilderness, and that they now have to atone for it until, etc. Isn't that terrible blindness? And what sense does it make to those who read Scripture? If that sin were really so great, why then did God subsequently confer so many blessings on the people of Israel? Why did he ever and again perform so many miracles through prophets and kings, also through peasants and women, as the books of Moses, Joshua, Judges, Kings, etc., testify? He would not have done any of this if he had not graciously forgiven all sin, except for this one, which was duly punished at the time. Why did he not forsake his people then because of this sin as he forsakes them now, instead of taking them, despite this sin, into the Promised Land, lavishing all good things on them, and elevating and honoring them above all the Gentiles? If God is withholding his Messiah now because of this sin (which was atoned for at the time) he might also have said then, "I will not lead you into the land nor honor you so highly as I promised; for you committed this sin which I will never forgive or forget."

But if no sin prevented God at that time from keeping his promise made to Abraham—as he never has forsaken his promise because of men's sin—why should he now delay so long with his Messiah by reason of this sin, in view of his glorious promise made to him that the throne of David and the sacrifices of the priests would not end before the Messiah came? Many other sins were committed at that time under Moses—the sins with Baal Peor, the sin of tempting God so often, etc., for which, as Moses' books attest, they were severely punished. Why do they not also mention those sins here? Dear friend, to such Jews you must say that this is foolishness, as they know, or ought to know.

Furthermore, at that time the Messiah had not yet been promised to David. For this reason their sinning with the calf cannot come into consideration here. Therefore let them name some other sin because of which they are suffering such misery and exile. If they should mention one or several, I ask you most kindly to inform me at once of this in writing. Then I, old fool and miserable Christian that I am, will immediately have a stone knife made and become a Jew. And I will not only circumcise that one member but also my nose and my ears. However, I am convinced that they can name none.

The Scriptures record that the Jews committed many more and graver sins before the Babylonian captivity than they can point to in connection with this Roman captivity. Yet the Babylonian captivity did not last more than seventy years, and at that time they were also very much comforted with the presence of prophets, princes, and the promise, as I shall show later. We find none of these in the Roman captivity; and yet we behold this terrible punishment. Whoever is able, let him say: Dear Jew, tell me, which sin is it, what is this sin, that prompts God to be angry with you so long and to withhold his Messiah?

In the second place, even if the Jews could name the sin—and it is quite indifferent whether they call it A or B (though they are able to do neither)—that still would not help them. They would still be caught in their lie. For in Jeremiah 31[:31-34] we find recorded: *"Behold, the days are coming, says the Lord, when I will make a new covenant with the house of Israel and the house of Judah, not like the covenant which I made with their fathers when I took them by the hand to bring them out of the land of Egypt, my covenant which they broke, though I was their husband, says the Lord. But this is the covenant which I will make with the house of Israel after those days, says the Lord: I will put my law within them, and I will write it upon their hearts; and I will be their God, and they shall be my people. And no longer shall each man teach his neighbor and each his brother, saying, 'Know the Lord,' for they shall all know me, from the least of them to the greatest, says the Lord; for I will forgive their iniquity, and I will remember their sin no more."*

This beautiful passage embraces many points, but since the Jews always flit and flutter from one subject to another when they feel themselves trapped, you must avoid all the others at this time and tenaciously stick to the issue for which this passage is now cited—namely, because the Jews claim that the promised Messiah's advent is being delayed as a result of their sin. Quite to the contrary, God here declares that he will make a new covenant or law, unlike Moses' covenant or law, and that he will not be prevented from doing this by the fact that they have sinned. Indeed, precisely because they failed to keep the first covenant, he wants to establish another, a new covenant, which they can keep. Their sin or their breaking of the previous covenant will not deter him. He will graciously forgive their sin and remember it no more.

You must base your argument on this passage and hold it before the Jews' eyes. For how do these things agree? How do they accord? The Jews say that the Messiah's advent is being impeded because they have not kept God's covenant but have sinned against it. God says, "No, I will not regard such sin. The fact that they did not keep my covenant will not hinder me. I am prompted to issue a new covenant all the more because they did not keep the old one, in order that such sin might be eternally forgiven and forgotten through the new covenant." Now it is time to pose the question: Who is lying here? God or the Jew? For they contradict one another. The Jew says "Yes," and God says "No." However, the question is quite superfluous, for it is proven that the Jews are lying and that their excuse that the Messiah is delayed because of their sin is worthless. God remains truthful when he declares that he is not stayed by any sin, but that he has held to his promise and the Messiah's coming, and that he still does so, regardless of their sin and their violation of his covenant.

. . .

Since it is clear and obvious that the Jews are unable to name a sin because of which God should delay so long with his promise and thus be a liar in this matter, and that even if they could mention one or more, God's word still stamps them as liars, since he assures them that he will never fail because of their sins in his promise to send the Messiah and to preserve the throne of David forever—it follows incontestably that one of the following two things must be true: either the Messiah must have come fifteen hundred years ago, or God must have lied (may God forgive me for speaking so irreverently!) and has not kept his promise. I repeat, either the Messiah must have come fifteen hundred years ago when the throne of David, the kingdom of Judah, the priesthood of Israel, the temple, and Jerusalem were still intact, when the law of Moses and the worship he instituted still endured, and the people were still living under their government in Jerusalem, before all of this had collapsed and been destroyed so miserably; or if not, God has lied. Those Jews who are still in possession of their reason cannot deny this. The hardened ones may wriggle and writhe, bend and twist with whatever artifices they may or can find, but their expedients and subterfuges are nothing over against such obvious truth.

The Messiah has come and God's promise has been kept and fulfilled. They, however, did not accept or believe this, but constantly gave God the lie with their own unbelief, etc. Is it any wonder that God's wrath destroyed them together with Jerusalem, temple, law, kingdom, priesthood, and reduced these to ashes, that he scattered them among all the Gentiles, and that he does not cease to afflict them as long as they give the lie to the divine promise and fulfillment and blaspheme them by their unbelief and disobedience? For they should have accepted the new covenant (as promised by Jeremiah) from the Messiah and received him. He was commissioned to teach them properly concerning the throne of David, the priesthood, the law of Moses, the temple, and all things. As Moses writes in Deuteronomy 18[15]: *"The Lord your God will raise up for you a prophet like me from among you, from your brethren—him you shall heed."* For God says that he will put his words in the prophet's mouth and speak with them.

. . .

But now in their last, Roman exile, there is none of this. There is no prophet, and they have no word from Scripture telling them how long this exile will endure. They must be so pitifully afflicted for an indefinite time, wandering aimlessly about without prophets or God's word. God never did this before, and he would not do it now if his Messiah had not come and his promise had not been fulfilled. For he promised that David's throne would not fail or the priestly sacrifices be discontinued; and yet both David's throne and Moses' altar, together with Jerusalem itself, have been destroyed and have lain desolate for fifteen hundred years. Meanwhile God keeps silent, as he never did in Egypt or in the other exile. Nor will he or can he do so, lest he be untrue to his promise.

. . .

Therefore those three punishments or exiles—in Egypt, in the wilderness, and in Babylon—cannot be compared with this last Roman exile. For in regard to the former, the sin is known, there are prophecies and promises, there are prophets and persons, for both the throne of David and the altar of Moses; and there is a definite time specified. In brief, where God is so disposed toward his people and where he deals thus with them and diligently keeps them and reassures them, one cannot say that he has forsaken them or has forgotten his divine promise. Nor can they be called forsaken, when God provided for the children of Israel in Egypt before they were born, determining the time for Abraham before he ever had a child. Read Jeremiah 30 and 31 and you will discover how God bemoans, like a weeping mother, the exile of his people in Babylon. He did this even before they went into exile and without any regard for their sin on account of which they were to be driven into exile.

Why, then, should God forget his promise so woefully in this exile or let it fail of fulfillment or be so hostile to them, since they have no sin which they can name, and yet this promise of the Messiah is the most glorious and the mightiest promise, upon which all other prophecy, promise, and the entire law are built? For the other promises such as those pertaining to Egypt, the wilderness, and Babylon, are to be esteemed very small in comparison with this chief promise of the Messiah. If God kept his less important promises there and then and comforted the people so heartily in lesser exiles; if he specified the time; if he proved himself their faithful God by means of persons and blessings and in every way, and always provided for them— how is it possible, how is it credible, how is it consistent that he would fail to keep, in this terrible, long, and great exile, his glorious promise given to David that his throne should remain established forever, as David exults in his last words (recorded in 2 Samuel in the first chapter [23:5]) and as we find in many other writings of the prophets, for example, in Isaiah and Jeremiah?

The Jews may say what they want about the sins for which they are suffering (for they are lying). God did not promise and pledge an eternal throne to their sin or their righteousness, but to David. Even if he were disinclined to keep this promise to the Jews because of their sin (which they cannot even name), he would not for that reason lie to David and fail him to whom he promised this. This is what David sings in Psalm 89. However, since David's throne, which God declares is not to be destroyed or fall, has been destroyed now for fifteen hundred years, it is incontrovertible that either the Messiah came fifteen hundred years ago and occupied the throne of his father David, and forever occupies it, or God has become a liar in his most glorious promise because of evil men and disobedient Jews. But this God did not want and never will want. No, the Jews are slandering God and deceiving themselves when they accuse God of breaking faith and trust with David because he did not send the Messiah in the manner they would have liked and as they prescribe and imagine him to be.

I know this argument is true. Where there are still reasonable Jews, it must move them, and it must even upset the obdurate ones a little, for they cannot bring any substantial evidence against it. But if it does not move them or make them waver, we have nonetheless substantiated our own faith, so that their foul and worthless lies and idle chatter cannot harm us. And if they do not stick to the point of the argument but evade the issue by resorting to other twaddle, as they like to do, let them go their way and you go yours. It only shows you how they are given to babbling and lying.
. . .

{Conclusion}
{LW 47:95–98}

And finally, to bring this letter to a close, I hope, my dear friend, that you will at least have been supplied with enough material to defend yourself against the Sabbatarians and to preserve the purity of your Christian faith. If you are unable to convert the Jews, then consider that you are no better than all the prophets, who were always slain and persecuted by this base people who glory solely in the boast that they are Abraham's seed, though they surely know that there have always been many desperate, lost souls also among them, so that they might well recognize that it requires more to be a child of God than just to be the seed of Abraham. Therefore neither does the law of Moses do them any good, for they have never kept it, as is shown by the aforementioned verse from Jeremiah 31, where God himself states this and bemoans it. Rather their disobedience does them harm. Even today they do not keep this law, nor can they keep it so long as Jerusalem does not become the seat of the Jews' kingdom and priesthood.

It is a known fact—and this they also admit in part—that they themselves no longer understand the law of Moses, especially certain passages in Leviticus and in other books. How, then, could they keep it even if they were now in Jerusalem? In brief, since these fifteen hundred years of exile, of which there is no end in sight, nor can there be, do not humble the Jews or bring them to awareness, you may with a good conscience despair of them. For it is impossible that God would leave his people, if they truly were his people, without comfort and prophecy so long. He never did this before. Moreover, he promised that he would do nothing without a prophecy preceding the event, as Amos says, *"Surely the Lord God does nothing without revealing his secret to his servants the prophets"* [Amos 3:7]. All estates, all governments, all the works of man must exist, occur, and continue in the word of God so that his people may know how they stand with God and what they are to do, to suffer, and to expect. This God has done from the beginning, and this he will do forever.

Because God for fifteen hundred years has failed to do this with the Jews but lets them live on and on in exile without any word or prophecy to them regarding it, it is evident that he has forsaken them, that they can no longer be God's people, and that the true Lord, the Messiah, must have come fifteen hundred years ago. What, do you suppose, might be the sin that continues to provoke such a terrible penalty and such silence of God other than their rejection, past and present, of the true Seed of Abraham and David, the dear Lord Messiah? They committed more terrible sins before the Babylonian captivity—the murdering of the prophets, etc.—than they can point to subsequently.

It does not make sense that they should suffer such misery for fifteen hundred years for unknown sins—sins which they cannot name—whereas they did not have to suffer more than seventy years for sins that were more obvious, terrible, murderous, and idolatrous. Furthermore, at that time they were not without prophets and without comfort, while in their present exile not even a fly flicks a wing for their consolation. If this is not being forsaken by God, then the devil, too, may boast that he is not forsaken by God.

If we reckon the time exactly, we find that their present exile under the Roman Empire is lasting longer than their former state and government in the land of

Canaan. Anyone may figure the time from the exodus from Egypt to the final destruction of Jerusalem, under which they still live, and he will arrive at the sum of approximately fifteen hundred and ten years. At present they have not lived many fewer years in exile; and in the end this will become a far longer period of time, since they neither have had nor will they have any prophet or prophecy regarding their exile's end. Is it credible that God should let his people live longer devoid of their dominion than in possession of it, longer without the law, temple, divine worship, Jerusalem, priesthood, kingdom, and country than with them?

This letter has grown in the writing. I was quite unaware of it, so quickly did my pen skim over the paper. For I have more thoughts on this subject than I have managed to express. Please be content with this for the time being, for the subject is far too big to be disposed of in a letter. I commend you to God. Amen.

Text #21

New Preface to Ezekiel (1541)

Language: German

Critical Edition: WA DB 11/1:395–405

English Translation: LW 35:284–93

Table Talk #5324

Language: German

Critical Edition: WA TR 5:58 (no. 5324)

English Translation: LW 54:408

In 1540 Luther announced that he intended to write a new preface to the German Bible to warn his readers against paying any attention to Rabbinic biblical interpretations. This is recorded in a Table Talk[1]:

> Nobody believes what labor it cost us—except those who work with us and hear about it, like George.[2] For the rabbis help us very little. I plan to put a new preface in the front of the Bible to warn everybody about the rabbis, for they are blinded and hardened. Even if they already have the book, as Isaiah said [Isa. 29:11–12], they are blind to it. This German Bible (this is not praise for myself but the work praises itself) is so good and precious that it's better than all other versions, Greek and Latin, and one can find more in it than in all commentaries, for we are removing impediments and difficulties so that other people may read in it without hindrance. I'm only concerned that there won't be much reading in the Bible, for people are very tired of it and nobody clamors for it any more.

The preface never materialized, but as part of the German Bible revision of 1541, Luther did compose an entirely new preface to Ezekiel specifically aimed at the Rabbis, the primary purpose of which was to debunk what he knew of Jewish interpretation of the book. Here we find an extended description of the relationship between the new (spiritual) and the old (bodily/physical/Mosaic) covenants. Regarding the Jews, Luther bluntly states: "The new covenant they do not want, the old they cannot have." Gentile Christians are the New Israel, that is, "the true Israelites" and "the new Jews," while Jewish messianic hope and the hope of a return to the land of Israel are utterly vain and lost. The latter is the message of Ezekiel's vision of the chariot, which signifies the destruction of Judaism and the Synagogue, for the rider on the chariot is Christ himself. Thus with Martin Brecht, it can be said that with this new preface Luther intended the "total repudiation of Jewish hopes."[3] For more on Luther's prefaces to the books of the Bible, see Text #15.

Excerpted below is the bulk of the Preface, excluding Luther's discussion of the Temple Vision in Ezekiel 40–48.

A New Preface to the Prophet Ezekiel (1541)
{LW 35:284–290}

St. Jerome and others write that it was, and still is, forbidden among the Jews for any man under thirty years of age to read the first and last parts of the Prophet Ezekiel and the first chapter of Genesis. To be sure, there was no need of this prohibition among the Jews, for Isaiah 29[:11-12] prophesies that the entire Holy Scriptures are sealed and closed to the unbelieving Jews. St. Paul says as much in 2 Corinthians 3[:14-16], that the veil of Moses remains over the Scriptures, so long as they do not believe in Christ.

Their works prove that too. For like filthy swine wallowing and rolling in a beautiful garden, they rip and torture the Scriptures in their interpretations of them. So it would be preferable if they were to quit meddling in the Scriptures, even though many of our own people cling so tightly to the rabbis and have such confidence in them, that they Judaize more than the ancient Jews themselves.

This vision in the first part of Ezekiel [1:4-28], however, is nothing else than a revelation of the kingdom of Christ in faith here upon earth, in all four corners of the whole world as said in Psalm 19[:4]: *In omnem terram.* This is how I understand it (let someone else improve on it). For no one can be a prophet, as St. Peter testifies, unless he have the Spirit of Christ [2 Pet. 1:21]. But to give an interpretation of the entire vision is too long a matter for a preface. To put it briefly: this vision is the spiritual chariot of Christ in which he rides here in the world, meaning thereby his entire holy church.

. . .

This vision, moreover (as Ezekiel himself shows in chapters 8–9), signified the end and destruction of the synagogue, or of Judaism, that is, of the priesthood, the worship, and the church organization instituted and given them by Moses. For all of these were instituted only until Christ should come, as St. Paul says in Romans 8[:2-3] and 2 Corinthians 3[:6], as Christ himself says in Matthew 11[:13], and as the Epistle to the Hebrews says repeatedly. The Jews have taken terrible offense at this; it has been a stumbling block to them even to this day.

Over against the blindness of the Jews, it should be known especially that all the prophecies which say that Israel and Judah shall return to their lands and possess them in a physical way forever, have been long since fulfilled, so that the hopes of the Jews are utterly vain and lost.

For this prophecy contains two things. The first is that Israel and Judah shall return to their land after their captivity. This came to pass through King Cyrus and the Persians, before the birth of Christ, at the time when the Jews returned to their land and to Jerusalem from all countries. They also came to Jerusalem every year to the feasts, even from foreign countries where they maintained their residence, drawing many Gentiles with them and to them.

But the hope of the Jews that there shall yet be another physical return, when all of them together shall come back into the land and set up again the old Mosaic order of things, this is something they have dreamed up themselves. There is not a letter in the prophets or in Scripture which says or signifies anything of the kind. It is written, indeed, that they shall return out of all lands whither they have been driven; not all of them, however, but only some of them out of all lands. There is a great difference between a return of all Jews and a return out of all lands. The return out of all lands is fulfilled; the return of all Jews was never prophesied, but rather the opposite, just as at Jerusalem, while it was yet standing, both before and after the captivity, not all the people were the people of God, but the majority of them were people of the devil, idolatrous murderers and the worst people on earth.

The second thing, and the best thing in this prophecy—that which the Jews will neither see nor heed—is that God promises to create something new in the land, to make a new covenant unlike the old covenant of Moses that they dream about. This is plain from Jeremiah 31[:31-32] and from many more passages. No longer are there to be two kingdoms but one kingdom, under their King David who is to come; and his shall be an everlasting kingdom, even in that same physical land.

This, too, has been fulfilled. For when Christ came and found the people of both Israel and Judah gathered again out of all lands so that the country was full, he started something new: he established the promised new covenant. He did this not at a spiritual place, or at some other physical place, but exactly in that same physical land of Canaan, and at that same physical Jerusalem—as had been promised—to which they had been brought back out of all lands.

And although the Jews did not want this covenant—or at least not many of them would accept it—it has, nevertheless, remained an everlasting covenant, and not only at Jerusalem and in that land. It has broken forth from there into all the four corners of the world, and remains to the present day, both at Jerusalem and everywhere. For the place, Jerusalem, is still there, and Christ is Lord and King there as he is in all the world. He helps and hears all who are there or who come there, as he does those in all the world. Meanwhile he lets Mohammed with his tyranny and the pope with his trickery do what they do; Christ is and remains Lord over all.

The Jews make a point of the name Israel and claim that they alone are Israel and that we are Gentiles. Now this is true so far as the first part of the prophecy and the old covenant of Moses are concerned, though this has long since been fulfilled. But according to the second part of the prophecy and the new covenant, the Jews are no longer Israel, for all things are to be new, and Israel too must become new. Those alone are the true Israel who have accepted the new covenant which was established and begun at Jerusalem.

For according to the old covenant I am no Israelite, or Jew. But I claim now that I am the son of St. Paul, and an Israelite or Benjamite. For Paul is my father, not the old Paul but the new Paul. He is still the old Paul, but out of the old Paul there has arisen a new Paul in Christ; and he has begotten me in Christ by the gospel, so that I am in his likeness according to the new covenant. Thus all the Gentiles who are Christians are the true Israelites and new Jews, born of Christ, the noblest Jew. Everything, therefore, depends upon the new covenant, which the Messiah was to found, making all things new, as he has done.

And this rule is to be noted well: when the prophets say of Israel that it is to return or to be gathered in its entirety, as in Micah 2[:12], Ezekiel 20[:40), etc., they are certainly speaking of the new covenant, and of the new Israel from which no one will be excluded, the everlasting kingdom of Christ. It cannot possibly be understood to mean the old Israel, for the majority of them remained in Assyria and Babylonia, both living and dead, and only a very few returned; Ezra [2:1–65] numbers them all.

The Jews, however, want to have a Messiah according to the old covenant and pay no attention to this new covenant. So they miss both covenants and hang between heaven and earth. The new covenant they do not want, the old they cannot have. Therefore the Scriptures are sealed against them, Isaiah 29{:11-12}, and they understand none of the prophets. Besides they are without any government, either physical or spiritual. The physical, earthly government they have not, for they have neither king nor lord, neither kingdom nor princedom; the spiritual too they have not, for they will not accept the new covenant, and must thus remain without a priesthood. In a word they not only despised this new covenant, but persecuted it. They tried to eradicate it, not wanting to put up with it; and on that account they have been destroyed, and their covenant along with them.

Even though Jerusalem and the whole ancient order could have remained, nevertheless, in order to fulfill the Scriptures, the new covenant would have had to come and make all things new, as it now is in Christendom. There would have had to be at Jerusalem an apostle, bishop, or preacher—as Christ himself made a beginning—who would have had to rule Christ's church there, preach the gospel, baptize, administer the sacrament, absolve, bind, etc. If the high priest—Caiaphas, or somebody else—had been unwilling to do this, an apostle would have had to do it, or one of the successors to the apostles, as has happened heretofore and must happen. Thus the eternal kingdom of Christ would have had to rule all the same, even in old Jerusalem as well as in all the world, as the prophecy intends and had promised. The old kingdom of Moses would then have remained as a temporal government.

For so the old, worldly, temporal government remains in all the world, and does not at all prevent the establishment upon earth of the new, spiritual, everlasting rule and kingdom of Christ under it and within it, a kingdom that has its own peculiar nature, as we clearly see. Especially is this the case where there are righteous kings and princes, who in their old government tolerate this new everlasting kingdom of Christ, or who themselves accept it, promote it, and desire as Christians to be in it. Otherwise the greater part of the kings, princes, and lords of the old government hate the new covenant and kingdom of Christ as poisonously and bitterly as the Jews at Jerusalem. They persecute it and would wipe it out; and, like the Jews, they go to destruction because of it. That is what happened to Rome; it will happen to others also. Christ's new kingdom must abide for it is promised it shall be an everlasting kingdom, and the old kingdom must perish in the end.

It is well to remember, too, that since God himself calls this kingdom a new kingdom, it must be a far more glorious kingdom than the old kingdom was or is. It was God's will to make it a far better kingdom than the old one. Even if this new kingdom had no other glory, this alone would be enough to make it glorious beyond measure: that it is to be an everlasting kingdom that will not come to an end like the old, worldly kingdom.

This everlasting kingdom, however, contains in addition such immeasurable, glorious blessings as forgiveness of sins, peace with God, security against everlasting death and all evil, communion with the Divine Majesty and with all angels and saints, joy and pleasure in the whole creation, even in a physical sense. For this same body, which is now the old body, shall also become new, together with the whole creation, as the soul has already begun to become new in faith.

Therefore the Jews do themselves wrong and injury when they desire through the Messiah not the new kingdom but the former, old, transitory kingdom, where they will possess silver, gold, riches, power, honor, pleasure, and joy according to the mortal flesh, all of which count before God as very minor things, indeed, as nothing at all. For if God had willed to promise such a kingdom, he would not have called it a new, different, and better kingdom.

Beyond the goods of this world nothing else can be called new and better, except only the spiritual, everlasting blessings in heaven, among which there can be nothing bad or evil. But among the earthly, old, temporal goods, however glorious they may be—as the Jews envision those coming from their Messiah—there must always be and remain much that is bad, much that is evil, at least death must be there, and the end of these goods.

These two things Ezekiel teaches us when he comforts the people concerning the return from Babylon, but even more when he prophesies the new Israel and the kingdom of Christ. That is his vision of the chariot, and also really his temple, in the last part of his book.

. . .

Text #22

Liscentiate Exam Heinrich Schmedenstede (1542)

Language:	Latin
Critical Edition:	WA 39/2: (185), 187–203
English Translation:	LW 34: (299), 303–21

The theses for this examination were composed by Luther himself. The "liscentiate" was the standard academic exam—originating in the Middle Ages and still in use in many European universities today—to qualify the already master's-level candidate for university teaching. With the *licentia docendi* in their particular area of expertise, the next step would then be the doctorate and regency (residency) at a university, and thus the qualification to examine other candidates. The term liscentiate in other contexts could refer also to the "license to practice," as in the field of law.

In concise fashion, the initial theses present Luther's understanding of the unity of the Testaments around the promise of the Seed and faith in that promise, which for Luther is the common characteristic of the people of God in both Testaments of the Christian Bible. This identity of faith is what enables Luther both to speak of the "Church" as being present in the Old Testament as well as to refer to the Old Testament saints as "Christians;" this he does throughout his Genesis lectures.

A persuasive case can be made to the effect that Gen. 3:15 *("I will put enmity between you and the woman, and between your seed and her seed; he will strike your head, and you will strike his heel")* was regarded by Luther as the single most important text in the Bible. In all editions of the Luther Bible, he included this marginal note for the reader of Gen. 3:15: "This is the first gospel and promise of Christ on earth, to the effect that he will overcome sin, death, and hell and save us from the power of the Serpent. In this Adam believed together with all of his descendents, (and) by which he became a Christian and was saved from his Fall."[1]

His interpretation of this one passage runs like a red thread throughout the Genesis lectures and functions as the lynchpin in his overall reading of the Christian Bible as a theological unity. For Luther, the seed of the woman is the Messiah/Son of God, and this text proclaims the promise of his coming. Those who belong to the Messiah/Son of God are those who trust in this promise. The serpent is Satan, and his seed represents those who belong to him. The Messiah/Son of God and Satan and those who belong to them are thus locked in perpetual struggle until the last day.

Presented below are the first twenty out of forty-six theses.

The Licentiate Examination of Heinrich Schmedenstede (July 7, 1542)
{LW 34:303–304}

The Theses

Master Heinrich of Lüneburg will respond to these theses for his diploma, with the Rev. Dr. Martin Luther presiding, next Friday at seven o'clock in the morning.

1. One and the same God has been worshiped from the beginning of the world in different ways through faith in the same Christ.

2. It is certain that Adam and Eve believed in the promised seed of the woman [Gen. 3:15], that is, in God who made the promise.

3. Abel in sacrificing pleased God [Gen. 4:4; Heb. 11:4], who promised the seed, in whom or in whose promise he believed.

4. Abraham, having been called out from the Chaldeans [Gen. 11:31; 12:1–3; Acts 7:4, Heb. 11:8], believed God, who promised the seed and who called him, and was justified.

5. Faith in the same promise was truly renewed to other people at different times;

6. Not indeed by human presumption, but by divine authority, which willed that the same promise should be renewed at different times and through different persons.

7. Briefly, whatever virtues or deeds were done by the pious before Christ were done through faith in his promise.

8. Just as whatever has been done by saints after Christ, has been done through faith in the fulfilled promise.

9. Those different ways of believing in the promised seed or in the same Christ in the course of time have come to an end.

10. Just as the Christian faith itself, renewed in the last period of the gospel, will cease at the end of the world.

11. So that statement most assuredly stands, "Jesus Christ is the same yesterday and today and forever," Hebrews 13[:8].

12. If Adam, Noah, and the other patriarchs had lived at the time of Abraham, who received the new promise, it would have been necessary for them to believe that Christ would be of the seed of Abraham or they would have lost God who promised the seed.

13. If Abraham had lived at the time of David, it would have been necessary for him to believe that Christ would be of the lineage of David, or he would have believed in vain in the seed of the woman.

14. If David had lived at the time of John the Baptist, it would have been necessary for him to believe in Jesus, the seed of his descendant, Mary, or he would have perished.

15. If John the Baptist had lived after the resurrection of Christ, no, rather in his own time, and would have believed that Christ would come or had not yet come, he would have been damned.

16. Therefore, the Jews believe in vain in God, who promises a Messiah, by which faith their fathers once believed correctly.

17. The Turks and other nations believe in vain in God the creator of the world, since they deny that he is the one who promises and proffers the seed; indeed, they blaspheme in saying that he is not the Father of Christ, the only-begotten Son.

18. The papists and sophists believe in vain in God the Father and all the other articles of our faith, since they reject the work of Christ completed for us.

19. For they deny that we are justified by faith alone, or what is the same thing, solely by Christ's completed work.

20. For solely by faith in Christ, once promised, now delivered, the whole church is justified, from the beginning of the world to the end.

. . .

Text #23

On the Jews and Their Lies (1543)

Language: German
Critical Edition: WA 53: (412), 417–552
English Translation: LW 47: (121), 137–306

This lengthy treatise is Luther's most infamous writing, and deservedly so. Though he states at the end that it caused him pain to write, he was nevertheless convinced that it needed to be written—riddled as it is with satire, anger bordering on rage, and pompous condescension—in order to unburden his own conscience regarding the Jewish question.

Occasion and Tenor

Though often characterized as the ravings of a sick old man, the treatise is a rhetorical tour-de-force and coheres as well with Luther's overall body of work concerning the Jews. One novel element in Luther's rhetorical arsenal here is his repeated invoking of the old stereotypical accusations against the Jews in terms of well-poisoning, ritual murder of Christian children, etc., which is not characteristic of his prior anti-Jewish writing.[1] Particularly odd (but perhaps particularly revealing) is Luther's way of writing as if Christians were the underdogs vis-à-vis the Jews.[2]

In 1542 Luther had received word once again from Count Schlink that his *Against the Sabbatarians* had generated a written rabbinic response. He expressly states that *On the Jews and Their Lies* was written to help Christians defend themselves against the claims made in the rabbinic response.[3] Over and again in the treatise it is clear that Luther is worried about Jews making inroads into the church, whether through conversion or Judaizing, and thus he writes to strengthen Christians against both. But behind this surface issue stands an additional item and that is Luther's claim to be in possession of new knowledge regarding Jewish blasphemy. During the late 1530's Luther had read *Victoria adversus impios Hebreos* ("Victory against the godless Hebrews") by the fourteenth-century Carthusian monk, Salvagus Porchetus, and *Der gantz Jüdisch glaub* ("The Entire Jewish Faith") by his own contemporary, Anthonius Margaritha, a Jewish convert. From the former Luther learned about the medieval Jewish text, *Toledot Yeshu* ("The History of Jesus"), which contained extremely unflattering stories about Jesus' birth and his secret power.[4] From the latter he learned about Jewish rituals and prayers, which according to Margaritha contained slanderous claims about Jesus, his mother, and all Christians.[5]

Toleration or Expulsion? The Proposals

Armed with his new knowledge, Luther took a definitive position on a major hot-button issue of the day, whether to tolerate or expel the Jews, whom he now calls "our plague, our pestilence, and our misfortune."[6] He states that his previous open stance toward the Jews was based on ignorance of their actual blasphemous practices: "What shall we Christians do with this rejected and condemned people, the Jews? Since they live among us, we dare not tolerate their conduct, now that we are aware of their lying and reviling and blaspheming. If we do, we become sharers in their lies, cursing, and blasphemy."[7]

Luther is here indebted to what he had learned from the Jewish convert, Margaritha, who had written: "This is what I say, that the more friendly, brotherly, and kindly a Christian treats a Jew, the more the Jew curses the Christian and his faith, mocks, and despises, and thinks to himself, this Christian knows that I am an enemy both to his God and to his faith, and that I curse and despise it. Therefore it must be from God that he loves me."[8] Luther's preferred solution is that Jews should live "where there are no Christians,"[9] and he makes his position clear: "In my opinion the problem must be resolved thus: If we wish to wash our hands of the Jews' blasphemy and not share in their guilt, we have to part company with them. They must be driven from our country. Let them think of their fatherland; then they need no longer wail and lie before God against us that we are holding them captive, nor need we then any longer complain that they are burdening us with their blasphemy and their usury. This is the most natural and the best course of action, which will safeguard the interest of both parties."[10]

If expulsion is not acceptable, then the civil authorities in Protestant territories must be urged to practice a sharp mercy toward the Jews so as to prevent them from continuing to blaspheme. This sharp mercy is itemized in two forms, one addressed to the civil authorities, and one to the pastors and preachers (who are to encourage the authorities to do their jobs):

To the Civil Authorities	To Pastors and Preachers
1. Burn down Synagogues	1. Burn down Synagogues
2. Destroy Jewish homes	2. Confiscate Prayer Books, Talmudic
3. Confiscate Prayer Books and Talmudic writings	writings, and the Bible
4. Forbid Rabbis to teach	3. Prohibit Jewish Prayer and
5. Abolish safe-conduct for Jews	Teaching
6. Prohibit Usury to the Jews	4. Forbid Jews to utter the name
7. Enforce manual labor on the Jews	of God publicly

Luther's unmistakeable intention was that the religious and social substructure of Jewish life in German Protestant lands be destroyed and that Jews would be forced to leave as a result. Most obscene is Luther's rationale for the burning of synagogues:

"This is to be done in honor of our Lord and of Christendom, so that God might see that we are Christians, and do not condone or knowingly tolerate such public lying, cursing, and blaspheming of his Son and of his Christians."[11] Though these proposals were not implemented, Luther did apparently succeed in persuading Elector John Frederick in May of 1543 to reinstate the edict of expulsion from Saxony that had been partially lifted in 1539.[12]

Justification and Structure

It is important to recognize that the first two-thirds of the treatise is designed to provide a biblical and theological rationale to justify the proposals. Under the rubrics of "Lies against Doctrine" and "Lies against Persons" Luther savages the Jews in three specific areas:

- Jewish boasts of being the sole people of God and their hatred of all other people
- Jewish willful resistence to the proper interpretation of Old Testament texts that prove that Jesus is the Messiah (This is by far the longest section in the treatise, and its main points are reiterated in the Addendum)
- Jewish curses and blasphemy against Jesus, Mary, and all Christians (Here the influence of Porchetus and Margaritha is most noteworthy)

The third area seems to be particularly neuralgic for Luther, as it leads directly into the Proposals. The excerpts below are drawn primarily from this section.

The treatise can be outlined as follows:

A. Lies against Doctrine or Faith	137–254
1. The False Boasts of the Jews	137–176
a. Descent from Abraham	
b. Circumcision	
c. Law of Moses	
d. Land—City—Temple	
2. Against Jewish Exegesis	176–254
a. Gen. 49:10	178–192
b. 2 Sam. 23:1-7	192–209
b¹. Jer. 33:17ff.	
b². Isa. 9:6	
c. Hag. 2:6-9	209–229
d. Dan. 9:24	229–254
B. Lies against Persons	254–267
1. Jesus	
2. Mary	
3. All Christians	

On the Jews and Their Lies (January 1543)

{Introduction to the Treatise}
{LW 47:137}

I had made up my mind to write no more either about the Jews or against them. But since I learned that these miserable and accursed people do not cease to lure to themselves even us, that is, the Christians, I have published this little book, so that I might be found among those who opposed such poisonous activities of the Jews and who warned the Christians to be on their guard against them. I would not have believed that a Christian could be duped by the Jews into taking their exile and wretchedness upon himself. However, the devil is the god of the world, and wherever God's word is absent he has an easy task, not only with the weak but also with the strong. May God help us. Amen.

. . .

{Lies against Persons}
{LW 47:254, 256–268}

In conclusion we want to examine their lies against persons, which, after all, do not make the doctrine either worse or better, whether the persons are pious or base. Specifically, we want to look at their lies about the person of our Lord, as well as those about his dear mother and about ourselves and all Christians. These lies are such as the devil resorts to when he cannot assail the doctrine. Then he turns against the person—lying, maligning, cursing, and ranting against him . . .

. . .

In the first place, they defame our Lord Jesus Christ, calling him a sorcerer and tool of the devil. This they do because they cannot deny his miracles. Thus they imitate their forefathers, who said, "He casts out demons by Beelzebub, the prince of demons" [Luke 11:15]. They invent many lies about the name of God, the tetragrammaton, saying that our Lord was able to define this name (which they call *Schem Hamphoras*),[13] and whoever is able to do that, they say, is also able to perform all sorts of miracles. However, they cannot cite a single instance of any men who worked a miracle worth a gnat by means of this *Schem Hamphoras*. It is evident that as consummate liars they fabricate this about our Lord. For if such a rule of *Schem Hamphoras* were true, someone else would have employed it before or afterward. Otherwise, how could one know that such power inhered in the *Schem Hamphoras*? But this is too big a subject; after this booklet is finished, I plan to issue a special essay and relate what Porchetus writes on this subject. It serves them right that, rejecting the truth of God, they have to believe instead such abominable, stupid, inane lies, and that instead of the beautiful face of the divine word, they have to look into the devil's black, dark, lying behind, and worship his stench.

In addition they rob Jesus of the significance of his name, which in Hebrew means "savior" or "helper." The name Helfrich or Hilfrich was common among the old Saxons; this is the equivalent of the name Jesus. Today we might use the name Hulfrich—that is, one who can and will help. But the Jews, in their malice, call him Jesu, which in Hebrew is neither a name nor a word but three letters, like ciphers or numeral letters. It is as if, for example, I were to take the three numeral letters C, L, and V as ciphers and form the word Clu. That is 155. In this manner they use the name Jesu, signifying 316.[14] This number then is to denote another word, in which *Hebel Vorik* is found. For further information on their devilish practices with such numbers and words, you may read Anthony Margaritha.[15]

When a Christian hears them utter the word "Jesu," as will happen occasionally when they are obliged to speak to us, he assumes that they are using the name Jesus. But in reality they have the numeral letters Jesu in mind, that is, the numeral 316 in the blasphemous word *Vorik*. And when they utter the word "Jesu" in their prayer, they spit on the ground three times in honor of our Lord and of all Christians, moved by their great love and devotion. But when they are conversing with one another they say, *Deleatur nomen eius*, which means in plain words, "May God exterminate his name," or "May all the devils take him."[16]

They treat us Christians similarly in receiving us when we go to them. They pervert the words *Seid Gott willkommen* [literally, "Be welcome to God"] and say, *Sched*[17] *wil k{o}m!* which means: "Come, devil," or "There comes a devil." Since we are not conversant with the Hebrew, they can vent their wrath on us secretly. While we suppose that they are speaking kindly to us, they are calling down hellfire and every misfortune on our heads. Such splendid guests we poor, pious Christians are harboring in our country in the persons of the Jews—we who mean well with them, who would gladly serve their physical and spiritual welfare, and who suffer so many coarse wrongs from them.

Then they also call Jesus a whore's son, saying that his mother Mary was a whore, who conceived him in adultery with a blacksmith. I have to speak in this coarse manner, although I do so with great reluctance, to combat the vile devil. Now they know very well that these lies are inspired by sheer hatred and spite, solely for the purpose of bitterly poisoning the minds of their poor youth and the simple Jews against the person of our Lord, lest they adhere to his doctrine (which they cannot refute). Still they claim to be the holy people to whom God must grant the Messiah by reason of their righteousness! In the eighth commandment, God forbade us to speak falsehoods against our neighbor, to lie, to deceive, to revile, to defile. This prohibition also includes one's enemies. For when Zedekiah did not keep faith with the king of Babylon, he was severely rebuked for his lie by Jeremiah and Ezekiel and was also led into wretched captivity because of it [Jer. 21:1ff.; Ezek. 12:1ff.].

However, our noble princes of the world and circumcised saints, against this commandment of God, invented this beautiful doctrine: namely, that they may freely lie, blaspheme, curse, defame, murder, rob, and commit every vice, however, whenever, and on whom they wish. Let God keep his own commandment: the noble blood and circumcised people will violate it as they desire and please. Despite this, they insist that they are doing right and good and meriting the Messiah and heaven thereby. They challenge God and all the angels to refute this, not to speak of the devil and the accursed Goyim who find fault with it; for here is the noble blood which cannot sin and which is not subject to God's commands.

What harm has the poor maiden Mary done to them? How can they prove that she was a whore? She did no more than bear a son, whose name is Jesus. Is it such a great crime for a young wife to bear a child? Or are all who bear children to be accounted whores? What, then, is to be said about their own wives and about themselves? Are they, too, all whores and children of whores? You accursed Goyim, that is a different story! Do you not know that the Jews are Abraham's noble blood, circumcised, and kings in heaven and on earth? Whatever they say is right. If there were a virgin among the accursed Goyim as pure and holy as the angel Gabriel, and the least of these noble princes were to say that she is an arch-whore and viler than the devil, it would necessarily have to be so. The fact that a noble mouth of the lineage of Abraham said this would be sufficient proof. Who dares contradict him? Conversely, any arch whore of the noble blood of the Jews, though she were as ugly as the devil himself, would still be purer than any angel if the noble lords were pleased to say this. For the noble, circumcised lords have the authority to lie, to defame, revile, blaspheme, and curse the accursed Goyim as they wish. On the other hand, they are privileged to bless, honor, praise, and exalt themselves, even if God disagrees with them. Do you suppose that a Jew is such a bad fellow? God in heaven and all the angels have to laugh and dance when they hear a Jew pass wind, so that you accursed Goyim may know what excellent fellows the Jews are. For how could they be so bold as to call Mary a whore, with whom they can find no fault, if they were not vested with the power to trample God and his commandment under foot?

Well and good, you and I, as accursed Goyim, wish to submit a simple illustration by means of which we, as benighted heathen, might comprehend this lofty wisdom of the noble, holy Jews a little. Let us suppose that I had a cousin or another close blood relative of whom I knew no evil, and in whom I had never detected any evil; and other people, against whom I bore a grudge, praised and extolled her, regarded her as an excellent, pious, virtuous, laudable woman, and said: This dunce is not worthy of having such a fine, honorable woman as his cousin; a she-dog or a she-wolf would be more fit for him. Then I, upon hearing such eulogies of my cousin spoken, would begin to say, against my own conscience: They are all lying, she is an arch-whore. And now I would, though lacking any proof, demand that everyone believe me, despite the fact that I was well aware of my cousin's innocence, while I, a consummate liar, was cursing all who refused to believe my lie—which I knew in my heart to be just that.

Tell me, how would you regard me? Would you not feel impelled to say that I was not a human being but a monster, a repulsive fiend, not worthy of gazing at sun, leaves, grass, or any creature? Indeed, you would consider me to be possessed by devils. I should rather treat my cousin's disgrace, if I knew of any, as though it were my own, and cover it up if it threatened to become public, just as all other people do. But although no one, including myself, knows anything but honorable things about her, I dare to step to the fore and defame my cousin as a scoundrel, with false slander, oblivious to the fact that this shame reflects on me.

That is the type of human beings—if I should or could call them that—which these noble, circumcised saints are. We Goyim, with whom they are hostile and angry, confess that Mary is not ours but rather the Jews' cousin and blood relative, descended from Abraham. When we praise and laud her highly, they proceed to defame her viciously. If there were a genuine drop of Israelite blood in such miserable Jews, do you not suppose that they would say: "What are we to do? Can she help it that her son provoked our ire? Why should we slander her? After all, she is our flesh and blood. It has undoubtedly happened before that a bad son issued from a pious mother." No, such human and responsible thoughts will not occur to these holy people; they must entertain nothing but devilish, base, lying thoughts, so that they may in that way do penance and merit the Messiah soon—as they have, of course, merited him now for fifteen hundred years.

They further lie and slander him and his mother by saying that she conceived him at an unnatural time.[18] About this they are most malicious and malignant and malevolent. In Leviticus 20[:18] Moses declares that a man must not approach a woman nor a woman a man during the female's menstrual uncleanness. This is forbidden on pain of loss of life and limb; for whatever is conceived at such a time results in imperfect and infirm fruit, that is, in insane children, mental deficients, demon's offspring, changelings, and the like—people who have unbalanced minds all their lives. In this way the Jews would defame us Christians, by saying that we honor as the Messiah a person who was mentally deficient from birth, or some sort of demon. These most intelligent, circumcised, highly enlightened saints regard us as such stupid and accursed Goyim. Truly, these are the devil's own thoughts and words!

Do you ask what prompts them to write this, or what is the cause of it? You stupid, accursed Goy, why should you ask that? Does it not satisfy you to know that this is said by the noble, circumcised saints? Are you so slow to learn that such a holy people is exempt from all the decrees of God and cannot sin? They may lie, blaspheme, defame, and murder whom they will, even God himself and all his prophets. All of this must be accounted as nothing but a fine service rendered to God. Did I not tell you earlier that a Jew is such a noble, precious jewel that God and all the angels dance when he farts? And if he were to go on to do something coarser than that, they would nevertheless expect it to be regarded as a golden Talmud. Whatever issues from such a holy man, from above or from below, must surely be considered by the accursed Goyim to be pure holiness.

For if a Jew were not so precious and noble, how would it be possible for him to despise all Christians with their Messiah and his mother so thoroughly, to vilify them with such malicious and poisonous lies? If these fine, pure, smart saints would only concede us the qualities of geese or ducks, since they refuse to let us pass for human beings! For the stupidity which they ascribe to us I could not assign to any sow, which, as we know, covers itself with mire from head to foot and does not eat anything much cleaner. Alas, it cannot be anything but the terrible wrath of God which permits anyone to sink into such abysmal, devilish, hellish, insane baseness, envy, and arrogance. If I were to avenge myself on the devil himself I should be unable to wish him such evil and misfortune as God's wrath inflicts on the Jews, compelling them to lie and to blaspheme so monstrously, in violation of their own conscience. Anyway, they have their reward for constantly giving God the lie.

In his Bible, Sebastian Münster relates that a malicious rabbi does not call the dear mother of Christ *Maria* but *haria*—i e , *sterquilinium*, a dung heap.[19] And who knows what other villainy they may indulge in among themselves, unknown to us? One can readily perceive how the devil constrains them to the basest lies and blasphemies he can contrive. Thus they also begrudge the dear mother Mary, the daughter of David, her right name, although she has not done them any harm. If they do that, why should they not also begrudge her, her life, her goods, and her honor? And if they wish and inflict all kinds of disgrace and evil on their own flesh and blood, which is innocent and about which they know nothing evil, what, do you suppose, might they wish us accursed Goyim?

Yet they presume to step before God with such a heart and mouth; they utter, worship, and invoke his holy name, entreating him to return them to Jerusalem, to send them the Messiah, to kill all the Gentiles, and to present them with all the goods of the world. The only reason that God does not visit them with thunder and lightning, that he does not deluge them suddenly with fire as he did Sodom and Gomorrah, is this: This punishment would not be commensurate with such malice. Therefore he strikes them with spiritual thunder and lightning, as Moses writes in Deuteronomy 28[:18] among other places: *"The Lord will smite you with madness and blindness and confusion of mind."* Those are, indeed, the true strokes of lightning and thunder: madness, blindness, confusion of mind.

Although these terrible, slanderous, blasphemous lies are directed particularly against the person of our Lord and his dear mother, they are also intended for our own persons. They want to offer us the greatest affront and insult for honoring a Messiah whom they curse and malign so terribly that they do not consider him worthy of being named by them or any human being, much less of being revered. Thus we must pay for believing in him, for praising, honoring, and serving him.

I should like to ask, however: What harm has the poor man Jesus done to these holy people? If he was a false teacher, as they allege, he was punished for it; for this he received his due, for this he suffered with a shameful death on the cross, for this he paid and rendered satisfaction. No accursed heathen in all the world will persecute and malign forever and ever a poor dead man who suffered his punishment for his misdeeds. How, then, does it happen that these most holy, blessed Jews outdo the accursed heathen? To begin with, they declare that Jerusalem was not destroyed nor were they led into captivity for their sin of crucifying Jesus. For they claim to have done the right thing when they meted out justice to the seducer and thus merited their Messiah. Is it the fault of the dead man, who has now met his judgment, that we Goyim are so stupid and foolish as to honor him as our Messiah? Why do they not settle the issue with us, convince us of our folly and demonstrate their lofty, heavenly wisdom? We have never fled from them; we are still standing our ground and defying their holy wisdom. Let us see what they are able to do. For it is most unseemly for such great saints to crawl into a corner and to curse and scold in hiding.

Now as I began to ask earlier: What harm has the poor Jesus done to the most holy children of Israel that they cannot stop cursing him after his death, with which he paid his debt? Is it perhaps that he aspires to be the Messiah, which they cannot tolerate? Oh no, for he is dead. They themselves crucified him, and a dead person cannot be the Messiah. Perhaps he is an obstacle to their return into their homeland? No, that is not the reason either; for how can a dead man prevent that? What, then, is the reason? I will tell you. As I said before, it is the lightning and thunder of Moses to which I referred before: *"The Lord will smite you with madness and blindness and confusion of mind."* It is the eternal fire of which the prophets speak: *"My wrath will go forth like fire, and burn with none to quench it"* [Jer. 4:4]. John the Baptist proclaimed the same message to them after Herod had removed their scepter, saying [Luke 3:17]: *"His winnowing fork is in his hand, and he will clear his threshing-floor and gather his wheat into his granary, but his chaff he will burn with unquenchable fire."* Indeed, such fire of divine wrath we behold descending on the Jews. We see it burning, ablaze and aflame, a fire more horrible than that of Sodom and Gomorrah.

Now such devilish lies and blasphemy are aimed at the person of Christ and of his dear mother; but our person and that of all Christians are also involved. They are also thinking of us. Because Christ and Mary are dead and because we Christians are such vile people to honor these despicable, dead persons, they also assign us our special share of slander. In the first place, they lament before God that we are holding them captive in exile, and they implore him ardently to deliver his holy people and dear children from our power and the imprisonment in which we hold them. They dub us Edom and Haman, with which names they would insult us grievously before God, and hurt us deeply. However, it would carry us too far afield to enlarge on this. They know very well that they are lying here. If it were possible, I would not be ashamed to claim Edom as my forefather. He was the natural son of the saintly Rebekah, the grandson of the dear Sarah; Abraham was his grandfather and Isaac his real father. Moses himself commands them to regard Edom as their brother (Deut. 23[:7]). They indeed obey Moses as true Jews!

Further, they presume to instruct God and prescribe the manner in which he is to redeem them. For the Jews, these very learned saints, look upon God as a poor cobbler equipped with only a left last for making shoes. This is to say that he is to kill and exterminate all of us Goyim through their Messiah, so that they can lay their hands on the land, the goods, and the government of the whole world. And now a storm breaks over us with curses, defamation, and derision that cannot be expressed with words. They wish that sword and war, distress and every misfortune may overtake us accursed Goyim. They vent their curses on us openly every Saturday in their synagogues and daily in their homes. They teach, urge, and train their children from infancy to remain the bitter, virulent, and wrathful enemies of the Christians.

This gives you a clear picture of their conception of the fifth commandment and their observation of it. They have been bloodthirsty bloodhounds and murderers of all Christendom for more than fourteen hundred years in their intentions, and would undoubtedly prefer to be such with their deeds. Thus they have been accused of poisoning water and wells, of kidnaping children, of piercing them through with an awl, of hacking them in pieces, and in that way secretly cooling their wrath with the blood of Christians, for all of which they have often been condemned to death by fire. And still God refused to lend an ear to the holy penitence of such great saints and dearest children. The unjust God lets such holy people curse (I wanted to say "pray") so vehemently in vain against our Messiah and all Christians. He does not care to see or have anything to do either with them or with their pious conduct, which is so thickly, thickly, heavily, heavily coated with the blood of the Messiah and his Christians. For these Jews are much holier than were those in the Babylonian captivity, who did not curse, who did not secretly shed the blood of children, nor poison the water, but who rather as Jeremiah had instructed them [Jer. 29:7] prayed for their captors, the Babylonians. The reason is that they were not as holy as the present-day Jews, nor did they have such smart rabbis as the present-day Jews have; for Jeremiah, Daniel, and Ezekiel were big fools to teach this. They would, I suppose, be torn to shreds by the teeth of today's Jews.

Now behold what a fine, thick, fat lie they pronounce when they say that they are held captive by us. Jerusalem was destroyed over fourteen hundred years ago, and at that time we Christians were harassed and persecuted by the Jews throughout the world for about three hundred years, as we said earlier. We might well complain that during that time they held us Christians captive and killed us, which is the plain truth. Furthermore, we do not know to the present day which devil brought them into our country. We surely did not bring them from Jerusalem.

In addition, no one is holding them here now. The country and the roads are open for them to proceed to their land whenever they wish. If they did so, we would be glad to present gifts to them on the occasion; it would be good riddance. For they are a heavy burden, a plague, a pestilence, a sheer misfortune for our country. Proof for this is found in the fact that they have often been expelled forcibly from a country, far from being held captive in it. Thus they were banished from France (which they call *Tsorfath*, from Obadiah [20]), which was an especially fine nest. Very recently they were banished by our dear Emperor Charles from Spain,[20] the very best nest of all (which they called *Sefarad*, also on the basis of Obadiah). This year they were expelled from the entire Bohemian crownland, where they had one of the best nests, in Prague. Likewise, during my lifetime they have been driven from Regensburg, Magdeburg, and other places.

If you cannot tolerate a person in a country or home, does that constitute holding him in captivity? In fact, they hold us Christians captive in our own country. They let us work in the sweat of our brow to earn money and property while they sit behind the stove, idle away the time, fart, and roast pears. They stuff themselves, guzzle, and live in luxury and ease from our hard-earned goods. With their accursed usury they hold us and our property captive. Moreover, they mock and deride us because we work and let them play the role of lazy squires at our expense and in our land. Thus they are our masters and we are their servants, with our property, our sweat, and our labor. And by way of reward and thanks they curse our Lord and us! Should the devil not laugh and dance if he can enjoy such a fine paradise at the expense of us Christians? He devours what is ours through his saints, the Jews, and repays us by insulting us, in addition to mocking and cursing both God and man.

They could not have enjoyed such good times in Jerusalem under David and Solomon with their own possessions as they now do with ours, which they daily steal and rob. And yet they wail that we have taken them captive. Indeed, we have captured them and hold them in captivity just as I hold captive my gallstone, my bloody tumor, and all the other ailments and misfortunes which I have to nurse and take care of with money and goods and all that I have. Alas, I wish that they were in Jerusalem with the Jews and whomever else they would like to have there.

Since it has now been established that we do not hold them captive, how does it happen that we deserve the enmity of such noble and great saints? We do not call their women whores as they do Mary, Jesus' mother. We do not call them children of whores as they do our Lord Jesus. We do not say that they were conceived at the time of cleansing and were thus born as idiots, as they say of our Lord. We do not say that their women are *haria*, as they do with regard to our dear Mary. We do not curse them but wish them well, physically and spiritually. We lodge them, we let them eat and drink with us. We do not kidnap their children and pierce them through; we do not poison their wells; we do not thirst for their blood. How, then, do we incur such terrible anger, envy, and hatred on the part of such great and holy children of God?

There is no other explanation for this than the one cited earlier from Moses—namely, that God has struck them with *"madness and blindness and confusion of mind."* So we are even at fault in not avenging all this innocent blood of our Lord and of the Christians which they shed for three hundred years after the destruction of Jerusalem, and the blood of the children they have shed since then (which still shines forth from their eyes and their skin). We are at fault in not slaying them. Rather we allow them to live freely in our midst despite all their murdering, cursing, blaspheming, lying, and defaming; we protect and shield their synagogues, houses, life, and property. In this way we make them lazy and secure and encourage them to fleece us boldly of our money and goods, as well as to mock and deride us, with a view to finally overcoming us, killing us all for such a great sin, and robbing us of all our property (as they daily pray and hope). Now tell me whether they do not have every reason to be the enemies of us accursed Goyim, to curse us and to strive for our final, complete, and eternal ruin!

From all of this we Christians see—for the Jews cannot see it—what terrible wrath of God these people have incurred and still incur without ceasing, what a fire is gleaming and glowing there, and what they achieve who curse and detest Christ and his Christians. O dear Christians, let us take this horrible example to heart, as St. Paul says in Romans 11, and fear God lest we also finally fall victim to such wrath, and even worse! Rather, as we said also earlier, let us honor his divine word and not neglect the time of grace, as Muhammad and the pope have already neglected it, becoming not much better than the Jews.

What shall we Christians do with this rejected and condemned people, the Jews? Since they live among us, we dare not tolerate their conduct, now that we are aware of their lying and reviling and blaspheming. If we do, we become sharers in their lies, cursing, and blasphemy. Thus we cannot extinguish the unquenchable fire of divine wrath, of which the prophets speak, nor can we convert the Jews. With prayer and the fear of God we must practice a sharp mercy to see whether we might save at least a few from the glowing flames. We dare not avenge ourselves. Vengeance a thousand times worse than we could wish them already has them by the throat. I shall give you my sincere advice:

{Luthers infamous "Proposals" now immediately follow.}

{Luther's Prayer for the Jews, LW 47:291–292}

These are the people to whom God has never been God but a liar in the person of all the prophets and apostles, no matter how much God had these preach to them. The result is that they cannot be God's people, no matter how much they teach, clamor, and pray. They do not hear God; so he, in turn, does not hear them, as Psalm 18[:26] says: *"With the crooked thou dost show thyself perverse."* The wrath of God has overtaken them. I am loath to think of this, and it has not been a pleasant task for me to write this book, being obliged to resort now to anger, now to satire, in order to avert my eyes from the terrible picture which they present. It has pained me to mention their horrible blasphemy concerning our Lord and his dear mother, which we Christians are grieved to hear. I can well understand what St. Paul means in Romans 10 [9:2] when he says that he is saddened as he considers them. I think that every Christian experiences this when he reflects seriously, not on the temporal misfortunes and exile which the Jews bemoan, but on the fact that they are condemned to blaspheme, curse, and vilify God himself and all that is God's, for their eternal damnation, and that they refuse to hear and acknowledge this but regard all of their doings as zeal for God. O God, heavenly Father, relent and let your wrath over them be sufficient and come to an end, for the sake of your dear Son! Amen.

. . .

Text #24

On the Ineffable Name and on the Lineage of Christ (1543)

Language:	German
Critical Edition:	WA 53: (573), 579–648
English Translation:	Here WA 53:579,2–580,9; 600,7–601,29 by Editors.[1]

As he had announced in *On the Jews and Their Lies*, Luther immediately set to work on a follow-up treatise, *On the Ineffable Name and On the Lineage of Christ*, making clear that he was not interested in debating with or trying to convert Jews, rather he writes to warn those in danger of becoming Jews. The treatise is saturated with fecal imagery and references to the Devil (a common association in Christian art and writing from the twelfth-thirteenth centuries onward), all of which is linked to the Jews: the Jews are the Devil's children, they worship the Devil, the Devil is their god, Jewish biblical interpretation is "Judas-piss," and so on. The crudeness of the treatise is approached perhaps only by *Against Hanswurst* (1541),[2] and two of Luther's close colleagues, Andreas Osiander and Justus Jonas, were deeply doubled by what he had written. Luther was cognizant of how such language sounded, and he excused himself with the following: "Oh, my God, my dear Creator and Father! [I trust that] you will graciously credit me that I have—most reluctantly—had to speak so shamefully about your divine majesty against your cursed enemies, Devils and Jews. You know that I have done this out of the flame of my faith and for the honor of your divine majesty. For this is a matter of utmost seriousness to me."[3]

The treatise contains a brief introduction followed by two main parts. In the introduction Luther speaks bluntly against the prospects of Jewish conversion and clarifies his understanding of the problematic text, Rom. 11:25-26. In part one he first presents his translation of a chapter from Porchetus's *Victory against the godless Hebrews*,[4] that is, the chapter in which Porchetus had summarized statements from the *Toledot Yeshu*[5] which portray Jesus—and Judas—as magicians empowered by knowledge of the correct pronunciation of the Tetragrammaton, the four-letter name of God. There then follows a scatological broadside against the Jewish exegetical practice of gematria[6] in general and its relevance to the *Shem Ha-Meforash* (The Ineffable Name of God) in particular. Part one concludes with two excursuses: an address to the civil authorities against toleration of the Jews, and an extended diatribe against reverencing the Tetragrammaton. Part two takes up the question of the true origins of Jesus and is devoted to demonstrating the Davidic lineage of Mary. This Luther accomplishes by harmonizing the competing genealogies in Matthew and Luke. Part two also concludes with two excursuses: on the relationship between the Old Testament and the New Testament, and an extended diatribe against rabbinic exegesis.

The Hebrew phrase, *Shem Ha-Meforash* (literally, "the fully articulated/explicated name"), as a designation of the Tetragrammaton goes back at least to the time of the Mishnah. In the Middle Ages Jewish mystical traditions significantly developed notions about the Name and the names of God. Via Margaritha[7] Luther had learned about the Jewish mystical practice of deriving the names of seventy-two angels from the Hebrew text of Exod. 14:19-21, each verse of which contains seventy-two letters. He regarded such a practice, as well any attempts to make exegetical or theological claims on the basis of the numerical values of Hebrew letters and words (gematria), as sheer nonsense and quintessentially rabbinic. In this treatise, Luther uses "Schem Hamphoras" as a blanket term to cover all such practices and proceeds to satirize Jewish reverence of the divine name in the most offensive manner. It is in this context that Luther—proudly—invokes the image of the *Judensau* in Wittenberg.

High on the exterior wall of St. Mary's Church in Wittenberg (the church where Luther preached most of his sermons), at the southeast corner (that is, facing Jerusalem), there is a small sandstone relief of an image that was popular in German churches from the twelfth-fifteenth centuries: the Jewish Sow. The image portrays a large sow with Jewish children sucking and a male Jew staring intently into the sow's behind. Luther invokes this image, which is still in place today, as the ideal illustration of the source of rabbinic knowledge in general and of the *Shem Hameforash* in particular.[8]

In the early 1980s, after an extended discussion about the *Judensau* image, the community of St. Mary's Church decided that the image should remain in place as a warning about the horrors of the recent past. In addition, a *Mahnung* (reminder/warning) was commissioned and placed on the ground directly beneath the *Judensau*, the inscription to which reads: "God's own name, the reviled *Shem Hameforash*, which the Jews prior to the Christians regarded as virtually unspeakably holy, died in six million Jews under the sign of a cross."

Excerpted below are the introduction to the treatise and Luther's discussion of the *Judensau*.

On the Ineffable Name and On the Lineage of Christ
[Introduction]
{WA 53:579,2–580,9}
In my most recent booklet I promised to write more about the lies and blasphemies that the frenzied, miserable Jews perpetrate about their *Shem Hamphoras*, about which Porchetus writes in his book, *Victoria*. Herewith I intend to have done just

that, in order to honor our faith and to oppose the Devil's lies of the Jews. I do this so that anyone who wants to become a Jew might see what kinds of beautiful articles they have to believe and adhere to if they want to be among the damned Jews.

As I pointed out in my previous booklet, it is not my intention to write against the Jews, as if I hoped to convert them. Therefore I did not call that book *Against the Jews*, but rather *On the Jews and Their Lies*, so that we Germans might know from history what a Jew is, and thus warn our Christians about them, as one would warn about the Devil himself, and also to strengthen and honor our faith. I do not write to convert the Jews, for that is about as possible as converting the Devil.

Just as we must teach and write about the Devil, hell, death, and sin, what they are and do, not so that we can turn the Devil into an angel, hell into heaven, death into life, sin into holiness, all of which is impossible, but rather so that we will beware of them, so I write about the Jews. For a Jew or a Jewish heart is as hard as wood, as hard as stone, as hard as iron, as hard as the Devil, so that it can in no way be moved. If Moses came with all the prophets and did all the miracles before their eyes so that they would leave their hardened reason behind—just as Christ and the Apostles did in their presence—it would all be in vain. Even if they were so gruesomely punished that the streets ran with blood, and one had to count their dead not in hundred thousands but in ten times a hundred thousand, as happened to Jerusalem under Vespasian and to Bittor under Hadrian,[9] nevertheless they would still claim to be right. If they had to be in misery another 1,500 years beyond the 1,500 they have already suffered, nevertheless God must be a liar while they are truthful.

In sum, they are Devil's children damned to hell. If there is anything human left in them, for that one this treatise might be useful. One can hope for the whole bunch as one wills, but I have no hope. I also know no biblical text [that supports such hope]. If we can't convert the large bunch of our Christians but must be content with a small little bunch, how much less is it possible to convert all these Devil's children. It amounts to nothing that some people derive from Romans 11[:25-26] the delusion that all Jews will be converted at the end of the world. St. Paul means something completely different.

. . .

{WA 53:600,7–601,29}

{After a satirical discussion of the medieval Kabbalistic practice of deriving the names of seventy-two angels from the text of Exod. 14:19-21, Luther continues:}

At this point you might well ask me: whence do the Jews get this high wisdom, such that the text of Moses, the holy innocent letters, should be divided into three verses and arithmetical or number-letters be made out of it? And also that they then name 72 angels and thus constitute the entire *Shem Hamphoras*? Leave me in peace about that. Ask the Rabbis and they will tell you all about it. Yes, before I become a Jew, I would like to hear your opinion in advance. For thereafter I know that I would have to believe the rabbis. But you have promised me the Jewish Catechism. Keep your promise.

Well, I do not know exactly whence they got it, but I can make a guess. Here in Wittenberg on our parish church there is a sow carved in stone. Under her, young piglets and Jews lie sucking. Behind the sow stands a rabbi who lifts the sow's right leg and with his left hand he pulls her rear over himself. He bends down and looks most studiously under her rear at the Talmud inside, as if he wanted to read and see something difficult and special. This is most likely where they got their *Shem Hamphoras* from. For previously there were very many Jews in these areas. This is proved by the names of towns and villages, and also of citizens and peasants, which are still in Hebrew today. So, an educated, honorable man, who was an enemy of the filthy lies of the Jews, had such an image made. Thus even today among the Germans it is said (to put it rudely) of one who has great wisdom without cause: "Where did he read that? Out of the rear of a sow!"

To this end, one could play around with the word, *Shem Hamphoras*, and make it, *Peres Shama* [i.e., "filth is there" or "filth is its name"], or master it artificially like [the Jews] do and make it *Shamha Peres* [i.e., "there is filth"] so that it sounds similar. As if a German would understand *Nerren* [fools] when hearing or reading *Neeren* [to feed], or "He has improved [*gebessert*] my property" as "He has wattered" [*gewessert*]. Thus the wretched, evil spirit mocks his captive Jews and lets them say *Shem Hamphoras* and believe and hope that there are great things associated with it. But he [actually] intends *Sham Haperes*, which means "Here is muck." Not the kind that's on the streets but the kind that comes out of the stomach. *Sham* means "here" or "there." *Peres* is what the sow and all animals have in their intestines, as Moses uses it in Leviticus {4:11ff; 8:17} where he commands that the sin offering be burned with skin and hair and all its *Peres*, manure, etc.

For the Devil has possessed and captured the Jews so that (as St. Paul says) [2 Tim. 2:26] they must follow his will and mock, lie, blaspheme, and even curse God and all that belongs to God. As a reward he gives them his mockery, the *Shamhaperes* [i.e., "there is the muck"], and helps them believe that this and all their lies and foolswork are a wonderful thing. They do not scream about such horrible captivity, nor do they beg with even the slightest sigh to get out of it. Rather they are happy to be in it, regard it as especially great freedom, and want us Christians to be in it with them. But they do scream about their Roman captivity, where they are not held captive by us but rather we by them, and this in our own country together with all our money and property! Because they are so well off, they treat us like the Devil treats them. They mock us to our disadvantage, just as the Devil mocks them to their eternal damnation.

Text #25

Josel of Rosheim: Letter to the Strasbourg City Council (1543)

Language:	German
Critical Edition:	Fraenkel-Goldschmidt, 400–8[1]
English Translation:	Fraenkel-Goldschmidt, 408–17[2]

Luther's two major anti-Jewish treatises of January and March 1543 did not go unnoticed in the German Jewish community, nor did the reinstatement of the edict of expulsion from Saxony (May 6, 1543) that had been partially lifted in 1539. On May 28 and July 11, 1543, Josel of Rosheim[3] sent letters to the Strasbourg City Council complaining about Luther's treatises, warning of their potential implications for the Jewish community, and seeking to prohibit the circulation of the treatises in areas under the Council's authority.[4] His first letter was provoked by *On the Jews and Their Lies*, while the second is aimed directly at *On the Ineffable Name*. The date of the latter is significant: the day after 9 Av, the annual commemoration of all calamities that have befallen the Jewish community. This second letter is presented below in its entirety.

Josel was worried about Luther, and rightly so. He had also lost any respect for Luther that he may previously have had. In his Hebrew work called the *Chronicle*, he plays with Luther's name in the same way that Luther had played with the name *Shem Ha-Meforash*, and refers to Luther as *Martin Lo Tohar* (Martin the unclean).[5] Josel's second letter is essential for understanding how Luther had come to be regarded in the German Jewish Community as well as for providing testimony to how Josel himself dealt with the anti-Jesus material in the *Toledot Yeshu* traditions. In addition, it must be said that Josel's letter gives the lie to the argument that Luther cannot be held accountable to "modern" standards of human dignity and decency, for his letter is an elegant, even noble, appeal to those very standards, as evidenced by his statement: "[F]or nowhere is it written that God forbids compassion."

Josel the Jew of Rosheim Responds to Martin Luther's Booklet against the Jews, July 11,1543

Most erudite, honourable, exalted, wise and gracious masters. In the first place, I humbly offer my services to Your Honours. Honourable Sirs, very recently I submitted to your Honours, both verbally and in writing, on behalf of many of my brethren and also of myself, a complaint expressing our grief and distress that various individuals are openly and complacently telling members of the common people that when they injure a Jew in his person or property they will be forgiven since Dr. Martin Luther has expressed this view in print [in his booklet], and has also instructed to preach to this effect [in the churches]. Consequently, I solicited your Honours, requesting that, insofar as possible, you would in accordance with divine law and justice extend to us protection and assistance in this matter, so as to ensure that there will be no further outbreaks of disorder and violence against all the laws of the public peace in the land. [And that moreover {such outbreaks}] contravene the freedoms which our lord the Emperor, may he be exalted, has accorded us, [whereby we are included under] the defense and protection of the Holy Roman Empire.[6] I also attached {to my letter} Your Honours' letters of recommendation and the one written by that most learned man, the late Dr. Wolf Capito,[7] with his own hand, and additional {documents?}. Your Honours have read the said Capito's [letter] with attention; you have that {letter}. And therefore, you have informed me that if anything should befall us, as a result {of Luther's tract}, you would be most distressed; you have also sent instructions to the potential danger spots, namely to Hochfelden, to prevent this from happening. In addition, you wished to show understanding, and therefore, for the meantime, without a new decree on your part, [the tract] is not to be printed within your jurisdiction, so that no person will oppress us on his own initiative, without the knowledge of the authorities. For this encouraging action, the unfortunate Jewish community expresses its heartfelt gratitude.

Your Honours, among other things, I made it clear that I have no wish to enter into any disputation whatsoever with the aforesaid Dr. Marti(n) Luther or with other persons on matters of faith, and that no such duty has been laid upon me by the Jewish community. However, in the year 307 {sic} {1537}, when you and the late aforesaid Dr. Capito gave me excellent letters of recommendation to the Elector, Duke Hans {Johannes} Frederick etc, and to Dr. Marti(n) Luther, [which included] a request that he should graciously hear my words on behalf of the Jewish community, and that in the framework of the law [the Torah?] he should deal compassionately with us unfortunate ones, we understood at that time that Jewish apostates or Mamelukes had turned the heart of Dr. Marti(n) Luther against us with lying words. Indeed he writes at the beginning of his booklet that he had never intended to work against us, but that after he was informed [of the aforesaid calumnies about the Jews], he proceeded to publish his booklet against us.

Honourable Sirs, and so with much toil and travail I journeyed up to seven miles into the [territory] of Meissen to the aforesaid Doctor; however, he did not wish to receive me but wrote me a letter, as you well know. I had indeed thought in my innocence that the aforesaid Doctor would not publish so hostile a book against us unfortunate ones, on the basis of tale bearing and incitement by those who wish us ill, apostates or Jews who are not apostates. I firmly believe that to seize a person's property or injure him bodily, or annul his rights and break his contract, without hearing his case and in violation of imperial or natural law before God and the world can never be considered just. Every person, whoever he is, should be granted the opportunity to have his claims and answers heard. Indeed, God himself, who knows the thoughts of every man, did not wish to destroy Sodom and Gomorrah until he had first informed Abraham of his intention. As He said: "I will go down and see whether they have behaved altogether according to the cry of it, which has reached me." [Genesis] 18:{21} etc. And when Abraham saw that God was so merciful and good, he spoke to Him as follows, as though he was not certain what He would do; he felt that God did not wish to punish them before they or their advocates would first receive an answer, whether they might yet be preserved through the {merits of the} righteous. He therefore arose and spoke cheerfully but also humbly, {and asked} whether if there were to be found in the city just ten righteous persons, would the Lord God pardon the whole city for their sakes.

How different is the conduct of Dr. Marti(n). He does not know the thoughts of any man—whether he is a believer, whether he is close or far from God—and yet, without giving them a hearing, he would dare to annihilate all of Jewry in this world and in the world to come, and would without hesitation deny them all hope or comfort in God—as though he was sent by God to preach these words. Howbeit, the prophets themselves, in spite of all their [the Israelites'] sins, did not condemn them for eternity, but after each punishment addressed them with words of comfort, {saying} that God in the end would alleviate {their sufferings} and not abandon them. Does he [Luther] not consider that there are even more than ten righteous Jews on earth, and that God may possibly derive satisfaction from them, and from our ancient forefathers in the past, for whose sakes He has preserved us the remaining ones? He has comforted us in all the prophecies of Isaiah[8] and Jeremiah, that ultimately He will redeem us and also deliver us that we may do His will. And therefore, no learned person has ever contended that we unfortunate Jews should be treated brutally, in such a tyrannical manner. If no faith is to be kept with us and the public peace *(Landfrieden)* does not include us because we do not wish to believe what Marti(n) Luther believes, there will be far-reaching consequences, for he {also} condemns persons who are far greater and more eminent and powerful than we unfortunate and persecuted ones; against them, too, he has hurled accusations that they serve the golden calf of Aaron, and that their fate will be even bitterer than ours.[9] I do not intend to discuss what he meant by this and I do not wish to poke my nose into this dispute and quarrel. However, I am compelled to mention this in order that Your Honours and all the higher and lower Estates will protect their subjects from such rash publications, and that they will not actually carry out his instructions, for he writes quite explicitly that if the authorities will not wish to see what is written in them, then every cleric will preach and acquaint the common man with this said program of his. I humbly ask the opinion of Your Honours, and of all discerning persons of whatever estate or rank, whether we unfortunate people are not obliged to complain about this and request protection and assistance.

I would also humbly bring to Your Honours' attention that the said Dr. Marti(n), not content with what he has already accused us of in the way of great iniquities, has now published another booklet, entitled *Shem Hamephoras,* in which he states that our forefathers wrote insulting things about your Messiah and your faith, things that undoubtedly these days only a few Jews know about. I myself—and I am an old man—can truthfully say that I have never read such things, save one time in Strasbourg, when I was at the home of the late Dr. Captor [Capito], in the presence of that learned printer Master Windlin Ayl. [Capito] told me that he had received a small book, along with other Hebrew works from Constantinople, in which some-one had written such offensive things about the Messiah that I do not now wish to repeat them or write them down.[10]

He {{Capito}}[11] said: {{"}}I have read through your Talmud, and have also perused all your books and commentaries as well as your prayer books, and had I found calumnies of the kind that there are in this booklet, I would not now support and aid you nor have such compassion for you. However, as I did not find anything like this in any place, I can only assume that perhaps in ancient times some person wrote whatever he pleased, as indeed it happens also in our days that people write things which are not to the liking of the community as a whole.[12] This booklet has now been stolen from me, which I regret very much, since, one of these days, some person might insult one of you on account of it, and it would be a disgrace if such libelous writings were to fall into the hands of the common people.{{"}} I rely on the words of this same trustworthy man, and Your Honours could have verified the matter with him.

Honourable Sirs, are we to blame that some person 1500 years ago, wrote books as the spirit moved him. That does not obligate us; we Jews have the Ten Command-ments and the Torah. In addition, we have the Prophets, and on them we rely, as also God has commanded us in Deuteronomy 17: "According to the law that they will teach you, and the judgement that they will tell you, you shall do; you shall not devi-ate from the word that they will tell you, to the right or to the left." And therefore, in accordance with God's command, [we follow] the sages as they have taught us the Torah, from that we will not deviate. Behold, seventy Elders sat in the Temple [in *lishkat ha-gazit,* "the Chamber of Hewn Stones"] and wrote many commentaries on the Torah, for the text is not always easy to comprehend. According to the {commentaries} of these elders, and of holy men, Daniel, Ezra and other great sages after them, the Talmud was compiled, {and it teaches us} how to keep the Torah, how to administer justice, law and order, how to observe the festivals and our laws, and how to pray with humility. However, the Talmud does not contain anything derogatory about anyone, despite what some claim against it.[13] I would like to prove to Your Honours in person, or to anyone who wishes to hear me, that the Talmudic commentary is valuable for {its description of} the true Messiah; however, at this point this is too lengthy a subject to set down in writing and therefore I have abandoned the idea.

It would have been preferable if Dr. Marti(n) had refrained from {writing} so libelous a booklet, since it is known that a scurrilous tract by so respected a man will undoubtedly be printed by someone, and then that same respected man will vent his wrath more on the printer than on the person {that is, himself} who conceived the work. Therefore, I find it strange [I am amazed] that so erudite a person permitted something of this kind to be printed; however, I am not criticizing him for this, but I want now speedily to respond to the said charges [that he made] against me and against my brethren.

Honourable Sirs, these calumnies and the other false accusations—as though we curse you, or insult your Messiah, or turn you away from your faith—these cruel slanders that he makes against us may have been taken from Antonius Margaritha. I refuted his {Margaritha's} words in the name of all Jewry at the Imperial Diet of Augsburg in [15]30, before our lord, His Majesty the Emperor, and all the delegates and counselors, with respect to these three aforesaid points. And that Jewish apostate was arrested and expelled from the city. I refer you for confirmation of this to the aforesaid delegates and to the Strasbourg city council.

Honourable Sirs, I have no time at present to explain this from the Bible; however, if God grants me life and years, I intend to prove truthfully and clearly from the Holy Scriptures that things are not as the said Dr. Marti(n) has asserted. I am hopeful that were he present he would not reject the truth, for he himself writes that he is now cognizant of things that he did not know twenty years ago, and therefore it is possible that he may learn additional things which likewise he did not know previously. Thus we all entreat in our prayers that God will have mercy on us and on all human beings, that His spirit will rest upon us so that we may truly recognize him, to do His Will in God's Name. Amen.

Honourable Sirs, my brethren have now been assaulted in a number of localities, in Meissen and within the jurisdictional authority of Braunschweig and its vicinity, on account of this booklet that was printed. In many places they have been cruelly oppressed, plundered, expelled, and injured in their persons and property, so I have been informed. Therefore, in the name of all the unfortunate Jews, I direct to you my humble request, that you will graciously consent to approach their Excellencies, the elector-princes of Saxony and Hesse.[14] They and their fathers, the late elector-princes, were always famous and esteemed for their benevolence and love of justice, and still are. Intercede with them, that they and the other members of the [Schmalkaldic] League, or each one individually, will show understanding, so that now, in these troubled times, they will continue to protect and deal mercifully with us unfortunate people as they did in the past, without any innovations, so that, contrary to former practice, we shall not be violently assaulted in the cities, market places and villages, or in the open fields.

However, if at the present time or in the future some person of high or low estate considers that he has charges against us, of the kind so extensively aired in Dr. Marti(n)'s booklet, I myself, the old man, am ready, dutifully and out of fear and love of God, and for the good of all mankind, to put myself willingly and gladly at the disposal of Your Honours, who are the delegates of the honourable city of Strasbourg, or in whatever way that will be appropriate, and give a suitable response to each and every point. This {I will do} without disputing anyone's belief and without offending Dr. Marti(n) or his followers, but solely, inasmuch as God gives me grace, to prove our righteousness and blamelessness, so that every person will remain in the divine and territorial peace and not be harmed. I wish also in this letter to declare before all men that I, who am an old man, have never heard of these matters. I therefore humbly beg and entreat Your Honours to graciously consent to write and intercede with your other neighbours and allies, that they should treat the unfortunate Jews compassionately; namely, that they should accord a charter of safe-passage and protection in every place under their government, as was the case until now, and that it should be transferred to me or to my representatives. This is in order that ignorant persons will not ruthlessly molest and rob these unfortunate people, for nowhere {is it written} that God forbids compassion. But with regard to cruelty, see Isaiah 36 [should read 47] on the King of Babylon, who was commanded by God to punish the Israelites for seventy years, and, notwithstanding this, He said afterward: "I was wroth with My people, I profaned My inheritance, and gave them into your hand; you showed them no mercy, you laid your yoke very heavily upon the aged, etc." And likewise there, in chapter 10, concerning the King of Assyria, He says: "Oh Assyria, the rod of My anger," and although the rod was ordained for them {the Jews} as a punishment from God, nevertheless, God was wroth with the chastiser and he was slain by his sons, as is written explicitly in 2 Kings [19:37]. And with those who stir up incitement He is even more incensed. Witness what befell those who incited the king that he should make Azariah and his companions abandon their religion and customs, until he threw them into the fiery furnace and God protected them there. But the instigators were burnt to death in the furnace, {see} Daniel, chapter 3. Witness what befell those who inclined the king to make Daniel abandon his religion and God's commandments, and he threw him into the lions' den, but God sealed the mouths of the lions; however, they ripped apart the bones of the men who had given {the king} the advice. There are many other stories that I will not mention on account of their length. However, this same mighty, eternal God still has the strength to open instantly in His mercy before the higher and lower Estates his great treasure trove—which is loving-kindness and fear of God, as we find in Isaiah 32 [33], "The fear of the Lord is his treasure, etc." In contrast, for the tyrannical inciters He opens the armoury of the weapons of his wrath, as we find explicitly in Jeremiah, chapter 50, that God opens for the inciter the armoury of the weapons of his wrath, etc. Concerning these two repositories, it behooves every person to entreat God with the utmost devotion that He will not allot him either too much or too little from each of them.

Therefore, whatever may befall us unfortunate people, we must bear it patiently in any event, but we appeal for God's mercy, that He will not inflict the weapons of His wrath upon us too harshly. We pray for this with all our strength, and cry out, for I myself know full well at the present time, that many of my unfortunate brethren, widows and orphans too, have no other hope than for the mercies of God on High, etc.

In good hope, that your Honours and all those whom these words reach, higher and lower Estates alike, will, out of their great intelligence, and for the reasons I have enumerated, protect us in their benevolence and let us unhappy ones be, and not institute any new measures against us, just as all the former emperors, kings, electors and princes of esteemed memory, and also the present ones and those who will come after them, upheld and do uphold {our privileges}, and [that {you will} permit us] to enjoy the same {rights}, as indeed Your Honours and all those mentioned above, out of your inborn sense of justice, know yourselves how to do so well.[15]

I request your Honours' kind response and attention to this matter. I shall not neglect to pray for you and for your said people, in my name and in that of my brethren, that God, will grant you a long, happy and peaceful rule.

Sent on the tenth of the eleventh month, in the year that we Jews reckon 5303 after the creation of the world.[16]

Your humble servant, Josel the Jew of Rosheim, in my name and in that of my brethren.

Text #26

On the Last Words of David (1543)

Language:	German
Critical Edition:	WA 54: (16), 28–100
English Translation:	LW 15: (xi), 265–352

The Last Words of David, 2 Samuel 23:1-7, was for Luther one of the premier christological passages in the Old Testament, and he referred to it constantly whenever christological interpretation of the Old Testament was at stake. For Luther David is not speaking in this passage about himself but rather about the Messiah in whom he believed. This treatise was written to defend that view and also to defend Luther's new translation of the passage that made this particular reading more explicit. Over the course of the treatise, Luther provides proof for the central Christian teachings and the litmus test for "orthodoxy" in line with the first ecumenical councils, namely, the doctrine of the Trinity, the Messiahship of Jesus, and the two natures of Christ, all based on the Old Testament (with significant help from the Gospel of John).

Over and above these doctrinal issues, Luther is at pains throughout the treatise to articulate his interpretive principles where the Old Testament is concerned, and thus the treatise amounts to a defense of his Old Testament hermeneutics as such. This brings him once again head to head with what he knows of Jewish biblical interpretation and contributes to the anti-Jewish character of the whole. For Luther, there could be no real common ground between Jewish and Christian readings of the Old Testament, because New Testament theology—Christology—trumps Old Testament Hebrew grammar, even at the level of translation: a truly radical philosophy. Because Jews are ignorant of theology—that is, because they reject Christ—Christians must be extremely wary of utilizing *any* Jewish/Rabbinic reading of an Old Testament text that has christological implications.[1] Over and again Luther states that the secret to Scripture and its interpretation is the message of Christ. His exegetical convictions are inseparably linked with his profound piety, which in turn was utterly and unmoveably shaped by his early "reformation experience." The treatise is structured according to Luther's treatment of specific biblical texts:

Excerpted below are the introduction and a series of passages highlighting Luther's Old Testament interpretational philosophy, then a broadside against the Jews and the Turks, and finally the conclusion to the treatise: the Jews as "Belial."

On the Last Words of David (August 1543)
{LW 15:267–270}

Saint Jerome reports that he was moved to translate the Bible anew from Hebrew into Latin by the sneering reproach of the enemies of Christ, the Jews, to the effect that Christians did not have the correct Bible in the version then in use throughout Christendom. The reason given was that a number of words and letters were faulty and altogether different from the Hebrew. Prior to this, others had been induced to translate the Bible for the same reason, for instance, Aquila, Theodotion, Origen, and others, until at that time there were up to six translations, which they called *Hexapla*. And in our day, too, so many are busying themselves with translating that history may repeat itself and there may be so many Bibles in the course of time and so many wiseacres who claim a mastery of the Hebrew tongue that there will be no end to it.

That will inevitably happen if we pay attention to what the Jews say and think of our Bible. After all, they are not in agreement among themselves, and they expound Scripture arbitrarily and quote out of context with their grammar. If we were to heed them, we could never acquire a uniform Bible, since every rabbi claims to be superior to the other. Furthermore, they all have to admit that the words in many a passage are incomprehensible to them. They are far from having one harmonious, perfect, and flawless Hebrew Bible, even from the point of view of grammar, to say nothing of theology, where they are so very incompetent.

Therefore such mockery of the Jews does not disturb me, and their opinion would not impel me to learn a single letter of the Hebrew language. The reason for that is this: We Christians have the meaning and import of the Bible because we have the New Testament, that is, Jesus Christ, who was promised in the Old Testament and who later appeared and brought with Him the light and the true meaning of Scripture. Thus He says in John 5{:46}: *"If you believed Moses, you would believe Me, for he wrote of Me."* Also Luke 24{:44-45}: *"'Everything written about Me in the Law, the Prophets, and the Psalms must be fulfilled.' Then He opened their minds to understand the Scriptures."*

For that is the all-important point on which everything depends. Whoever does not have or want to have this Man properly and truly who is called Jesus Christ, God's Son, whom we Christians proclaim, must keep his hands off the Bible—that I advise. He will surely come to naught. The more he studies, the blinder and more stupid will he grow, be he Jew, Tartar, Turk, Christian, or whatever he wants to call himself. Behold, what did the heretical Arians, Pelagians, Manichaeans, and innumerable others among us Christians lack? What has the pope lacked? Did they not have the sure, clear, and powerful Word of the New Testament? What do the factions of our day lack? Do they not have the New Testament, clear and reliable enough? If the New Testament had to be translated in accord with each such stupid devil's mind, how many New Testaments, do you suppose, would we have to have?

If I were offered free choice either to have St. Augustine's and the dear fathers', that is, the apostles', understanding of Scripture, together with the handicap that St. Augustine occasionally lacks the correct Hebrew letters and words—as the Jews sneeringly accuse him, or to have the Jews' correct letters and words—which they, in fact, do not have everywhere—but minus St. Augustine's and the fathers' understanding, that is, with the Jews' interpretation, it can be easily imagined which of the two I would choose. I would let the Jews with their interpretation and their letters go to the devil, and I would ascend into heaven with St. Augustine's interpretation without their letters. For even if St. Augustine cannot say *Kikaion*, as the Jews do, but says *cucurbita* instead in Jonah 4{:6}, cannot say *venient Hemdath* but says *veniet Desideratus* instead in Hag. 2{:7}, and many similar things, yet his faith on that account breaks neither neck nor limb, for he knows "the Valiant One," who is called "Way, Truth, and Life" [John 14:6], of whom, as I said, the prophets foretell and testify.

Furthermore, since the Jews repudiate this Christ, they cannot know or understand what Moses, the prophets, and the psalms are saying, what true faith is, what the Ten Commandments purport, what tradition and story teach and prove. But according to the prophecy in Is. 29[:12], Scripture must be to them what a letter is to an illiterate. Indeed, he may see the letters, but he is ignorant of their significance. As the German riddle says: A field of white is sable sown, And men pass by to see what's grown; But many view a growth unknown. However, anyone conversant with and exercised in the art of reading lets his eyes run over a page and catches the meaning even if he does not closely observe every letter and word. Before the other has spelled out one word, he has perused the entire letter. Likewise, a musician may sing the whole song before another discerns and discovers whether so or fa is to be sounded in a key.

Just consider that excellent man Lyra. He is a good Hebraist and a fine Christian. What good work he produces when he, in accord with the New Testament, opposes the Jewish concept. But whenever he follows his Rabbi Solomon,[2] how meaningless and unimpressive it sounds; it has neither hands nor feet, despite his good command of words and letters. Still he surpasses all the others, both the old and the new Hebraists, who follow the rabbis altogether too strictly. Indeed, in translating and expounding, one need not intentionally strain oneself to transmit the concept of the rabbis and grammarians to us Christians. It is all too prone to stick to us of itself, automatically, just like pitch and glue, even if we deliberately guard against it. For the letters and the stories of the others blind the eyes and induce us occasionally to lose sight of the meaning of Christ where we should not, and thus the Jewish concept insinuates itself unawares, as every translator without exception has experienced. I, too, was not exempt from it.

In brief, if we do not apply all diligence to interpret the Hebrew Bible, wherever that is feasible, in the direction of the New Testament, in opposition to the interpretation of the rabbis, it would be better to keep the old translation (which, after all, retains, thanks to the New Testament, most of the good elements) than to have so many translations just because a few passages presumably have a different reading or are still not understood. This only confuses the memory of the reader, hinders his study, and leaves him in greater uncertainty than he was before.

To illustrate this, I have decided to discourse on the last words of David, not according to the German translation, in which I followed all the others to avoid the impression that I considered myself the only smart person. No, now I am going to be stubborn and follow none but my own spirit. He who dislikes this may ignore it. It is not the first time that I wrote something displeasing to others. I thank God that I am inured to that. I, on the other hand, do not approve of everything written by others either. Let everyone see how he may build on the foundation with gold or wood, silver or hay, gems or straw. The Lord's Day will bring this to light [cf. 1 Cor. 3:12–13].

. . .

{LW 15:286–287}

{1 Chron.} 17:17{b}. *Thou hast regarded me as in the form of a Man who is God the Lord on high.*[3]

The translation of these words by almost all other Hebraists is far different. Several, however, and among these Bernhard Ziegler,[4] bear witness to me that this passage may and must be translated grammatically as I did. With these words David clearly states that his Son, the Messiah, will surely be true Man, in form, manner, and size like any other man, and yet up above and on high, where there is no manner of men, where only God is and governs, He is to be God the Lord. That is, I say, clearly the opinion of David tersely expressed. In view of this, he says above: "Whither, whither are you, dear God, taking me?" And here: "Why do you regard me, unworthy human being that I am, that my son should be King in Your eternal kingdom?" David knows full well that no other than the true God is entitled to be King in God's eternal kingdom. And since the son of David is man and a person apart from the Father, who installs him in His kingdom, and since there cannot be two gods or more than one God, David here concludes that his Son, the Messiah, must be true and natural God, and yet none other God than the Father, but a separate Person in the same one inseparable Godhead, and that the Holy Spirit, who as true God speaks these words through Nathan and David concerning the Father and the Son, is the third Person in the same one Godhead.

That is the doctrine and the belief of the New Testament, namely, that Jesus of Nazareth, David's and the Virgin Mary's Son, is true Man and God's natural, eternal Son, one God and three distinct Persons together with the Father and the Holy Spirit. And since David's words in this passage amply reflect that meaning in accord with the general usage of the Hebrew tongue, we Christians must not seek or heed any other significance in them but regard this as the only correct one and look upon all other interpretations as worthless human imagination. The New Testament cannot err, nor can the Old Testament where it {rhymes} and agrees with the New Testament.

You may feel tempted to ask here: "If the words of David and Nathan reveal the doctrine of Christ's deity so clearly, how do you explain that neither the holy fathers nor any other teacher discovered or ever mentioned this, and that you recent and young Hebraists just became aware of this now? Why do the Jewish rabbis not discern this?" We reply: After the days of the apostles the knowledge of the Hebrew language was scant and deficient. The dear fathers and teachers contented themselves with the New Testament, in which they found this doctrine and all others in great abundance. The prophets and apostles, however, did perceive the truth of this very well, as we shall hear later. It is perfectly natural that the rabbis did not see this; for he who is blind sees nothing. In Is. 6[:9] the prophet says of them: *"See and see, but do not perceive."* And whoever must learn from them will surely also become blind. To be sure, we, too, would not be able to see it if we could not look the Old Testament straight into the eye because we are illumined by the New Testament. For the Old Testament is veiled without the New Testament [2 Cor. 4:3-4].

. . .

{LW 15:298–299}

[W]e want to discourse further on David's last words before we conclude them and take leave of them. This we do for the strengthening of our faith and in defiance of all devils, Jews, Mohammedans, papists, and all other enemies of this Son of David.

In the first place we want to give Moses, the fountainhead, the source, the father, and teacher of all prophets, a hearing. We want to test him to see whether we find him to be a Christian, whether he supports our position, since Christ Himself mentions him by name and says in John 5[:46]: *"Moses wrote of Me."* And if he wrote of Christ, he must, of course, have prophesied and proclaimed Him and enjoined all prophets who followed him to write and to preach of Christ. This they have done diligently, so that all Jews, young and old, know that a Messiah was to come. But

Moses lies buried and is hidden from them, and no one knows where he is interred. Therefore we shall authorize and commission two faithful and reliable legates, or ambassadors to look for him, find him, rouse him, and fetch him hither. These two are the evangelist John and the apostle Paul. I wager that these two will hit the mark and not miss. However, I do not want you to forget what I said earlier, namely, that I would like to discuss here the proposition: Wherever the Hebrew text readily yields to and {rhymes} with the New Testament, this is and must be the only right interpretation of Scripture. All else, whatever Jews, Hebraists, and anybody else may babble against this to make it agree with their stippled, tormented, and coerced grammar, we must certainly consider sheer lies.

. . .

{LW 15:339}

Thus all of Scripture, as already said, is pure Christ, God's and Mary's Son. Everything is focused on this Son, so that we might know Him distinctively and in that way see the Father and the Holy Spirit eternally as one God. To him who has the Son Scripture is an open book; and the stronger his faith in Christ becomes, the more brightly will the light of Scripture shine for him.

{LW 15:342–344}

{After a lengthy presentation of Old Testament proofs for the doctrine of the Trinity and the two natures of Christ, Luther concludes against the Jews (and Turks) and their interpretations.}

Reason admittedly does not find that in its Bible, that is, in its chimney flue, its dreamland. Nor do the Jews find this in their Bible, that is, in the Talmud, under the sow's tail, where they study their *Schamhaperes.*[5] Neither does Mohammed find it in his Bible, that is, in his bed of harlotry; for that is where he did most of his studying. Thus this contemptible, filthy fellow boasts that God, that is, the devil, had endowed him with so much physical strength that he could bed with as many as 40 women and yet remain unsatisfied. Indeed, his choice book, the Koran, smells and savors of his studies in that Bible, the carnality of harlots. He looked for and found the spirit of his prophecy in the right spot, that is, in the *mons Veneris.* And it is surely not surprising that he who pores over such books knows nothing of God, or Messiah. Thus they also do not know what they are saying and what they are doing.

Thanks and praise be to God in all eternity that we Christians know that Messiah is God's one eternal Son, whom He sent into the world to take our sins upon Himself, to die for us, and to vanquish death for us. Thus Is. 53{:6, 10}: *"All we like sheep have gone astray . . . and the Lord has laid on Him the iniquity of us all. . . . He made Himself an offering for sin, etc."* Therefore we exult and rejoice that God's Son, the one true God together with the Father and the Holy Spirit, became man, a servant, a sinner, a worm for us; that God died, and bore our sins on the cross in His own body;

that God redeemed us through His own blood. For God and Man are one Person. Whatever the Man does, suffers, and speaks, that God does, suffers, and speaks; and, conversely, what God does and speaks, that the Man does and speaks. He is both God's and Mary's Son in one undivided Person and in two distinct natures. The devil and his pander and whoremaster Mohammed and his *Schamhaperists*, the Jews, may be offended at this; they may blaspheme and curse (whoever cannot refrain), but all of them will tremble eternally for this in the depth of hell with howling and gnashing of teeth. God willing, that day is not far removed. Amen.

For the time being I will discontinue here discoursing on these sublime doctrines on the basis of the Old Testament. I hope that this may suffice to exhort our Hebraists to wrest the Old Testament from the rabbis wherever possible, regardless of their interpretations, commentaries, or grammars. These rabbis are very often at variance with one another and do not know where they stand. They are prone to equivocate with words and sentences to suit their stupid interpretation, even though the letter harmonizes readily with the New Testament, and it is certain that Jesus Christ is Lord over all. To Him Scripture must bear witness, for it is given solely for His sake. It was not my intention to quote the New Testament extensively this time since all of this has been proven there so clearly for approximately 1500 years. (That is the reason, too, why the Jews reject the New Testament.) This is particularly clear in the Gospel of St. John, in which practically every other word, as it were, proclaims that Jesus is God and Man in one Person. This same John, together with the other apostles, evangelists, and many thousands of their disciples, were also Jews, or Israel and Abraham's seed by birth, much more purely and more definitely than the present-day Jews, or Israel, are. No one knows who the latter are or whence they came.[6]

Now, if we are willing to believe the Jews, or Israel, it is far more reasonable to give those Jews, or Israel, credence, who have for approximately 1,500 years to date governed the church publicly in all the world, who have overcome devil, death, and sin, who have interpreted the writings of the prophets, and who have continuously worked miracles through their disciples. I repeat that it is far more meet that we believe such true and acknowledged Jews and Israelites than these false and unknown Jews or Israelites, who have wrought no miracle these 1,500 years, who have interpreted no writings of the prophets, who have perverted everything, who have done nothing in the open but underhandedly and clandestinely, like children of darkness, that is, of the devil, have practiced nothing but blasphemy, cursing, murder, and lies against the true Jews and Israel, that is, against the apostles and prophets. And they continue this daily and thus prove that they are not Israel or Abraham's seed but venomous and devilish foes of the true Israel and Abraham's children and in addition despoilers, robbers, and perverters of Holy Scripture. Therefore it behooves us to recover Scripture from them as from public thieves wherever grammar warrants this and {rhymes} with the New Testament. The apostles furnish us with many precedents for this.

I shall now come back to the last words of David, with which I began this booklet. In this way I shall bind the beginning and the end of this wreath together. I have digressed and meandered enough. Others can and will, I hope, improve on this and diligently seek and find the Lord Jesus in the Hebrew Old Testament; for He lets Himself be found there very readily, especially in the Psalter and in Isaiah. Try it according to the rule given above, and I am sure that you will agree with me and thank God.

. . .

{LW 15:351–352}

{2 Sam.} 23:6. *But the sons of Belial are all like thorns that are thrown away; for they cannot be taken with the hand;* 23:7. *but the man who touches them arms himself with iron and the shaft of a spear, and they are utterly consumed with fire in their dwelling.*

Here David is prophesying of the Jews who would not accept this Lord and Messiah. He calls them בל יעל, or, as we are accustomed to say, "Belial." In German that means *unnütz* ("worthless") or *schädlich* ("harmful"). In worldly government we call such people worthless and base knaves who are bent on working harm. But David is here speaking in the spirit and about the kingdom of Christ. For there it is the vogue to esteem the enemies of Christ's kingdom, such as Jews, heretics, heathen, highly. For even today Jews, Mohammed, pope, and factious spirits imagine they render God the greatest service when they inflict harm on the true Christians. They resent being called בל יעל; they want to be regarded as the worthiest. Thus Jer. 23[:32] says about the false prophets: *"They do not profit this people at all,"* that is, they are the most pernicious when they would be the most useful. In brief, the Christians are "Belial" and children of the devil; these, however, are the only children of God. Whatever they do is right—until God expels them and consumes them with the fire of His wrath. This we witness in the present-day Jews. What a terrible fire of divine wrath has overtaken them!

David likens them to the thistles among the grain in the field, which, in my opinion, the Lord Jesus calls ζιζάνια in Matt. 13[:25]. We translated that into German with the word *Unkraut* ("tares"). Ambrose in his Hexaemeron says: "Degenerating from wheat seed to its own kind." In German we call these *Trespen* ("bromegrass"). But Christ is here speaking of a more noxious plant, one that is uprooted in the harvest and destroyed by fire, and He uses practically the same word as David does, who also separates his thistles and burns them with fire. Therefore ζιζάνια must be what David here calls קוֹץ, the large, noisome, thorny thistles or the other type of thistles which our peasants call *toll Graet* ("deadly nightshade"), which are sorted out with scythes, sickles, rakes, and pointed sticks in the harvesttime, for this cannot be done with the bare hand. They serve no other purpose than to be burned. Bromegrass, however, is used as fodder for the cattle. Thus the hardened Jews are such evil, prickly thistles and *toll Graete*. Neither God's benefactions nor His miracles could convert them and cannot convert them now; but with the iron and spear of the Romans they were ejected and consumed with physical fire together with their city in their own dwelling. Over and above that, wherever they are in exile, they are still burning within themselves with the spiritual fire of divine wrath. Thus David foretold its destruction and final perdition to this people, which was imposed on them because they would not accept this King. The Lord prophesied the same in Luke 19[:43–44]; Dan. 9[:26]; and Zech. 14[:2].

Let this be my translation and exposition of David's last words according to my own views. May God grant that our theologians boldly apply themselves to the study of Hebrew and retrieve the Bible for us from those rascally thieves. And may they improve on my work. They must not become captive to the rabbis and their tortured grammar and false interpretation. Then we will again find and recognize our dear Lord and Savior clearly and distinctly in Scripture. To Him, together with the Father and the Holy Spirit, be glory and honor in eternity. Amen.

Text #27

Two Letters to Katharina Luther (1546)

February 1, 1546

Language:	German
Critical Edition:	WA Br 11:275–76
English Translation:	LW 50:290–92

February 7, 1546

Language:	German
Critical Edition:	WA Br 11:286–87
English Translation:	LW 50:301–4

In two of Luther's last remaining letters to his wife Katharina, the matter of the Jews is at the forefront of the issues he wants to share with her, alongside reports on his consumption of beer and wine, his health, and his bowel movements. Responding to her recent letters,[1] Luther playfully fuels his wife's worries with the depiction of a substantial presence of Jews in and around Eisleben, implying that they have the ability to cause physical harm, even to Luther's person.

The two letters below from February 1546 were sent from Eisleben, Luther's birthplace, where he had arrived with his three sons on January 28 to help settle a dispute between the four Counts of Mansfeld over mining rights in Eisleben, a dispute that also involved members of Luther's own family.[2] He would die on February 18 without seeing the resolution to the dispute that wore him out—just as had the long travel, the bad weather and his many ailments, some of which he blamed most acutely on the Jews. Clearly irritated by the number of Jews living around the town—apparently unharmed and protected by the widow Countess Dorothea of Mansfeld (Solms)—Luther wants to give a serious boost to the Saxon Elector's decree of 1543 and have the Jews expelled for good from this area. In his second letter he boasts of what he had done, out of necessity: "Today I made my opinion known in a sufficiently blunt way if anyone wishes to pay attention to it." Fully aware of the influence he has from the pulpit, Luther implicates himself as a willing and leading contributor to the anti-Jewish political developments of his time.[3] What relationship there may have been, if any, among the frustrations caused by his evident sexual impotence, the difficulties involved with the release of his bowels, and the expulsion of the Jews of Eisleben, requires a different type of analysis.

To Mrs. Martin Luther
{LW 50:290–292}
[Eisleben,] February 1, 1546

To my dearly beloved mistress of the house, Catherine Luther, a doctor, the lady of Zölsdorf [and] of the pig market, and whatever else she is capable of being

Before all else, grace and peace in Christ, and my old, poor, and, as Your Grace knows, powerless love. Dear Katie. Yes, on the way, shortly before Eisleben, I became dizzy. That was my fault. Had you been here, however, you would have said that it was the fault of the Jews or their god. For shortly before Eisleben we had to travel through a village in which many Jews are living, [and] perhaps they have attacked me so painfully. At this time over fifty Jews reside here in the city of Eisleben.[4] It is true that when I passed by the village such a cold wind blew from behind into the carriage and on my head through the beret, [that it seemed] as if it intended to turn my brain to ice. This might have helped me somewhat to become dizzy. But thank God now I am well, except for the fact that beautiful women tempt me so much that I neither care nor worry about becoming unchaste.

After the main issues have been settled, I have to start expelling the Jews. Count Albrecht is hostile to them and has already outlawed them. But no one harms them as yet. If God grants it I shall aid Count Albrecht from the pulpit, and outlaw them too.[5]

I am drinking beer from Naumburg which tastes to me almost like the beer from Mansfeld which you praised to me. It agrees with me well and gives me about three bowel movements in three hours in the morning. The day before yesterday your little sons drove to Mansfeld because John of Jena so humbly begged them to do so. I do not know what they are doing there. If it were cold they could join the people who are freezing; however, since it is warm they certainly could do or endure anything else, as they are pleased.

With this I commend you and the whole house to God; give my greetings to all the table companions.

February 1, 1546

Your loving Martin Luther, who has grown old

To Mrs. Martin Luther
{LW 50:301–304}
[Eisleben,] February 7, 1546

To my dear mistress of the house, Catherine Ludher, a doctor, the lady of the pig market at Wittenberg—placed into the hands of, and at the feet of, my gracious lady

Grace and peace in the Lord! You, dear Katie, read John and the *Small Catechism*, about which you once said: Everything in this book has been said about me. For you prefer to worry about me instead of letting God worry, as if he were not almighty and could not create ten Doctor Martins, should the old one drown in the Saale, or burn in the oven, or perish in Wolfgang's bird trap. Free me from your worries. I have a caretaker who is better than you and all the angels; he lies in the cradle and rests on a virgin's bosom, and yet, nevertheless, he sits at the right hand of God, the almighty Father. Therefore be at peace. Amen.

I think that hell and the whole world must now be empty of all devils, who, perhaps for my sake, have congregated here at Eisleben, so hard has this affair run aground. There are also Jews here, about fifty in one house, as I have written to you previously. Now it is said that in Rissdorf—close to Eisleben, where I became ill during my journey—there are supposedly about four hundred Jews living and working. Count Albrecht, who owns all the area around Eisleben, has declared that the Jews who are caught on his property are outlaws. But as yet no one wants to do them any harm. The Countess of Mansfeld, the widow of Solms,[6] is considered to be the protector of the Jews. I do not know whether this is true. Today I made my opinion known in a sufficiently blunt way if anyone wishes to pay attention to it. Otherwise it might not do any good at all.[7] You people pray, pray, pray, and help us that we do all things properly, for today in my anger I had made up my mind to grease the carriage. But the misery of my fatherland, which came to my mind, has stopped me.

I have also now become a jurist, but this will not be to their advantage. It would have been better had they let me remain a theologian, for if I meddle with them, should I live, I will turn out to be a goblin who by God's grace will attack vigorously their haughtiness. They behave as if they were God; certainly they had better abandon this attitude soon, before their god turns into a demon, as happened to Lucifer, who because of his haughtiness simply was unable to remain in heaven. Well, God's will be done.

Please let Master Philip read this letter, for I have no time to write to him. [Instead I wrote to you, however,] so that you could comfort yourself with the knowledge that I would love you if I could, as you know, and as Melanchthon perhaps also knows as far as his wife is concerned, and as he well understands.

We are living well here; for each meal the city council gives me one half *Stübig* of Italian wine which is very good. Sometimes I drink it with my companions. The native wine is also good, and the beer of Naumburg is very good, except I think that because of its pitch it congests my chest. In all the world the devil has spoiled the beer for us with pitch, and among you people [he has spoiled] the wine with sulphur. But here the wine is pure, if one disregards the particular quality of the native wine.

So that you do not get confused, you should know that all the letters you had written have arrived here; today those have arrived which you wrote last Friday and sent along with Master Philip's letters.

February 7, 1546

Your loving Martin Luther, Doctor

Text #28

An Admonition against the Jews (1546)

Language:	German
Critical Edition:	WA 51:195–96
English Translation:	LW 58:458–59[1]

During his last days in his hometown of Eisleben,[2] Luther preached four sermons at St. Andrew's Church (January 31; February 2, 7, and 14), the last sermons of his life. It was most likely to his second last sermon, from February 7, that Luther added an afterward, *Admonition against the Jews*. In terms of this particular type of sermonic speech, Christopher Brown states: "In genre, the 'Admonition' is a specimen of Luther's practice of exhorting the congregation from the pulpit on some matter of contemporary concern after the sermon proper."[3] As is clear from his recent letters to Katharina, the existence of Jews in and around Eisleben caused him deep distress. He had promised his wife to put an end to it with the primary means available to him: the pulpit. On February 7 he wrote his wife: "Today I made my opinion known in a sufficiently blunt way if anyone wishes to pay attention to it."[4] In light of what is known of the biblical texts Luther used for his last two sermons (Matt. 13:24–30; Matt. 11:25–30) and of the reports of the weakness that interrupted his final sermon, these words to Katharina are the best evidence that the *Admonition* belongs with the February 7 sermon.[5] The *Admonition*, which (barring [immediate?] conversion) forcefully advocates the expulsion of the Jews so as to avoid being implicated in—and thus contaminated by—Jewish blasphemy, stands as Luther's final word on the Jewish question.[6] He died on February 18, 1546, a bitter—and proud—enemy of the Jews.

Admonition against the Jews
{LW 58:458–459}

Now that I have been here and preached to you for a while, it is time for me to go home and perhaps never preach to you again. Therefore, I want to leave you with this blessing and prayer: that you remain diligent in the Word of God's grace that your preachers and pastors faithfully teach you, and that you may become accustomed to praying God to protect you from all wise and prudent ones [Matt. 11:25] who despise the doctrine of the Gospel, for they have often done much harm and would like to do still more.

More than others, you still have Jews in your land who do great harm. Now, we want to deal with them in a Christian manner and, in the first place, to offer them the Christian faith, so that they will receive the Messiah, who is after all their kinsman, born of their flesh and blood, and the true seed of Abraham, of whom they boast. I am afraid, however, that Jewish blood has now become more diluted and impure. You should first invite them to turn to the Messiah and be baptized so that people can see that they are serious. If not, we will not tolerate them, for Christ has commanded us to be baptized and believe in Him.[7] Although we are not yet able to believe as strongly as we ought, nevertheless God bears with us patiently.

Now, the way things stand with the Jews is this: that they daily blaspheme and slander our Lord Jesus Christ. Since they do this, and we know about it, we should not tolerate it. For if I tolerate in my midst someone who slanders, blasphemes, and curses my Lord Christ, then I make myself a participant in the sins of another [1 Tim. 5:22]. But if I already have enough sins of my own, then you lords should not tolerate them but drive them away. If, however, they convert, give up usury, and receive Christ, then we will gladly regard them as our brothers.

Otherwise, it will not work, for they have gone too far. They are our open enemies; they do not cease to blaspheme our Lord Christ; they call the Virgin Mary a whore and Christ, the child of a whore. Us they call changelings and abortions, and if they could kill us all, they would gladly do so. And they often do, especially those claiming to be doctors, even if they do help on occasion, for it is the devil who lends his help and seal. They are also practitioners of the medicine used in Italy, where poison is administered to kill someone in an hour, a month, a year, even ten or twenty years. This is the art they have mastered.[8]

Therefore, do not be troubled for them, for they do nothing else among you than to blaspheme our dear Lord Christ abominably and to seek after our body, life, honor, and property. Yet we want to exercise Christian love toward them and pray for them to convert and receive the Lord, whom they should properly honor more than we do. If anyone refuses to do this, let there be no doubt that he is an incorrigible Jew who will not cease to blaspheme Christ, to suck you dry, and (if he can) to kill you.[9]

Therefore, I beseech you not to participate in the sins of others. You have enough to pray from God, that He might be merciful to you and preserve your government, even as I still pray daily and hide myself under the shield of the Son of God [Ps. 91:1]. Him I regard and honor as my Lord; to Him I must run and flee if the devil, sin, or other misfortune assails me. For He is my Shield, as broad as heaven and earth, and the Hen under whose wings I crawl before God's wrath [Ps. 91:4; Matt. 23:37].

For this reason I can have neither fellowship nor patience with the stubborn blasphemers and slanderers of this dear Savior.

This is the final warning I wanted to give you, as your countryman: that you should not participate in the sins of others.[10] For I would give good and faithful advice both to the lords and to their subjects. If the Jews will be converted to us and cease their blasphemy, and whatever else they have done to us, we will gladly forgive them. But if not, then neither should we tolerate or endure them among us.

Afterword

Martin Luther never danced at a Jewish wedding. He never broke bread at Passover. He never shared a cup of Sabbath wine. He never studied Torah with a rabbi. He never held in his arms a newly circumcised Jewish boy. He never saw the anguish of expelled Jewish families vandalized at the hands of an irate Christian mob. He never smelled the smoke of burning Jewish martyrs. He never met Josel of Rosheim, who came to ask for his help.

History has recognized the merits of Josel, an eloquent and compassionate Jewish man, widely respected by his contemporaries as the spokesperson for the whole of German Jewry. Josel had written to Luther in the spring of 1537 in hope of securing a letter of recommendation to the Saxon elector, so that he himself could intercede with the elector regarding safe travel for Jews through Saxony. Such safe travel was crucial for Jews for the conduct of business, marriage arrangements, and religious celebrations. Had Luther encountered this man of integrity and learning and heard first-hand of his honorable, humanitarian intentions, this meeting could have been a turning point. Instead, Luther closed his door. He was not interested in conversation about the serious matters at stake. When looking for decisive moments in Luther's development, this is surely one, with broad ramifications for himself and his followers. It is decisive for us today, as well, whether we follow his path of "no conversation" or take a different route and dare to be confronted with views and experiences that may shape and change us and our basic beliefs in a fundamental way.

It is appropriate to wonder how Luther might have been different had he benefitted from actual regular benevolent encounters with Jewish people, like Josel. There is substantial evidence from Luther's own biography for how his experiences with the many people he encountered—and debated—were important ingredients in his theological argumentation. His capacity for great anger and deep compassion were often poignantly stirred by the people he met. But this is a question that cannot be answered.

The text samples included in this volume speak their own troubling and saddening language. They reveal the intensity, passion, and consistency with which Luther wrote about the Jews, in ways that are unacceptable from our contemporary perspective. In our post-Holocaust context, and knowing more than Luther did about just how far human beings—including Christians—can go down the road of Jew-hatred, we are following tracks that are shameful and that require honest remembering. Because of the atrocities of the Nazi era, and because of ongoing expressions of anti-Semitism in our time as well, it is only proper to bring to continued inspection and prayerful reflection words such as Luther's, so that we better continue to tell the truth, repent, and strive for justice and protection of the dignity of life, in accordance with the worthy principles of our respective religions.

Remembering and truthtelling are part of keeping ourselves honest and in touch with reality. We know, and we want our children to know, that the expulsions, the pogroms, and the Holocaust really did happen, just as unspeakable violence really happens today. In the same manner, the remains of teachings that in any way have been employed by Christians for ill and violence toward others must be scrutinized and purged. Remembering and re-examining the foundations of Christian beliefs as well as their significance and impact over time is an essential, ongoing task for each new generation. Without such historical scrutiny there can be no valid claims for contemporary theological relevance.

It is our human responsibility to remember what has happened, to try to understand why, and to ask how things could have been different. It is our Christian responsibility to reassess the structures of our beliefs and the effects of these beliefs on others. It is both a human and a Christian responsibility to take an active role for the sake of the future and begin by rejecting dehumanizing views and actions. We recognize from Luther's own words how tainted and unacceptable some of his views are; at the same time, we wish to reclaim from his teachings that which continues to be life-giving and honorable, and which steers us to become better stewards of the divine gift of life.

Without implying Luther as the father of modern anti-Semitism or as the exceptional culprit in all the crimes of Christians against Jews, we can continue to try to locate Luther in his own specific place in the long spectrum of Christian and Jewish relations. Based on what we know about the reality Luther lived in, we can recognize the odds that were against him in terms of the stimuli and streams of influences that shaped him in his time and place. We can also observe the choices he himself made, and deliberately so.

The focus of this volume has been on Luther's own words regarding the Jews and Judaism in light of what we know about his interactions and the lives of Jews in the Holy Roman Empire. While the topic has generated a plethora of expectations and approaches, this volume invites readers to observe how Luther's understanding of and feelings toward the Jews and Judaism were fundamental for his reading of the Bible, and vice versa. Consequently, his theology—including its most celebrated manifestations—is based on the very principles and perspectives he developed when deliberating on the "Jewish question" as an essential part of his biblical hermeneutics. The same can be said about his piety: Luther's faith is fundamentally shaped against the mirror of how he understood Jewish religiosity and who the "Jew" was in his imagination.

The text samples in this book illustrate amply how Luther's theology and biblical interpretation are impossible to understand fully apart from his understanding of Judaism. Readers are, thus, invited to reflect carefully on the basics of Luther's most renowned theological principals and insights: What are the essential ingredients in Luther's Christology and doctrine of justification? Are his anti-Jewish arguments central for his theological constructions on faith? Can we safely excise the anti-Jewish elements from his theology and still uphold his teaching on justification by grace through faith apart from works, without implying a denigrating assessment of Judaism? Taking these questions seriously may suggest a need for a paradigm shift in how we approach, assess, and employ Luther's theology.

Readers are further invited to investigate these matters for themselves and grapple with their bearing on Lutheran—or any Christian—theology and spirituality today. What can we do with this information? Is there any positive benefit to gain? How do these revelations from Luther illuminate the basics of our contemporary beliefs? What needs purging and what is worthy of continued embrace? How can wrestling with this difficult material make us better preachers and theologians, and better human beings?

By highlighting the power and danger of Luther's words, on the one hand, and by recognizing the ongoing stains of Christian proclamation, on the other, we hope to stir compassionate, constant reorientation in our ways of relating to one another and especially to the "other" we seek to know and love. We are convinced that honest study of Luther brings a heightened cautiousness about the reality-altering power of words—for better and for worse—and makes us more deliberate about the words we use and how. With the memory of those violated and killed in the name of the Christian God, we can reflect on the fundamentals of our beliefs and about our experiences of God, and continue to imagine and implement better ways of protecting the dignity of human life. We can reassess what of the "tainted greatness"[1] of Luther we choose to embrace and transmit to our children, and what not. While learning from Luther, we can pray to learn from past mistakes and open the doors in our hearts and minds respectfully to one another. We can be open to correction and become inspired and redirected in our mutual search for better understanding and living out divine truths, something Luther devoted his life to. Driven by his passions, he closed important doors that have begun to open. Let this volume be an invitation to open new doors, and pray that we so gain more illumination in our common human [and Christian] concerns.

Chronology

It can be argued that the very basics of the Christian belief system incorporate anti-Jewish perspectives that have been tragically acted out in Christian tradition from liturgy to social order. Through the centuries, Jewish people have been subjected to random and organized violence—pogroms, trials, massacres and burnings, destruction of property, synagogues, books and lives—at the hands of the Christian majority in Europe.

At a Glance

The Middle Ages brought the Crusades, forced baptisms, and ritual murder accusations (two of the earliest and most famous being the 1144 case of William of Norwich and the 1475 case of Simon of Trent).

In addition to the frequent defamation of the Jews in Christian art and literature (including the *Judensau* in thirteenth-century German churches), organized efforts were made to separate Jews from their Christian neighbors with distinct clothing or a badge and requiring Jews to live in separate walled areas, known as ghettoes (Fourth Lateran Council of 1215). Forced baptism continued to take place, regardless of the church's caution against it (as articulated in the papal bull "Sicut Judaeis," from the twelfth century onward). Special "Jewish laws" were issued to organize, restrict and, also, protect the lives and rights of Jews.

Local and nationwide expulsions were a common occurrence in the centuries leading up to the Reformation century, with several peaks: 1380–1391, 1420–1429, 1440–1459, 1470–1479, 1490–1499, 1510–1519. Earlier, Jews were expelled from France in 1182, in 1290 from England, and in 1306, 1322, 1394 from France. In 1491 Jews were expelled from Geneva, and in 1492 from Spain. The sixteenth-century reforms brought no change in this regard, as revealed by the following examples from the history of expulsions.

In the fourteenth-fifteenth centuries, Jews were expelled from Palatine, Goslar, Austria, Brandenburg, Cologne, Saxony, Speyer, Mainz, Augsburg, Bavaria, Frankonia, Hildesheim, Göttingen, Mainz, Tirol, Helmstadt, Hesse, Salzburg, Mainz, Saxony,

Magdeburg, Württemberg, Würzburg, Mecklenburg, Magdeburg, Nürnberg, Esslingen, and Ulm.[1]

In the sixteenth century, Jews were expelled from, for example, Berlin, Braunschweig, Strasbourg, Regensburg, Zurich, Freiburg, Hagenau, Saxony, Württemberg, Hesse, Goslar, Genova, Bavaria, Prague, Papal States, Brunswick, Hannover.

In the seventeenth-eighteenth centuries, Jews were expelled from, for example, Worms, Kiev, Ukraine, Hamburg, Lithuania, Vienna, Vilna, Russia, Bohemia, Moravia, Bordeaux, Warsaw, Alsace, Lübeck, Austria, Romania, Slovakia, Bavaria.

In the fourteenth through the twentieth centuries, different violent acts (burning, slaughter, mob attacks, pogroms, and large-scale discrimination) took place in, for example, Posen, Poland, Prague, Rome, Austria, Toledo, Cracow, Southern Germany, Venice, Seville, Vilna, Lisbon, Kiev, France, Munich and Breslau, Uzbekistan, Bucharest. The Holocaust in Europe took place in 1938–1945.

The timetable below maps out selected anti-Jewish acts and other significant events parallel to Luther's lifespan and (some of his) activities.

Timetable

Years	Luther's Life and Works	Contextual Developments
1400s	Luther would come to know of this and similar stories; his arch-opponent Johann Eck would write about this particular case	1475 The case of missing Simon of Trent: ritual murder accusation against the Jews
	1483 Martin Luther born	
1500–1519	These mass expulsions were "big news" and something Luther would become aware of	1491 Jews expelled from Geneva
		1492 Jews expelled from Spain
	1505 Luther joins the Augustinian Order in Erfurt (from where Jews were expelled in 1458, and 900 Jews had burned themselves in 1349)	1509 The Reuchlin–Pfefferkorn Affair: confiscation of Jewish Books in Cologne
	Luther knew about the controversy, taking later the side against the confiscation	1510 Josel of Rosheim: spokesperson for Jewry in Lower Alsace
	Luther would come to know only from distance about Josel, who later used his influence to prevent publication of Luther's damaging works	1510 Trial and temporary expulsion of Jews in Braunschweig; host desecration charges
		1510 Expulsion of Jews from Berlin
	Luther knew of these slandering descriptions of Judaism	Pfefferkorn's *Der Juden Spiegel* 1507, *Handt Spiegel* 1511, *Brantspiegel* 1512, Reuchlin's *Augenspiegel* 1511
	1512 Luther to Wittenberg: Professor of Bible	

	1513–1515 *Lectures Dictata super Psalterium*	
	1515–1516 *Lectures on Romans*	Erasmus Novum instrumentum 1516
	1516–1517 *Lectures on Galatians*	
	1517–1518 *Lectures on Hebrews*	
	1517 *Disputation against Scholastic Theology*	
1520–1530	1517 *Ninety-Five Theses*	1519 Expulsions of Jews in Regensburg
	1518 *Heidelberg Disputation* and Debate with Cajetanus	
	1519 Leipzig debate with Eck, and Karlstadt	
	1518–1521 *Operationes in Psalmos*	1520 Emperor Charles V coronation
	1520 Three reformation treatises: *To Christian Nobility of the German Nation; The Babylonian Captivity of the Papacy; The Freedom of a Christian*	1521 Reforms in Wittenberg: Clergy marriage, New Mass, Iconoclasm, Common Chest, Anti-usury regulations
		1522 March Turmoil in Wittenberg
	1521 Luther excommunicated; March-May, Diet of Worms; June, Luther outlawed	
	1522 Luther in Wartburg hiding; New Testament translation, September and December—Luther to Wittenberg: *Invocavit sermons*	1523 Diet of Nuremberg
		1523 July 1, first protestants burnt in Brussels
	1523 *That Jesus Christ Was Born a Jew*	1524 Philip of Hesse and the expulsion edict
	1523–1525 *Lectures on Deuteronomy*	1524–1525 Peasants' riots and slaughter
	1524–1526 *Lectures on Minor Prophets*	
	1524 Luther abandons his monastic habit	
	1524 Writes to the princes, against radicals, to the councilmen	1526 Diet of Speyer
	1524–1525 Translation of psalms; hymns	1527 Demands of Jews to be expelled from Prague (also 1507)
1531–1540	1525 April, reply to the "robbing" peasants	
	1525 Marriage with Katharina von Bora; Treatise *On the Bondage of the Will*	1529 Posing martyrs
		1529 Diet of Speyer: birth of "protestants"
	1527 Against Fanatics	1529 Marburg Colloquy: issue of Lord's Supper
	1528 Daughter Elizabeth born and dies	1530 Diet of Augsburg, debate between a Jewish convert and a professing Jew
	1528 *Concerning Christ's Supper*	
	1529 *Catechisms; On War against the Turks*	
		1530 Jews not allowed to travel through in Strasbourg
	Daughter Magdalena born	1530s Anabaptist activity in Moravia

1530 Luther's father dies	1531 Smalcaldic league formed
	1531 Melanchthon's Apology of CA
	1532 Religious peace in Nuremberg
	1532 Philip of Hesse: gives Jews six more years in Hesse, with restrictions on usury and business
1531 Luther's mother dies	1534–1535 Anabaptists' "kingdom" in Munster
	1536 –1539 Philip of Hesse and Martin Bucer debate on the "Judenordnung" in Hesse
1534 *German Bible*	1536 August 6, 1536 Elector of Saxony forbids Jews to settle or travel in Saxony
	1536 Wittenberg Concord
1535–1545 *Lectures on Genesis*	1536 Calvin meets cardinal Farissol in Ferrara –c. 3000 Jews in Ferrara
	1536/37 Josel of Rosheim, with a letter from Capito (April 26, 1537), asks to meet with Luther to plead his case for the Jews with the elector
1537 Luther ill, Schmalcald Articles Luther replies to Josel, June 11 Disputations on biblical law	1537 Bundestag at Smalcalden
1538 *Against the Sabbatarians*	
1539 1541 Revised bible translation	1539 Assembly of princes in Frankfurt: emperor modifies regulations on Jews' travel; mentions the request of Josel
Antinomian controversies	
Luther is aware of these developments in Hesse, while involved—albeit less publically—in the elector's decisions about Jewish rights in Saxony	1539 Judenordnung in Hesse (Martin Bucer and Philip of Hesse). {{Jews forbidden to curse Jesus or Christianity; life after Talmud, disputations on religion, and new synagogues forbidden; required to attend sermons; permission for commerce; Jews to appoint their own supervisors and pay protection fees to the prince. Death penalty for sexual relations with a Christian woman or trading stolen goods, and prohibition of trade with nonresidential Jews.}}
1541–1547	
1541 New preface to Ezekiel Luther on a preaching tour In their thinking about the Jews, the arch-enemies Eck and Luther find common ground	1540 Jesuit order approved—efforts for reforming the Catholic church
	1540/1541 Philip of Hesse, defender of Jews: bigamy charges—loss of Protestant leader
	Religious colloquies in Hagenau, Worms, Regensburg
	1540–1541 Tittingen Libel: Jews accused of kidnapping and mutilating a three-year-old peasant's son Michael from Sappenfeld

1541 Johannes Eck argues for the story of Simon of Trent as a Jewish ritual murder, in response to Andreas Osiander's opposite argument

1541 Toleration of Jews discussed at Regensburg imperial diet. {{The 1530 privileges returned; the rule for a Jewish badge lifted; Josel of Rosheim present}}

1541 Josel's "Letter of Consolation to Hessian Jewry" {{To comfort and furnish Jews with the foundations of their faith, with advise on Gentile relations, wise ruling, financial concerns and business affairs, with a section on false accusations against the Jews; basic rights.}}

1541 The Diet of Naples. Expulsion of Jews from Spain

1541–1542 Expulsion of Jews from Prague

1542 The Smalcald league in war

1542 Luther's will to Katharina
Luther's daughter Magdalena dies

1543 On the Jews and their Lies; On the Ineffable Name and Christ's Lineage; On the Last Words of David

1543 New restrictions on Jews in Saxony, May 6: elector restores the 1536 decree, cancels 1539 modifications. {{Jews not allowed to live or travel in Saxony, or practice business or trade.}}

After 1543, Josel of Rosheim writes to the city council of Strasbourg: his request not to publish Luther's 1543 texts granted

Catholics attack Luther's 1543 texts

1544 Book of Sermons, and Hauspostille

1544–1545 Diet of Worms. {{Religious schism, usury condemned, with Luther's 1543 works. Josel of Rosheim complains about the persecution of Jews in Saxony and Hesse; emperor orders punishment for anyone hurting a Jew.}}

1544 April 3, Imperial court order: a special charter of rights. {{Protection of travel, no obligation to wear a badge, right for money lending; articles against closing synagogues and forbidding attacks on Jews and their expulsion.}}

1545 Autobiographical Preface to Luther's Latin Works

1546 Eine Vermahnung Wider Die Juden, February

1546 February 18, Luther dies

1546 Braunschweig expulsion of Jews

1546–1547 Smalcaldic War 1546–1557

{{Josel of Rosheim; the elector of Saxony's loss and capture considered a sign of divine punishment for betraying the Jewish people.}}

1553 Talmud burned in Rome, Barcelona, Venice

1554 Talmud in the Index list

1555 Diet of Augsburg: cuius regio eius religio

1580 The Book of Concord unites Lutherans; no article on Jews

Declaration of ELCA to the Jewish Community

The Church Council of the Evangelical Lutheran Church in America on April 18, 1994, adopted the following document as a statement on Lutheran-Jewish relations:

In the long history of Christianity there exists no more tragic development than the treatment accorded the Jewish people on the part of Christian believers. Very few Christian communities of faith were able to escape the contagion of anti-Judaism and its modern successor, anti-Semitism. Lutherans belonging to the Lutheran World Federation and the Evangelical Lutheran Church in America feel a special burden in this regard because of certain elements in the legacy of the reformer Martin Luther and the catastrophes, including the Holocaust of the twentieth century, suffered by Jews in places where the Lutheran churches were strongly represented.

The Lutheran communion of faith is linked by name and heritage to the memory of Martin Luther, teacher and reformer. Honoring his name in our own, we recall his bold stand for truth, his earthy and sublime words of wisdom, and above all his witness to God's saving Word. Luther proclaimed a gospel for people as we really are, bidding us to trust a grace sufficient to reach our deepest shames and address the most tragic truths.

In the spirit of that truth-telling, we who bear his name and heritage must with pain acknowledge also Luther's anti-Judaic diatribes and the violent recommendations of his later writings against the Jews. As did many of Luther's own companions in the sixteenth century, we reject this violent invective, and yet more do we express our deep and abiding sorrow over its tragic effects on subsequent generations. In concert with the Lutheran World Federation, we particularly deplore the appropriation of Luther's words by modern anti-Semites for the teaching of hatred toward Judaism or toward the Jewish people in our day.

Grieving the complicity of our own tradition within this history of hatred, moreover, we express our urgent desire to live out our faith in Jesus Christ with love and respect for the Jewish people. We recognize in anti-Semitism a contradiction and an affront to the Gospel, a violation of our hope and calling, and we pledge this church to oppose the deadly working of such bigotry, both within our own circles and in the society around us. Finally, we pray for the continued blessing of the Blessed One upon the increasing cooperation and understanding between Lutheran Christians and the Jewish community.

Abbreviations

Luther's Works

AWA	Archiv zur Weimarer Ausgabe. Cologne: Böhlau, 1981–.
LW	Luther's Works—American Edition. 55 vols. Ed. Jaroslav Pelikan and Helmut T. Lehman. St. Louis: Concordia; Minneapolis: Fortress Press, 1955–2002.
WA	D. Martin Luthers Werke: Kritische Gesamtausgabe. 67 Vols. Weimar: H. Böhlau, 1883–1997.
WABr	D. Martin Luthers Werke: Kritische Gesamtausgabe: Briefwechsel. 18 Vols. Weimar: H. Böhlau, 1930–1985.
WADB	D. Martin Luthers Werke: Kritische Gesamtausgabe: Deutsche Bibel. 12 Vols. Weimar: H. Böhlau, 1906–1961.
WATr.	D. Martin Luthers Werke: Kritische Gesamtausgabe: Tischreden. 6 Vols. Weimar: H. Böhlau, 1912–1921.

Other

ADLIF	Anti-Defamation League, Interfaith Focus
AHR	American Historical Review
ARG	Archiv für Reformationsgeschichte
BBG	Basler Beiträge zur Geschichtswissenschaft
BCCT	Brill's Companions to the Christian Tradition
BET	Beiträge zur evangelischen Theologie
BHR	Bibliothèque d'Humanisme et Renaissance
BHT	Beiträge zur historischen Theologie
BÖT	Beiträge zur ökumenischen Theologie
BibSym	Biblia et Symbiotica
BibSac	Biblia Sacra
CJ	Concordia Journal
Cross Curr.	Cross Currents
CurTM	Currents in Theology and Mission
CTM	Concordia Theological Monthly
EvTh	Evangelische Theologie
FF	Face to Face
FKG	Forschungen zur Kirchen- und Geistesgeschichte

HCMR	History of Christian–Muslim Relations
HTR	*Harvard Theological Review*
HUS	*Harvard Ukrainian Studies*
Int	Interpretation
JA	*Jahrbuch für Antisemitismusforschung*
JAAR	*Journal of the American Academy of Religion*
JBL	*Journal of Biblical Literature*
JC	Judentum und Christentum
JCC	Jewish Culture and Contexts
JSS	*Jewish Social Studies*
JQR	*Jewish Quarterly Review*
KZ	*Kirchliche Zeitschrift*
LCC	Library of Christian Classics
LTJ	*Lutheran Theological Journal*
LQ	*Lutheran Quarterly*
MT	*Modern Theology*
MTZ	*Münchener theologische Zeitschrift*
NAWG	Nachrichten der Akademie der Wissenschaften zu Göttingen Philologisch-Historische Klasse
NSGTK	Neue Studien zur Geschichte der Theologie und der Kirche
NTT	*Nederlands Theologisch Tijdschrift*
PAAJR	*Proceedings of the American Academy for Jewish Research*
PIASH	*Proceedings of the Israel Academy of Sciences and Humanities*
PMS	Patristic Monograph Series
PTS	Patristische Texte und Studien
PT	*Political Theology*
RBS	Resources for Biblical Study
SCEH	Studies in Central European Histories
SCES	Sixteenth Century Essays and Studies
SCJ	*Sixteenth Century Journal*
SEJ	Studies in European Judaism
SFSHJ	South Florida Studies in the History of Judaism
SHCT	Studies in the History of Christian Thought
SJC	Studies in Judaism and Christianity
SKI	Studien zu Kirche und Israel
SMHR	Spätmittelalter, Humanismus, Reformation
SMRT	Studies in Medieval and Reformation Thought
SRR	*Seminary Ridge Review*
TSMEMJ	Texts and Studies in Medieval and Early Modern Judaism
VCSS	Variorum Collected Studies Series
VTSup	Supplements to Vetus Testamentum
TZ	*Theologische Zeitschrift*
ZBK	*Zeitschrift für bayerische Kirchengeschichte*
ZGL	*Zeitschrift für germanistische Linguistik*
ZTK	*Zeitschrift für Theologie und Kirche*

Notes

Introduction—*Brooks Schramm*

1. Heiko A. Oberman, *The Roots of Anti-Semitism: In the Age of Renaissance and Reformation*, trans. James I. Porter (Philadelphia: Fortress Press, 1984), 46.

2. Thomas Kaufmann, "Luther and the Jews," in *Jews, Judaism, and the Reformation in Sixteenth-Century Germany*, ed. Dean Phillip Bell and Stephen G. Burnett, SCEH 37 (Leiden: Brill, 2006), 99. Hereinafter references to this volume will be cited as Bell and Burnett.

3. Heiko A. Oberman, *Luther: Man between God and the Devil*, trans. Eileen Walliser-Schwarzbart (New York: Image, 1992), 296.

4. On Margaritha, see Michael Walton, *Anthonius Margaritha and the Jewish Faith* (Detroit: Wayne State University Press, forthcoming 2012).

5. Heinrich Bornkamm, *Luther and the Old Testament*, trans. Eric W. and Ruth C. Gritsch, ed. Victor I. Gruhn (Mifflintown: Sigler, 1997), 1.

6. Though Luther did not write to or for Jewish readers, his rhetorical style is often "as if" Jews are in his audience.

7. WA 40/3:730,17–19.

8. This argument is developed at length in *On the Jews and Their Lies*, Text #23.

9. The most comprehensive, and aggressive, example of this genre of Jewish anti-Christian writing is the *Sefer Nizzahon Vetus* ("The old 'Book of Victory'"), the definitive treatment of which is David Berger, *The Jewish-Christian Debate in the High Middle Ages: A Critical Edition of the Nizzahon Vetus* (Philadelphia: Jewish Publication Society, 1979). On the general topic of medieval Jewish anti-Christian polemic, see Hanne Trautner-Kromann, *Shield and Sword: Jewish Polemics against Christianity and the Christians in France and Spain from 1100–1500* (Tübingen: Mohr, 1993).

10. Quoted in Peter von der Osten-Sacken, *Martin Luther und die Juden: Neu untersucht anhand von Anton Margarithas "Der gantz Jüdisch glaub" [1530/31]* (Stuttgart: Kohlhammer, 2002), 223.

11. Kaufmann, "Luther and the Jews," 72.

12. Wilhelm Maurer, "Die Zeit der Reformation," in *Kirche und Synagoge: Handbuch zur Geschichte von Christen und Juden: Darstellung mit Quellen*, 2 vols., ed. Karl Heinrich Rengstorf and Siegfried von Kortzfleisch (Stuttgart: Klett, 1968), 1:379.

13. For further explication of this point, see the fine discussion by Leonard M. Hummel, "'Wrath Against the Unrighteous': The Place of Luther's Lectures on Romans in his Understanding of Judaism," *SRR* 11, no. 1–2 (2008–09): 64–82.

14. The German linguist, Dietz Bering, has demonstrated that Luther's polemical vocabulary utilized against the Jews, the Pope, and the Turk is essentially identical. See idem, "Gibt es bei Luther einen antisemitischen Worschatz? Zur Widerlegung einer politischen Legende," *ZGL* 17 (1989): 137–61. On the critique of Bering's conclusions, see Osten-Sacken, *Martin Luther,* 26–27.

15. See Kaufmann, "Luther and the Jews," esp. 72.

16. This practical distinction between the Turks and the Jews in Luther's thought is captured nicely by Scott Hendrix: "The advances of the Ottoman Turks into central Europe did raise legitimate anxiety, but the concern of Luther and other reformers about the Jewish presence in Europe was irrational." Idem, "Martin Luther, reformer," in *The Cambridge History of Christianity,* vol 6: *Reform and Expansion 1500–1660,* ed. R. Po-chia Hsia (Cambridge: Cambridge University Press, 2007), 6:18.

17. See Text #7.

18. See Osten-Sacken, *Martin Luther und die Juden,* 32–33.

19. See Text #6.

20. LW 13:23.

21. Osten-Sacken, *Martin Luther und die Juden,* 15.

22. For the statistics in this section, see Siegfried Raeder, "The Exegetical and Hermeneutical Work of Martin Luther," in *Hebrew Bible/Old Testament: The History of its Interpretation,* vol. 2: *From the Renaissance to the Enlightenment,* ed. Magne Sæbo (Göttingen: Vandenhoeck & Ruprecht, 2008), 363–406; Bornkamm, *Luther and the Old Testament,* 269–83.

23. Salo W. Baron, *A Social and Religious History of the Jews,* vol. 13: *Inquisition, Renaissance, and Reformation* (New York: Columbia University Press, 1969), 13:220.

24. *Luther's Works* 58: *Sermons 5,* ed. Christopher Boyd Brown (St. Louis: Concordia, 2009), 407.

25. It is reasonable to think that "some of Luther's concern to find the single proper meaning for each biblical verse is a reflection of his life-long work as a Bible translator." Stephen Burnett, private communication.

26. See Scott H. Hendrix, "Luther against the Background of the History of Biblical Interpretation," *Int* 37, no. 3 (1983): 229–39.

27. On this whole discussion, see Osten-Sacken, *Martin Luther und die Juden,* 38–40, 228–30.

28. On the highly selective use of rabbinic materials by Luther, and indeed by the entire circle of Hebraists at Wittenberg, see Stephen Burnett, "Reassessing the 'Basel-Wittenberg Conflict:' Dimensions of the Reformation-Era Discussion of Hebrew Scholarship," in *Hebraica Veritas? Christian Hebraists and the Study of Judaism in Early Modern Europe,* ed. Allison P. Coudert and Jeffrey S. Shoulson, JCC (Philadelphia: University of Pennsylvania Press, 2004), 181–201.

29. LW 1:296.

30. WA 53:644, 30–645,5.

31. LW 54:226.

Introduction—*Kirsi Stjerna*

1. For general observations about the paradigm shift in studying European Jewish history, see Debra Kaplan, *Beyond Expulsion: Jews, Christians, and Reformation Strasbourg* (Palo Alto: Stanford University Press, 2011), 1–11.

2. See Text #24.

3. Carter Lindberg, private communication.

4. See Petra Schöner, "Visual Representations of Jews and Judaism in Sixteenth-Century Germany," in Bell and Burnett, 387, 373, 390–91.

5. See Edith Wenzel, "The Representation of Jews and Judaism in Sixteenth-Century German Literature," in Bell and Burnett, 395, 399.

6. Ibid., 415–16. In the short narratives for entertainment and edification, the birth of the Messiah and the "wisdom berries" were popular.

7. Chava Fraenkel-Goldschmidt, *The Historical Writings of Joseph of Rosheim: Leader of Jewry in Early Modern Germany*, ed. Adam Shear, trans. Naomi Schendowich, SEJ 12 (Leiden: Brill, 2006), 30. Blood libels were a prelude for witch hunts and witchcraft trials; in both cases, proceedings involved inquisitional courts, and death was often at stake (idem, 27–28).

8. On Miracle Stories and Passion Plays, see Wenzel, "The Representation of Jews," 399–407; on trials, see R. Po-chia Hsia, *The Myth of Ritual Murder: Jews and Magic in Reformation Germany* (New Haven: Yale University Press, 1990).

9. Wenzel, "The Representation of Jews," 329.

10. In his "Refutation of a Jew-Book in Which a Christian. . . . Claims that Injustice Is Done the Jews in the Accusation that They Murder Christian Children . . ." the Catholic professor Johann Eck (1486–1543), in response to Lutheran pastor Andreas Osiander's (1496–1552) anonymous treatise, argues for the death of Simon of Trent (1475) as a Jewish ritual murder. See Wenzel, "The Representation of Jews," 411. On Eck, see Robert Bireley, "The Catholic Reform, Jews, and Judaism in Sixteenth-Century Germany," in Bell and Burnett, 250.

11. For example, the Tittingen Libel: When a three-year-old boy, Michael, son of a peasant in the village of Sappenfeld, disappeared on March 14, 1540, two weeks before Easter, rumors followed about Jews having abducted him. Not wanting to lose the revenue from the Jews' taxes, the financially strapped Lutheran Count Otto did not allow Jewish homes to be searched. The boy's stabbed body was found April 2, with his foreskin slit and a cross cut on his shoulder. The Jews were expelled from the region in 1555. See Fraenkel-Goldschmidt, *The Historical Writings*, 244–48.

12. Wenzel, "The Representation of Jews," 408–9. The best known ritual murder accusation comes from Trent 1475 (mentioned above with Eck): A little boy, Simon, son of a tanner, went missing. After his body was found, it reportedly bled in the presence of Jewish persons who were then interrogated. Charges were brought against the entire Jewish community and trials with torture-secured confessions. Even though Pope Pius IV had spoken out against such accusations, stories of Jewish ritual murders were printed in publications like those of the saints' lives, books of martyrs, and catechisms, until forbidden by the Second Vatican Council (1962–1965). See Wenzel, "The Representation of Jews," 409–10, 412.

13. Carter Lindberg, private communication.

14. In both witch courts and blood libel trials, forced confessions and testimonies of seemingly unreliable people (criminals, prostitutes, vagrants, etc.) could be used, because of the gravity of the crime. Whether the accused confessed or denied, punishment by death could hardly be avoided, especially with accompanying accusations of witchcraft and demonic involvement. According to court records, regardless of initial denial of accusations, the unbearable process led to confessions of guilt and sometimes implication of accomplices. The testimony of even a single person could start the notorious trial process with the "almost inevitable" outcome, unless it was stopped from the outset. See Fraenkel-Goldschmidt, *The Historical Writings*, 28–31.

15. Exceptional from the Jewish side is the record of the traveling Josel of Rosheim, who successfully intervened on behalf of individuals and entire communities. From the Lutheran side, Andreas Osiander as a rare theologian wrote—anonymously—against ridiculous accusations of Jews' ritual murders. On trials that frequently pit different authorities against each other, see Hsia, *The Myth of Ritual Murder.*

16. Dean Bell, private communication.

17. The peak times for European expulsions were 1380–1389, 1420–1429, 1440–1459, 1470–1479, 1490–1499, 1510–1519. See Dean Phillip Bell, "Jewish Settlement, Politics, and the Reformation," in Bell and Burnett, 432.

18. Kaplan, *Beyond Expulsion*, 10.

19. See Bell, "Jewish Settlement," 431–34, 436; also Christopher Ocker, "German Theologians and the Jews in the Fifteenth Century," in Bell and Burnett, 33–35.

20. For a case study on Strasbourg, see Kaplan, *Beyond Expulsion.*

21. "In several principalities, the rulers published special laws (*Judenordnungen*) defining the legal status, rights, and obligations of the Jews." Fraenkel-Goldschmidt, *The Historical Writings*, 11.

22. On Hesse, see Bell, "Jewish Settlement," 441–49; also Fraenkel-Goldschmidt, *The Historical Writings*, 340–56.

23. On Braunschweig, see Bell, "Jewish Settlement," 438–41. On the rise of Lutheranism and expulsions, see Jay Berkovitz, "Jewish Law and Ritual in Early Modern Germany," in Bell and Burnett, 482–83.

24. On Saxony, see Fraenkel-Goldschmidt, *The Historical Writings*, 232–39. The May 6, 1543 decision (cancelling 1539 modifications and returning to the 1536 decree) decrees that because of Jews' dishonest business, continuing efforts to "pursue trades and practice the medical arts," trying to "lead the people astray with lying words and curses directed against the true Messiah," and leading and getting into disputations regarding their "perverted faith," Jews were not allowed to live or travel through Saxony or practice their trade (idem, 236–237).

25. "When the medieval urban Jewish communities disappeared through expulsions, Jewish life gradually shifted to the countryside, often with only one or two Jewish families residing in local villages. This new demographic reality became the norm in the Empire through the mid-seventeenth century, and necessitated a conceptual and physical restructuring of the Jewish community." Kaplan, *Beyond Expulsion*, 6–7.

26. Ibid., 10.

27. Bell, "Jewish Settlement," 427–28. For example, Braunschweig had one hundred Jews before 1546.

28. The following information mostly from Bell, "Jewish Settlement," 426–31.

29. See David B. Ruderman, *Early Modern Jewry: A New Cultural History* (Princeton: Princeton University Press, 2010); Dean Philip Bell, *Jewish Identity in Early Modern Germany: Memory, Power, and Community* (Burlington: Ashgate, 2007); Kaplan, *Beyond Expulsion*, "Introduction."

30. See Bell, "Jewish Settlement," 426–27.

31. Ibid., 428–29.

32. See Bell, "Jewish Settlement," 427; Bireley, "The Catholic Reform," 255. For example, by 1600 about 2,200 or more Jews apparently resided in Frankfurt.

33. In 1522 Prague had 600 Jews, in 1541 about 1,200, and by 1600 about 6,000. By 1702 at least 11,527 Jews lived in Prague. In the smallish town of Ferrara, Italy, about 3,000 Jews, refugees from France and Spain or Portugal, resided there under the protection of the duchess Renata d'Este [Calvin's associate]). Bell, "Jewish Settlement," 427.

34. See Andreas Pangritz, "Once More: Martin Luther and the Jews," in *Remembering for the Future: The Holocaust in an Age of Genocide*, vol. 2: *Ethics and Religion*, ed. John K. Roth et al. (New York: Palgrave, 2001), 613–14 [603–17]. For example, by 1339 members of the Wittenberg Jewish community were allowed to return.

35. The University of Erfurt where Luther studied, just as the *Augustinerkloster* he joined as a monk, were located in the old Jewish part of town, in close proximity to the former Old Synagogue. Luther's daily life in Erfurt centered in an area that had been built by a Jewish population well integrated in the affairs of the society, and even defended at times by its Christian citizens who resisted the territorial rulers' order to expel Jews.

36. See Steven Rowan, "Luther, Bucer and Eck on the Jews," *SCJ* 16, no. 1 (1985): 83–84; Leonard Swidler, *After the Absolute: The Dialogical Future of Religious Reflection* (Minneapolis: Fortress Press, 1990), 116–17; Mark R. Cohen, *Under Crescent and Cross: The Jews in the Middle Ages* (Princeton: Princeton University Press, 1994), 129–30.

37. Kaplan, *Beyond Expulsion*, 1–11; Bell, "Jewish Settlement."

38. Especially after the Crusades, imperial protection was needed not only for Jews but also women, merchants, and clerics. Without a "coherent" Jewish policy, some Emperors defended Jewish rights more consistently, whereas others persecuted them. Though Jews had a better chance of fairer treatment in imperial courts (which served the benefit of the Empire), they were not free of anti-Jewish prejudice. Legally the status of the Jews remained profoundly inferior. See Fraenkel-Goldschmidt, *The Historical Writings*, 11–13; Bireley, "The Catholic Reform," 254; Cohen, *Under Crescent and Cross*, 47, 51.

39. See Bireley, "The Catholic Reform," 254. The imperial law was designed to maintain public peace and forbid violence. Special protection for Jews was needed especially in unstable times, such as after the Black Death, when Jews were increasingly pushed into the countryside. Christian nobility could give letters of protection and a safe place (with conditions) within their estate. See Fraenkel-Goldschmidt, *The Historical Writings*, 10–13.

40. See Ruderman, *Early Modern Jewry*, 78–79.

41. As the emperor began to lose his centralized authority, and in competition with local princes and cities, no single authority prevailed over the others, e.g., in relation to the Jews. See Ocker, "German Theologians," 34–35. Referring to a climate of "fiscal terrorism," Cohen, *Under Crescent and Cross*, 50–51, argues: "Thus, Jews, while benefiting from fair treatment in municipal courts, and often acquiring some form of official mem-

bership in the town, continued to occupy a marginal place compared to Christians, with their full citizenship. In extreme cases, municipal authorities requested from an overlord the right not to tolerate the Jews in their midst. Increasingly as the Middle Ages wore on, towns decided to do away with the 'Jewish problem' altogether by the draconian act of expulsion. In a word, marginality degenerated into exclusion."

42. At Worms in 1157 Fredrick I had issued a charter guaranteeing Jewish freedom of travel, the inviolability of property, fair treatment, protection from forced baptism, the right to sell wine, medicines, etc, and Jewish autonomy in internal Jewish disputes. See Cohen, *Under Crescent and Cross*, 43–44.

43. See Fraenkel-Goldschmidt, *The Historical Writings*, 293–98; Bireley, "The Catholic Reform," 254.

44. Clarification from Debra Kaplan, personal communication.

45. See Bireley, "The Catholic Reform," 253, 255; Rowan, "Luther, Bucer, and Eck on the Jews," 84–85.

46. See Bireley, "The Catholic Reform," 256; also 253, 255–56; Rowan, "Luther, Bucer and Eck on the Jews," 84–85; Edward A. Synan, *The Popes and the Jews in the Middle Ages* (New York: Macmillan, 1965).

47. See Carter Lindberg, "No Greater Service to God than Christian Love: Insights from Martin Luther," in *Social Ministry in the Lutheran Tradition*, ed. Foster R. McCurley (Minneapolis: Fortress Press, 2008), 50–68.

48. On the exploitation of Jews as vulnerable "money sponges," see Jonathan Elukin, *Living Together, Living Apart: Rethinking Jewish-Christian Relations in the Middle Ages* (Princeton: Princeton University Press, 2007), 116–17; Rowan, "Luther, Bucer, and Eck on the Jews," 83–84; Fraenkel-Goldschmidt, *The Historical Writings*, 21–23, 485; Bireley, "The Catholic Reform," 249–68. Expulsions often happened at the times of calm, the time of reorganizing societal systems, including finances (Elukin, 117).

49. After the authority of the pope and the emperor crumbled with the rise of individual states and rulers and the Protestants, the Jews lost their most consistent, symbolic, protectors.

50. See Synan, *The Popes and the Jews*, passim, for more on medieval popes and the Jews.

51. The text for the "Constitution for the Jews" (*Sicut Judaeis non*) quoted here was issued by Innocent III in 1199, with his words of introduction and conclusion, whereas an older text dates from Alexander III (1159–1181). The text (with *italics* by editors) is from Synan, *The Popes and the Jews*, 229–32.

52. See Cohen, *Under Crescent and Cross*, 36–38: "We wish, however, to place under the protection of this decree only those [Jews] who have not presumed to plot against the Christian faith."

53. The thirteenth century saw movement away from the original *Sicut Judaeis*: e.g., the bull, *Turbado corde* ("With a troubled heart") from Clement IV in 1267, speaks of the importance of finding Christian heretics and professing Jews, to prosecute them as heretics. Cohen, *Under Crescent and Cross*, 39.

54. Ibid., 36–38.

55. During periods of calm, Jewish businesses provided Christian households with luxury goods. On "tolerance of practical rationality," see Elukin, *Living Together, Living Apart*, 124. See also Kaplan, *Beyond Expulsion*, 1–2, 4–5, 7.

56. Ruderman, *Early Modern Jewry*, 63. The requirement (from the second half of the sixteenth century) for European Jews to live in separate areas called ghettos was to "shield catholic society from Jewish 'contamination.'" At the same time, in Venice the ghetto system actually "fashioned for the first time a Jewish community, Jewish institutions, and even 'the reconstruction of Jewishness'" (Ruderman, 62–63).

57. Cohen, *Under Crescent and Cross*, 42.

58. See Schöner, "Visual Representations of Jews," 360–61.

59. Ibid., 360. For example, the Phrygian cap, a broad brimmed hat tapered from above and curving to the forehead, and a conical hat, the *pileus cornutus*, were common. It is telling that these indicators are absent from Jewish art and self-portrayals (Ibid., 363).

60. Cohen, *Under Crescent and Cross*, 42.

61. Christian Hebraists were a particularly susceptible group of being labeled "Jew friends." See Text #2.

62. See Text #7.

63. See Text #20.

64. For example, Melanchthon, ambiguously, called Jews by the worst possible names while admiring the scholarship of Jews, whom he considered God's people and thus to be defended. Bucer, also ambivalent, appreciated Hebrew scholarship and used Jewish commentators but campaigned against the Jews in Hesse, in conflict with Duke Phillip. Zwingli, using anti-Jewish stereotypes, was interested in biblical Judaism and its continuity, and, regardless of his anti-rabbinic sentiments, developed constructive perspectives on the Old Testament, promoting friendly treatment of Jews toward the goal of their conversion. Calvin had little to do with or say about the Jews—Geneva had expelled its Jews by his time—but from a theological perspective he found it helpful to distinguish between the Jewish people and Jewish persons. Osiander, the most complex of the reformers, preached anti-Jewish sermons but defended Jews in writing (anonymously), stirring a debate with Eck.

65. See Joy Kammerling, "Andreas Osiander, the Jews, and Judaism," in Bell and Burnett, 219–47.

66. Ibid., 227.

67. Ibid., 238.

68. Ibid., 231–47, on Osiander. On Eck, for whom "Lutheranism was the new Judaism," see Rowan, "Luther, Bucer, and Eck on the Jews," 86–87.

69. See Rowan, "Luther, Bucer and Eck on the Jews," 84–85, 89–90.

70. See Text #8.

71. See Maria Diemling, "Anthonius Margaritha on the 'Whole Jewish Faith:' A Sixteenth-Century Convert from Judaism and his Depiction of the Jewish Religion," in Bell and Burnett, 303–33; Yaacov Deutsch, "Von der Juden Ceremonien: Representations of Jews in Sixteenth-Century Germany," in Bell and Burnett, 335–56. Margaritha provided a systematic description of Jewish ritual life (including explanation of holidays, life cycle, etc.) and (for the first time in German) translations of Jewish prayers, without addressing Jewish faith or beliefs as such. The book contributed to increased interest of Christians in Jewish religious practice (Deutsch, 343).

The Text Selections

1. See Susan C. Karant-Nunn, "Condemnation of the Jews," in *The Reformation of Feeling: Shaping the Religious Emotions in Early Modern Germany* (Oxford: Oxford University Press, 2010), 133–57, 299–305.

Text #1. First Psalms Lectures (1513–1515)

1. See Peter von der Osten-Sacken, *Martin Luther und die Juden: Neu untersucht anhand von Anton Margarithas "Der gantz Jüdisch glaub" [1530/31]* (Stuttgart: Kohlhammer, 2002), 58–65.

2. See Walter Bienert, *Martin Luther und die Juden: ein Quellenbuch mit zeitgenössischen Illustrationen, mit Einführungen und Erläuterungen* (Frankfurt am Main: Evangelisches, 1982), 26.

3. LW 10:6; WA 3:12,29–31; 55/1:6,26–28.

4. With the reference to "Jewish treachery," Luther is invoking language used in the traditional Good Friday Latin liturgy; it was also a standard and favored label for Jews utilized by Christian anti-Jewish polemicists for well over a thousand years prior to Luther.

5. Throughout the text selections, material between { } is by Editors.

6. WA 55/2:575 locates after ★ below.

7. For the background to this section, see the narrative in 1 Sam. 6.

Text #2. Letter to George Spalatin (1514)

1. Preserved Smith, ed., *Luther's Correspondence and Other Comtemporary Letters*, vol. 1: *1507–1521* (Philadelphia: Lutheran Publication Society, 1913), 23–24.

2. Chava Fraenkel-Goldschmidt, *The Historical Writings of Joseph of Rosheim: Leader of Jewry in Early Modern Germany*, ed. Adam Shear, trans. Naomi Schendowich, SEJ 12 (Leiden: Brill, 2006), 116.

3. Heiko A. Oberman, *The Roots of Anti-Semitism: In the Age of Renaissance and Reformation*, trans. James I. Porter (Philadelphia: Fortress Press, 1984), 46.

Text #3. Lectures on Romans (1515–1516)

1. Wilhelm Pauck, ed., *Lectures on Romans: Martin Luther*, LCC 15 (Philadelphia: Westminster, 1961).

2. LW 35:365.

3. LW 35:380.

4. From the 1545 Luther Bible.

5. LW 34:337. For Luther's complete discussion, see *Preface to the Complete Edition of Luther's Latin Writings* [1545], LW 34:336–37.

6. The phrase "of unbelief" is not in LW but is inserted by the editors from WA 56:113,12.

7. The old covenant did not take away but increased sin, and the power of men could not take it away; therefore only the new covenant, that is, grace through faith in Christ takes away sin. Moreover, God takes away sin, when He bestows faith, for sins are forgiven to believers. Thus he is trying to say: "This will be a covenant of taking away and forgiving sins, just as the first covenant was one of adding and nonforgiveness." It can also be understood as: "When I will take away their sins," that is, when they acknowledge through faith that I am the one who does it, admitting that it is vain for them to think they can do it themselves. Yet the meaning is the same.

8. This word of the apostle warns us that in this succession of statements there lies hidden something that is more profound than we can comprehend, namely, that he has said "until the full number of the Gentiles come in" (v. 25), "in order that they also may receive mercy" (v. 31), and "that He may have mercy upon all" (v. 32). And in all of these statements he is making the point that God willed that evil should come in order that out of it He might cause the good to take place. But why this happens this way to those people and at the same time both good and evil do not befall the same people is "unsearchable." For these statements cause us great wonder: "They have fallen in order that they might be saved," and "they do not believe in order that they might believe."

Text #4. Lectures on Galatians (1519)
1. LW 54:20.
2. LW 31: (17), 25–33; (3), 9–16; (35), 39–70.

Text #5. Second Psalms Lectures (1519–1521)
1. The *Second Psalms Lectures* will be translated in their entirety in the New Series of Luther's Works from Concordia Publishing House.
2. LW 44: (115), 123–217; 36: (3), 11–126; 31: (327), 333–77.
3. See Siegfried Raeder, "The Exegetical and Hermeneutical Work of Martin Luther," in *Hebrew Bible/Old Testament: The History of Its Interpretation*, vol. 2: *From the Renaissance to the Enlightenment*, ed. Magne Sæbo (Göttingen: Vandenhoeck & Ruprecht, 2008), 2:375.
4. Osten-Sacken, *Martin Luther und die Juden*, 88. WA 5:534,11–540,3.
5. Translation of Ps. 14:7 by editors.
6. A temporal reference to the time between the death of Emperor Maximilian on January 12, 1519, and the coronation of Carl V on October 26, 1520.

Text #6. Magnificat (1521)
1. See Text #7.

Text #7. That Jesus Christ Was Born a Jew (1523)
1. See Thomas Kaufmann, "Luther and the Jews," in *Jews, Judaism, and the Reformation in Sixteenth-Century Germany*, ed. Dean Phillip Bell and Stephen G. Burnett, SCEH 37 (Leiden: Brill, 2006), 81–82.

Text #8. Letter to the Baptized Jew, Bernard (1523)
1. Preserved Smith and Charles M. Jacobs, eds., *Luther's Correspondence and Other Contemporary Letters*, vol. 2: *1521–1530* (Philadelphia: Lutheran Publication Society, 1918), 2:185–87.
2. See Martin Brecht, *Martin Luther*, 3 vols., trans. James L. Schaff (Minneapolis: Fortress Press, 1985–), 2:112–13; 3:335; LW 50:144–45.
3. WABr 5:452 (no. 1632).
4. As Luther did with Michael the Jew from Posen before his baptism in 1540. See Brecht, *Martin Luther*, 3:339; WATr 5:83 (no. 5354).
5. After hearing such stories the frustrated Luther snaps that future Jewish converts should be dunk in the Elbe and cautions his friend Amsdorf actually not to baptize a Jew because "they are rogues." Brecht, *Martin Luther*, 3:335, 437.

Text #9. Lectures on Deuteronomy (1525)
1. LW 9:63. The matter is made more complicated for the English reader because of the translator's decision to capitalize Old Testament and New Testament.

2. See especially Text #10.

3. See Text #23.

Text #10. Sermon: How Christians Should Regard Moses (1525)

1. LW 46: (3), 8–43; 46: (45), 49–55; 46: (57), 63–85.

Text #11. Lectures on Zechariah (1525/1526)

1. WA 23: [477] 485–664; LW 20:153–347.

2. See Text #12 for further explication.

3. Osten-Sacken, *Martin Luther und die Juden*, 113.

Text # 12. Sermon on Jeremiah 23:5-8 (The Visit of Three Jews) (1526)

1. Ibid., 103–10. The other occurrences, in chronological order, are:

Lectures on Isaiah, LW 16:227 [1527–1530] = WA 31/2:162,28–29

Table Talk, WATr 3:370, 9–21 (#3512) [1536]

Against the Sabbatarians, LW 47:65–66 [1538] = WA 50:313, 1–6 (esp. 5–6)

Table Talk, WATr 4:619,20—620,15 (#5026) [1540]

Table Talk, WATr 4: 517,4–20 (#4795) [1541/2]

On the Jews and Their Lies, LW 47:191–192 [1543] = WA 53:461,28–462,5

On the Ineffable Name, Falk, 173 [1543] = WA 53:589,12–19 (esp. 16–19)

2. Thomas Kaufmann, "Luther and the Jews," 73–74.

3. See Text #7.

4. See Deut. 21:23.

5. A Hebrew/Aramaic wordplay.

6. That is, "young woman" rather than "virgin."

7. A Hebrew scholar and colleague of Luther's.

Text #13. Commentary on Psalm 109 (1526)

1. Mary's interest in Luther's teachings originated from her Lutheran sister Isabella, the wife of the Danish King Kristian II, until suffocated by pressure from her Catholic brother Ferdinand; later, as a regent for the Netherlands, she opted for leniency towards Protestant uprisings. On her attitudes towards the Jews little is known, but in 1527, soon after Luther's mail, demands for the expulsion of Jews in Bohemia intensified.

2. See Text #7.

3. Brecht, *Martin Luther*, 3:334.

4. WA 38:54,24–27.

5. A clear exaggeration on Luther's part, which has led to many misconceptions about Luther's relationships with Jews.

6. A Germanized pronunciation of Hebrew תלוי from Deut. 21:23.

Text #14. Lectures on Isaiah (1527–1530)

1. LW 17:3.

2. LW 16:3.

3. See Andrew Colin Gow, *The Red Jews: Antisemitism in an Apocalyptic Age 1200–1600*, SMRT 55 (Leiden: Brill, 1995).

Text #15. Preface to Daniel (1530)

1. A key witness to Luther's growing "end-of-the-world" mindset is his *Computation of the Years of the World*, which he wrote in 1541 and then revised in 1545: WA 53: (1), 22–181.

2. The material between asterisks was replaced in the new 1541 Preface.

3. The material between asterisks was replaced in the new 1541 Preface.

Text #16. Letter to Josel of Rosheim (1537)

1. See partial translation in LW 47:62.

2. For example, in Hesse, the debate over the lot of the Jews in 1538–1539 between Martin Bucer and a committee of evangelical preachers seeking enforced expulsion and the more lenient Philip of Hesse (who had continued to permit Jewish residence in Hesse during 1532–1538), resulted in 1539 in a tightened *Judenordung*.

3. See Brecht, *Martin Luther*, 3:336.

4. For Josel and his life's work and influence, the indispensable study is Fraenkel-Goldschmidt, *The Historical Writings of Joseph of Rosheim*.

5. The imperial diets were particularly important for Jews, whose rights were typically addressed at these gatherings of the German imperial estates, who would negotiate among themselves and with the Emperor about the economic advantages of either allowing or forbidding Jewish business or residence in any given territory (Ibid., 1–5). At these meetings where Jews would serve as a "bargaining chip" towards economic gain for the Emperor, Josel spoke with integrity and courage, and, in addition to hindering total expulsions, saved many lives.

6. Ibid., 35: "Apparently he {i.e., Josel} was not yet aware that the Elector's decision itself was almost certainly prompted by Luther's negative attitude toward the Jews."

7. WABr 8:76–78 (no. 3152).

8. See Text #20.

9. See Text #7.

10. Elector John Frederick of Saxony, 1532–1547.

11. George, Albertine Duke of Saxony, 1500–1539.

12. *That Jesus Christ Was Born a Jew* (1523), Text #7.

13. See Numbers 22–24.

Text #17. Lectures on Genesis 12 (1537)

1. LW 4:351–52.

2. See, for example, the concluding prayer in "Barekh" of the Passover Haggadah.

Text #18. The Three Symbols of the Christian Faith (1538)

1. The biblical quote has been altered to reflect Luther's usage, WA 50:279,12.

2. The word in question is the Tetragrammaton, the four-letter name of God. All caps are supplied here and below by the editors based on WA, because this is crucial to Luther's argument.

3. Luther's German text is plural here, WA 50:280,30.

4. Altered here and below from WA 50:281,17–18.

Text #19. Lectures on Genesis 17 (1538)

1. While the practice of circumcision among Christians became commonplace in the United States during the twentieth century, it would have been an utter aberration in Luther's Germany.

2. LW 3:77.

3. See the Table Talk #356 (1532), LW 54:51–52.

Text #20. Against the Sabbatarians (1538)

1. On these four treatises, Texts #20, #23, #24, #26, as well as Text #7, see now Thomas Kaufmann, *Luthers "Judenschriften": Ein Beitrag zu ihrer historischen Kontextualisierung* (Tübingen: Mohr, 2011).

2. The count wrote to Luther already in 1532 and may be referring to the short-lived Anabaptist-Sabbatarian faction in Silesian Slovakia and Moravia (led by Oswald Glait and Andreas Fischer), active in the 1530's and persecuted from 1535 on. See LW 47:59–60; Daniel Liechty, *Sabbatarianism in the Sixteenth Century: A Page in the History of the Radical Reformation* (Berrien Springs: Andrews University Press, 1993).

3. These small groups that celebrated the Jewish Sabbath and interpreted Scripture with strong eschatological expectations were small minorities susceptible to the persecution of Anabaptist believers and other minority groups.

4. See Brecht, *Martin Luther*, 3:338; Walter Homolka, Walter Jacob, and Esther Seidel, eds., *Not by Birth Alone: Conversion to Judaism* (Herndon: Cassell, 1997), 25.

5. Kaufmann, "Luther and the Jews," 89. Luther mentions Sabbatarian groups in a 1532 Table Talk, and then again in his Lectures on Genesis with a reference to the Jews and "their apes, the Sabbatarians": "In our time there arose in Moravia a foolish kind of people, the Sabbatarians, who maintain that the Sabbath must be observed after the fashion of the Jews. Perhaps they will insist on circumcision too, for a like reason." LW 2:361; cf 47:60.

6. See Text #23.

7. Brecht, *Martin Luther*, 3:339.

8. See Introduction to Text #12.

Text #21. New Preface to Ezekial (1541)

1. Table Talk No. 5324 (Between October 19 and November 5, 1540), LW 54:408.

2. George Rörer, Luther's personal secretary.

3. Brecht, *Martin Luther*, 3:340.

Text #22. Liscentiate Exam Heinrich Schmedenstede (1542)

1. LW DB 8:45.

Text #23. On the Jews and Their Lies (1543)

1. Virtually all of these old accusations were collected and used by Luther's archenemy, Johann Eck, in his contemporary anti-Jewish treatise, *Ains Judenbüechlins Verlegung* ("Refutation of a Jew-Book") [1541].

2. See especially LW 47:263.

3. An intriguing possibility for Luther's knowledge of these pertinent rabbinic exegetical arguments is that he could have recently read Sebastian Münster's *Messiahs of the Christians and Jews*. If so, this would also have given him access to portions of the medieval Jewish anti-Christian work, *Sefer Nizzahon Vetus*. See Stephen G. Burnett, "Reassessing the 'Basel-Wittenberg Conflict,'" in *Hebraica Veritas? Christian Hebraists and the Study of Judaism in Early Modern Europe*, ed. Allison P. Coudert and Jeffrey S. Shoulson, JCC (Philadelphia: University of Pennsylvania Press, 2004), 193, 201n.84; Kaufmann, "Luther and the Jews," 90, 92–93.

4. See Text #24. Porchetus's work was printed in Paris in 1520, and Luther had his own copy (see WA 60:236–39).

5. Margaritha's book (first published 1530) contained the first translation into German of substantial portions of the Jewish daily morning prayer service. Margaritha's book belonged to a stream of distorted mirrors, which while having the appearance of objectively offering valuable "firsthand" ethnographic information, also managed to fuel the worst fears of Christians about Jews and their faith practices. See Stephen G. Burnett, "Distorted Mirrors: Antonius Margarita, Johann Buxtorf and Christian Ethnographies of the Jews," *SCJ* 25 (1994): 275–87.

6. LW 47:275.

7. LW 47:268.

8. Quoted in Kaufmann, "Luther and the Jews," 93 n.79.

9. LW 47:277.

10. LW 47:287–88.

11. LW 47:268.

12. Brecht, *Martin Luther*, 3:349, notes that on the day the edict was issued, May 6, 1543, Luther was a guest of the Elector.

13. See Text #24.

14. That is, the numerical equivalent of the Hebrew name, יֵשׁוּ, Yeshu.

15. Margaritha has called to Luther's attention the *'Aleinu* prayer, the concluding prayer for all standard Jewish prayer services. In a portion of the prayer that is based on Isa. 30:7 and 45:20, Jews give thanks to God that, unlike the Gentiles, they do not worship "hével va-riq" (vanity and emptiness) nor do they pray to "el lo' yoshía" (a god who does not save). The numerical equivalent of "va-riq" (and emptiness) is 316, the same as that of "Yeshu." Interestingly, Margaritha does not draw any connection between "Yeshu" and "lo' yoshía" (he does not save).

16. Margaritha's text records, accurately, a standard Jewish curse against a wicked person: "yímach shemo" (may his name be erased).

17. Rabbinic Hebrew for "demon."

18. This charge is not in Margaritha.

19. *Maria = Haria* is an Aramaic wordplay from harya' = "excrement" or "shit." See Table Talk #5462 (1542; WATr 5:166,31) where Luther translates *haria* as "scheishaus"; LW 54:426 euphemizes with "stinkpot."

20. Luther should have referred to Ferdinand and Isabella.

Text #24. On the Ineffable Name and on the Lineage of Christ (1543)

1. At present the only English translation of the complete treatise is in Gerhard Falk, *The Jew in Christian Theology* (Jefferson: McFarland, 1992) [163], 166–224. There are, however, numerous errors.

2. LW 41: (179), 185–256.

3. WA 53:605, 8–13; cf. Falk, *The Jew in Christian Theology*, 186.

4. See Introduction to Text #23.

5. A medieval German-Jewish anti-Christian text. See Text #25.

6. See below.

7. See WA 53:594 n.7.

8. An inscription, "Rabbini. Schem HaMphoras." was added above the image long after Luther's death, but clearly under the influence of this treatise.

9. A reference to the fall of Bethar at the end of the Bar Kokhba revolt, 135 CE.

Text #25. Josel of Rosheim: Letter to the Strasbourg City Council (1543)

1. Fraenkel-Goldschmidt, *The Historical Writings of Joseph of Rosheim*.

2. Used with permission of Brill.

3. See Text #16.

4. Josel's letters hardly imply that the Strasbourg city council was a known friend of the Jews. While the city did enjoy the reputation of being one of the more hospitable places in terms of religious difference, it had already banned Jews in 1391, who nevertheless continued to be present in city life and business. One obvious reason why Josel approaches leaders in Strasbourg is that the city hosted some of the most productive and "free" publishing houses of the time.

5. See Section #22 of the *Chronicle* in Fraenkel-Goldschmidt, *The Historical Writings*, 328–31.

6. In the Holy Roman Empire, even in the so called "free cities," the Emperor saw himself as the highest overlord for and the protector of the Jews—a source of important imperial tax revenue. In the absence of a uniform policy, gaining the Emperor's ear was crucial, especially so in the battle against the Lutherans, who did not enjoy imperial, or papal recognition until the 1555 Peace of Augsburg.

7. See introduction to Text #16.

8. On the seven Sabbaths between 9 Av and Rosh Hashanah the prophetic readings are taken from Isaiah 40ff. and emphasize God's message of comfort to Israel. Josel likely has these very readings in mind.

9. Josel is implying the large-scale negative impact of Luther's having advocated the circumvention of imperial law, with its stipulations for protection of the Jews. Thus Luther is not only standing against the Pope, he is presenting a danger to the wellbeing of the entire empire.

10. Josel is referring here to the *Toledot Yeshu*, a medieval German-Jewish anti-Christian treatise. See Fraenkel-Goldschmidt, *The Historical Writings*, 412, n. 20 for an excellent discussion of the matter.

11. In this text, {{ }} are insertions of the Editors. { } are from Fraenkel-Goldschmidt.

12. An astute observation from Josel that not all Christian communities acted the same way in regards to their Jewish neighbors, and that what is said in writing is never the comprehensive picture of reality.

13. See Peter Schäfer, *Jesus in the Talmud* (Princeton: Princeton University Press, 2007).

14. Josel names the territories that were the most powerful supporters of the Reformation. It is noteworthy that Josel had also challenged the "crown" theologians in both Hesse and Saxony—Martin Bucer and Luther—whose princes were much more amicable towards the Jews than their theologians were.

15. Josel's request about prohibiting the printing of Luther's 1543 works in Strasbourg was successful, whereas the city magistrates ignored his plea for intervention with the leaders of the Smalcaldic League and other territorial rulers' orders about the Jews, as that was a matter pertaining to the larger issue of Jewish rights in the Holy Roman Empire. See Debra Kaplan, *Beyond Expulsion: Jews, Christians, and Reformation Strasbourg* (Palo Alto: Stanford University Press, 2011), 104–5.

16. 10 Av 5303 = 11 July 1543.

Text #26. On the Last Words of David (1543)

1. Luther's rigid stance in this regard is evident throughout his Genesis lectures.

2. Rabbi Solomon son of Isaac (1040–1105), "Rashi," was the greatest of all the medieval Jewish commentators. He wrote a commentary on the entire Hebrew Bible as well as on the entire Babylonian Talmud. The biblical commentary of Nicholas of Lyra (1270–1349), together with Sebastian Münster's *Biblia hebraica latina* (1534/1535), were Luther's primary conduits into rabbinic exegesis.

3. This is Luther's new translation. The Hebrew text is most likely corrupt.

4. Hebrew professor in Leipzig and close confidant of Luther in the Old Testament translation project.

5. See Text #24.

6. A noteworthy, though not common, polemical claim of Luther's, which anticipates an all-too-typical contemporary anti-Jewish slander, to the effect that there is no connection between present-day Jews and the Jews of antiquity.

Text #27. Two Letters to Katharina Luther (1546)

1. None of Katharina's letters to her husband have survived.

2. The pro-Reformation Counts Albrecht and Gebhard, and their cousins Philip and John George of Mansfeld, were in a constant power struggle with one another. Luther and Melanchthon had already traveled to Eisleben in December 1545 to intervene in the dispute over mining rights, but the trip was cut short when Melanchthon became ill.

3. See Text #28.

4. The number seemed high to Luther whose Wittenberg did not have a recognizable Jewish community. By the mid-sixteenth century most Jews had moved to the safer rural areas, such as Eisleben, which had received Jewish refugees as a result of the expulsion ordered by the Archbishop of Magdeburg in 1493. Luther's insinuation of the Jews "possibly" being the cause behind his sudden illness draws on common medieval superstitions suggesting active Jewish engagement in causing physical harm for innocent Christians.

5. Count Albrecht, 1480–1560. Luther's "promise" to use the pulpit in this way is a reminder of the role played by Protestant preaching in the development of anti-Jewish political policy in the sixteenth century. The statement also reveals Luther's seriousness. When the gospel and Christian lives were at stake, Christians had a duty to interfere in matters otherwise considered to belong to the realm of the secular authority, such as expulsions of the Jews.

6. Countess Dorothea of Mansfeld (1493–1578), daughter of Count Philip of Solms and (from 1521) second wife of Ernst II of Mansfeld-Voderort (1479–1531).

7. In this private letter to his wife, Luther sums up the conclusions he recently made in his 1543 explicitly anti-Jewish publications, with no indication that there would be any discord in these matters between the spouses, or with his closest colleague, Melanchthon.

Text #28. An Admonition against the Jews (1546)

1. Used with permission of Concordia Publishing House.

2. See Text #27.

3. LW 58:404.

4. See Text #27.

5. See the discussion by Brown in LW 58:400–404.

6. Brown points to a sharp, unresolved tension in Luther. In his February 7 sermon on the Parable of the Wheat and the Tares, Luther advocates the public toleration of heresy, while in the Admonition he advocates the expulsion of Jews precisely on the grounds of blasphemy. See LW 58:405, 408–9.

7. In his earlier writings he made the point about Christian education and examination of the convert's faith being more important than a hasty baptism. But here the logic of the Admonition gives this language the character of a "final offer."

8. At the end of his rope, Luther gives voice to some of the worst fears of Christians about what Jews could do to harm them, and this without any criticism whatsoever.

9. Even here the words "Christian love" are evoked as Luther remains true to his conviction that conversion to Christ is the only way for Jews to be saved by the message of God's love, while God's wrath and death fall upon those who resist. That has been Luther's repeated warning, articulated now with new urgency: The Jews are out to kill Christians.

10. This statement reveals the seriousness of the matter to Luther and his spiritual and pastoral concern: he is addressing a sin, an evil, which he regards as his pastoral duty. Passivity in this regard would imply complicity.

Afterword

1. This is the provocative phrase of Carter Lindberg, "Tainted Greatness: Luther's Attitudes toward Judaism and Their Historical Reception," in *Tainted Greatness: Antisemitism and Cultural Heroes*, ed. Nancy A. Harrowitz (Philadelphia: Temple University Press, 1994), 15–35.

Chronology

1. Dean Phillip Bell, "Jewish Settlement, Politics, and the Reformation," in *Jews, Judaism, and the Reformation in Sixteenth-Century Germany*, ed. Dean Phillip Bell and Stephen G. Burnett, SCEH 37 (Leiden: Brill, 2006), 421–50.

Bibliography

General Works on Luther

Brecht, Martin. *Martin Luther.* 3 vols. Translated by James L. Schaff. Minneapolis: Fortress Press, 1985, 1990, 1993.

Ebeling, Gerhard. *Luther: An Introduction to His Thought.* Translated by R. A. Wilson. Philadelphia: Fortress Press, 1970.

Gritsch, Eric W. *Martin, God's Court Jester: Luther in Retrospect.* Philadelphia: Fortress Press, 1983.

Hendrix, Scott H. *Luther.* Abingdon Pillars of Theology. Nashville: Abingdon, 2009.

———. "Martin Luther, Reformer." In *The Cambridge History of Christianity.* Vol. 6: *Reform and Expansion 1500–1660*, edited by R. Po-chia Hsia, 3–19. Cambridge: Cambridge University Press, 2007.

Kaufmann, Thomas. *Martin Luther.* Munich: Beck, 2006.

Kittelson, James M. *Luther the Reformer: The Story of the Man and His Career.* Minneapolis: Augsburg, 1986.

Kolb, Robert. *Martin Luther as Prophet, Teacher, Hero: Images of the Reformer, 1520–1620.* Grand Rapids: Baker, 1999.

Leppin, Volker. *Martin Luther.* Darmstadt: Wissenschaftliche, 2006.

Lohse, Bernhard. *Martin Luther's Theology: Its Historical and Systematic Development.* Translated and edited by Roy A. Harrisville. Minneapolis: Fortress Press, 1999.

Lull, Timothy F., ed. *Martin Luther's Basic Theological Writings.* 2nd ed. Minneapolis: Fortress Press, 2005.

Oberman, Heiko A. *Luther: Man between God and the Devil.* Translated by Eileen Walliser-Schwarzbart. New York: Image, 1992.

Whitford, David M. *Luther: A Guide for the Perplexed.* London: T&T Clark, 2011.

Readers and Sourcebooks

Appold, Kenneth G. *The Reformation: A Brief History*. Malden: Wiley-Blackwell, 2011.

Bagchi, David, and David C. Steinmetz, eds. *The Cambridge Companion to Reformation Theology*. Cambridge: Cambridge University Press, 2004.

Hillerbrand, Hans J. *The Division of Christendom: Christianity in the Sixteenth Century*. Louisville: Westminster John Knox, 2007.

———, ed. *The Protestant Reformation*. Rev. ed. New York: Harper Perennial, 2009.

Hsia, R. Po-chia, ed. *The Cambridge History of Christianity*. Vol 6: *Reform and Expansion, 1500–1660*. Cambridge: Cambridge University Press, 2007.

Janz, Denis R., ed. *A Reformation Reader: Primary Texts with Introductions*. 2nd ed. Minneapolis: Fortress Press, 2008.

Lindberg, Carter. *The European Reformations*. 2nd ed. Malden: Wiley-Blackwell, 2010.

———, ed. *The Reformation Theologians: An Introduction to Theology in the Early Modern Period*. Malden: Blackwell, 2002.

McGrath, Alister E. *Reformation Thought: An Introduction*. 3rd ed. Malden: Blackwell, 1999.

Pettegree, Andrew, ed. *The Reformation World*. New York: Routledge, 2000.

Works on Luther and the Jews

Ages, Arnold. "Luther and the Rabbis." *JQR* 58, no. 1 (1967): 63–68.

Arnold, Matthieu. "Luther et les Juifs: État de la Question." *Positions Luthériennes: Revue trimestrielle* 50 (2002): 139–65.

Bäumer, Remigius. "Die Juden im Urteil von Johannes Eck und Martin Luther." *MTZ* 34 (1983): 253–78.

Bell, Dean Phillip. "Martin Luther and the Jews: The Reformation, Nazi Germany, and Today." In *The Soloman Goldman Lectures*. Vol. 7, edited by Dean Phillip Bell, 155–87. Chicago: Spertus Institute of Jewish Studies, 1999.

Bienert, Walther. *Martin Luther und die Juden: ein Quellenbuch mit zeitgenössischen Illustrationen, mit Einführungen und Erläuterungen*. Frankfurt am Main: Evangelisches, 1982.

Brosseder, Johannes. *Luthers Stellung zu den Juden im Spiegel seiner Interpreten: Interpretation und Rezeption von Luthers Schriften und Äusserungen zum Judentum im 19. und 20. Jahrhundert vor allem im deutschsprachigen Raum*. B T 8. Munich: Max Hueber, 1972.

Cohen, Carl. "Die Juden und Luther." *ARG 54* (1963): 38–51.

———. "Martin Luther and His Jewish Contemporaries." *JSS* 25 (1963): 195–204.

Edwards, Mark U., Jr. *Luther's Last Battles: Politics and Polemics, 1531–1546*. Minneapolis: Fortress Press, 2005 (1983).

———. "Martin Luther and the Jews: Is There a Holocaust Connection?" *FF* 10 (1983): 24–25.

———. "Toward an Understanding of Luther's Attack on the Jews." In *Christians, Jews, and Other Worlds: Patterns of Conflict and Accommodation*, edited by Philip F. Gallagher, 1–19. Lanham: University Press of America, 1988.

Erling, Bernhard. "Martin Luther and the Jews, in Light of his Lectures on Genesis." In
    Israel, the Church, and the World Religions Face the Future, edited by John Todd, François
    Refoulé, and Landrum Rymer Bolling, 129–47. Jerusalem: Ecumenical Institute for
    Theological Research, 1984.

Falk, Gerhard. *The Jew in Christian Theology: Martin Luther's Anti-Jewish "Vom SchemHam-
    phoras."* Jefferson: McFarland, 1992.

Friedlander, Albert H. "Martin Luther und wir Juden." In *Die Juden und Martin Luther—
    Martin Luther und die Juden: Geschichte, Wirkungsgeschichte, Herausforderung*, edited by
    Heinz Kremers, 289–97. 2nd ed. Neukirchen-Vluyn: Neukirchener, 1987.

Gräßel, Michael. *Kontinuität und Diskontinuität in Martin Luthers Stellung zum Judentum.*
    Munich: GRIN, 2007.

Gritsch, Eric W. "Luther and the Jews: Toward a Judgment of History." In *Stepping-Stones
    to Further Jewish-Lutheran Relationships: Key Lutheran Statements*, edited by Harold H.
    Ditmanson, 104–19. Minneapolis: Augsburg, 1990.

Gritsch, Eric W. *Martin Luther's Anti-Semitism: Against His Better Judgment.* Grand Rapids:
    Eerdmans, 2011.

Hagen, Kenneth. "Luther's So-called *Judenschriften*: A Genre Approach." *ARG* 90 (1999):
    130–58.

Hillerbrand, Hans J. "Martin Luther and the Jews." In *Jews and Christians: Exploring the
    Past, Present, and Future*, edited by James H. Charlesworth, 127–50. New York: Cross-
    road, 1990.

Hummel, Leonard M. "'Wrath against the Unrighteous': The Place of Luther's Lectures
    on Romans in His Understanding of Judaism." *SRR* 11, no. 1–2 (2008–2009): 64–82.

Junghans, Helmar. "Martin Luther und die Juden." In *Spätmittelalter, Luthers Reformation,
    Kirche in Sachsen: Ausgewählte Aufsätze*, edited by Michael Beyer and Günther Warten-
    berg, 297– 322. Leipzig: Evangelische, 2001.

Kaufmann, Thomas. "Luther and the Jews." In *Jews, Judaism, and the Reformation in Six-
    teenth-Century Germany*, edited by Dean Phillip Bell and Stephen G. Burnett, 69–104.
    SCEH 37. Leiden: Brill, 2006.

———. *Luthers "Judenschriften": Ein Beitrag zu ihrer historischen Kontextualisierung.* Tübingen:
    Mohr, 2011.

———. *Luthers "Judenschriften" in ihren historischen Kontexten.* NAWG I, no. 6. Göttingen:
    Vandenhoeck & Ruprecht, 2005.

Kleiner, John W. "Martin Luther and the Jews." *Consensus* 19, no. 1 (1993): 109–26.

Kremers, Heinz, et al., eds. *Die Juden und Martin Luther—Martin Luther und die Juden:
    Geschichte, Wirkungsgeschichte, Herausforderung.* 2nd ed. Neukirchen-Vluyn: Neukirch-
    ener, 1987.

Lewin, Reinhold. *Luthers Stellung zu den Juden: Ein Beitrag zur Geschichte der Juden in
    Deutschland während des Reformationszeitalters.* NSGTK 10. Berlin: Trowitzsch, 1911;
    reprint, Aalen: Scientia, 1973.

Lindbeck, George. "Martin Luther and the Rabbinic Mind." In *Understanding the Rabbinic Mind: Essays on the Hermeneutic of Max Kadushin*, edited by Peter Ochs, 141–64. Atlanta: Scholars, 1990.

Lindberg, Carter. "Tainted Greatness: Luther's Attitudes toward Judaism and Their Historical Reception." In *Tainted Greatness: Antisemitism and Cultural Heroes*, edited by Nancy A. Harrowitz, 15–35. Philadelphia: Temple University Press, 1994.

Maser, Peter. "Luthers Schriftauslegung in dem Traktat 'Von den Juden und ihren Lügen' (1543): Ein Beitrag zum 'christologischen Antisemitismus' der Reformation." *Judaica* 29 (1973): 71–84, 149–67.

———. "Erbarmen für Luther? Zu zwei neuen Büchern über den Reformator und die Juden." *Judaica* 39 (1983): 166–78.

Maurer, Wilhelm. "Die Zeit der Reformation." In *Kirche und Synagoge: Handbuch zur Geschichte von Christen und Juden: Darstellung mit Quellen*. 2 vols. Edited by Karl Heinrich Rengstorf and Siegfried von Kortzfleisch, 1:375–429. Stuttgart: Klett, 1968.

———. *Kirche und Synagoge: Motive und Formen der Auseinandersetzung der Kirche mit dem Judentum im Laufe der Geschichte*. Stuttgart: Kohlhammer, 1953.

McNutt, James E. "Luther and the Jews Revisited: Reflections on a Thought Let Slip." *CMT* 38, no. 1 (2011) 40–47.

Meier, Kurt. "Zur Interpretation von Luthers Judenschriften." In *Vierhundertfünfzig Jahre lutherische Reformation, 1517–1967: Festschrift für Franz Lau zum 60. Geburtstag*, edited by James Atkinson et al., 233–51. Göttingen: Vandenhoeck & Ruprecht, 1967.

Nestigen, James Arne. "Luther, Judaism, and Cultural Tolerance." *Dialog* 35 (Summer 1996): 166–73.

Oberman, Heiko A. "Die Juden in Luthers Sicht." In *Die Juden und Martin Luther—Martin Luther und die Juden: Geschichte, Wirkungsgeschichte, Herausforderung*, edited by Heinz Kremers et al., 136–62. 2nd ed. Neukirchen-Vluyn: Neukirchener, 1987.

———. "From Luther to Hitler." In *The Two Reformations: The Journey from the Last Days to the New World*, edited by Donald Weinstein, 81–85, 212. New Haven: Yale University Press, 2003.

Oberman, Heiko A. "Luthers Stellung zu den Juden: Ahnen und Geahndete." In *Leben und Werk Martin Luthers von 1526 bis 1546: Festgabe zu seinem 500 Geburtstag*, 2 vols., edited by Helmar Junghans, 1:519–30, 2:894–904. Göttingen: Vandenhoeck & Ruprecht, 1983.

Osten-Sacken, Peter von der. *Martin Luther und die Juden: Neu untersucht Anhand von Anton Margarithas "Der gantz Jüdisch glaub" (1530/31)*. Stuttgart: Kohlhammer, 2002.

Pangritz, Andreas. "Once More: Martin Luther and the Jews." In *Remembering for the Future: The Holocaust in an Age of Genocide*, Vol. 2: *Ethics and Religion*. Edited by John K. Roth et al., 603–17. New York: Palgrave, 2001.

Pawlikowski, John T. "Martin Luther and Judaism: Paths toward Theological Reconciliation." *JAAR* 43, no. 4 (1975): 681–93.

Reu, Michael. "Luther and the Jews." *KZ* 66 (1942): 588–610.

Rogge, Joachim. "Luthers Stellung zu den Juden." *Luther* 40 (1969): 13–24.

Rowan, Steven. "Luther, Bucer, and Eck on the Jews." *SCJ* 16, no. 1 (1985): 79–90.

Roynesdal, Olaf. *Martin Luther and the Jews.* Ph.D. Dissertation. Marquette University. Milwaukee: 1986.

Rubenstein, Richard L. "Luther and the Roots of the Holocaust." In *Persistent Prejudice: Perspectives on Anti-Semitism*, edited by Herbert Hirsch and Jack D. Spiro, 31–41. Fairfax: George Mason University Press, 1988.

Rupp, Ernest Gordon. "Martin Luther and the Jews." *NTT* 31, no. 2 (1977): 121–35.

Schmidt, Johann M. "Martin Luther's Attitude toward the Jews and Its Impact on the Evangelical Church in Germany in the Beginning of the Third Reich." In *Proceedings of the Ninth World Congress of Jewish Studies*, 157–64. Jerusalem: World Union of Jewish Studies, 1986.

Schramm, Brooks. "Populus Dei: Luther on Jacob and the Election of Israel (Gen 25)." In *The Call of Abraham: Essays on the Election of Israel in Honor of Jon D. Levenson*. Edited by Gary A. Anderson and Joel S. Kaminsky. Notre Dame: University of Notre Dame Press, 2012.

Schreiner, Stefan. "Was Luther vom Judentum wissen konnte." In *Die Juden und Martin Luther—Martin Luther und die Juden*, edited by Heinz Kremers et al., 58–71. 2nd ed. Neukirchen-Vluyn: Neukirchener, 1987.

Schubert, Anselm. "Fremde Sünde: Zur Theologie von Luthers späten Judenschriften." In *Martin Luther: Biographie und Theologie*, edited by Dietrich Korsch and Volker Leppin, 251–70. SMHR 53. Tübingen: Mohr, 2010.

Sherman, Franklin. "On the Jews and Their Lies: Introduction." LW 47:123–36.

Siirala, Aarne. "Luther and the Jews." *Lutheran World: Publication of the Lutheran World Federation* 11, no. 3 (1964): 337–57.

Späth, Andreas. *Luther und die Juden.* BibSym 18. Bonn: Kultur und Wissenschaft, 2001.

Stöhr, Martin. "Luther und die Juden." In *Christen und Juden: Ihr Gegenüber vom Apostelkonzil bis heute*, edited by Wolf-Dieter Marsch and Karl Thieme, 115–40. Göttingen: Vandenhoeck & Ruprecht, 1961.

Sucher, C. Bernd. *Luthers Stellung zu den Juden: Eine Interpretation aus germanistischer Sicht.* Nieuwkoop: de Graaf, 1977.

Tjernagel, Neelak S. *Martin Luther and the Jewish People.* Milwaukee: Northwestern, 1985.

Wallmann, Johannes. "Luthers Stellung zu Judentum und Islam." *Luther* 57 (1986): 49–60.

———. "The Reception of Luther's Writings on the Jews from the Reformation to the End of the Nineteenth Century." In *Stepping-Stones to Further Jewish-Lutheran Relationships: Key Lutheran Statements*, edited by Harold H. Ditmanson, 120–44. Minneapolis: Augsburg, 1990.

Waschke, Ernst-Joachim. "Martin Luther und die Juden oder: Von einem Irrweg in der Theologie." In *Judentum seit der Zeit des Zweiten Tempels in Geschichte, Literatur und*

Kult: Festschrift für Thomas Willi, edited by Julia Männchen und Torsten Reiprich, 371–83. Neukirchen-Vluyn: Neukirchener, 2007.

Wenzel, Edith. "Martin Luther und der mittelalterliche Antisemitismus." In *Die Juden in ihren mittelalterlichen Umwelt*, edited by Alfred Ebenbauer and Klaus Zatloukal, 301–19. Vienna: Bölau, 1991.

Martin Luther, the Bible, and the Jewish People

Abrahams, Israel. *Jewish Life in the Middle Ages*. New York: Atheneum, 1969.

Abulafia, Anna Sapir. *Christians and Jews in Dispute: Disputational Literature and the Rise of Anti-Judaism in the West (c. 1000–1150)*. VCSS. Aldershot: Ashgate, 1998.

Alfonsi, Petrus. *Dialogue against the Jews [Dialogus contra Iudaeos]*. Translated by Irven M. Resnick. Washington, DC: Catholic University of America Press, 2006.

Bagchi, David. "The German Rabelais? Foul Words and the Word in Luther." *Reformation and Renaissance Review: Journal of the Society for Reformation Studies* 7, no. 2–3 (2005): 143–62.

Bardtke, Hans. *Luther und das Buch Esther*. Tübingen: Mohr, 1964.

Baron, Salo W. *A Social and Religious History of the Jews*. Vol. 13: *Inquisition, Renaissance, and Reformation*. New York: Columbia University Press, 1969.

Beck, James. "The Anabaptists and the Jews: The Case of Hätzer, Denck, and the *Worms Prophets*." *Mennonite Quarterly Review* 75, no. 4 (2001): 407–27.

Bein, Alex. *Die Judenfrage: Biographie eines Weltproblems*. 2 vols. Stuttgart: Deutsche, 1980.

Beintker, Horst J. Eduard. "Luther und das Alte Testament." *TZ* 46, no. 3 (1990): 219–44.

Bell, Dean Philip. *Jewish Identity in Early Modern Germany: Memory, Power, and Community*. Burlington: Ashgate, 2007.

———. "Jewish Settlement, Politics, and the Reformation." In *Jews, Judaism, and the Reformation in Sixteenth-Century Germany*, edited by Dean Phillip Bell and Stephen G. Burnett, 421–50. SCEH 37. Leiden: Brill, 2006.

———, and Stephen G. Burnett, eds. *Jews, Judaism, and the Reformation in Sixteenth-Century Germany*. SCEH 37. Leiden: Brill, 2006.

Ben-Sasson, Haim Hillel. "Disputations and Polemics." *Encyclopedia Judaica*. Vol 6. Jerusalem: Keter, 1971.

———. "Jewish-Christian Disputation in the Setting of Humanism and Reformation in the German Empire. *HTR* 59 (1966): 369–90.

———. "The Reformation in Contemporary Jewish Eyes." *PIASH* 4 (1969–1970): 239–326.

Berger, David. The Jewish-Christian Debate in the High Middle Ages: A Critical Edition of the *Nizzahon* on Vetus. Philadelphia: Jewish Publication Society, 1979.

Berkovitz, Jay. "Jewish Law and Ritual in Early Modern Germany." In *Jews, Judaism, and the Reformation in Sixteenth-Century Germany*, edited by Dean Phillip Bell and Stephen G. Burnett, 481–502. SCEH 37. Leiden: Brill, 2006.

Bireley, Robert. "The Catholic Reform, Jews, and Judaism in Sixteenth-Century Germany." In *Jews, Judaism, and the Reformation in Sixteenth-Century Germany*, edited by Dean Phillip Bell and Stephen G. Burnett, 249–68. SCEH 37. Leiden: Brill, 2006.

Boendermaker, J. P. "Martin *Luther*—ein semi-iudaeus: Der Einfluss des Alten *Testaments* und des jüdischen Glaubens auf *Luther* und seine Theologie." In *Die Juden und Martin Luther—Martin Luther und die Juden*, edited by Heinz Kremers et al., 45–57. 2nd ed. Neukirchen-Vluyn: Neukirchener, 1987.

Boettcher, Susan. "Preliminary Considerations on the Rhetorical Construction of Jews in Lutheran Preaching at Mid-Sixteenth Century." In *Bundeseinheit und Gottesvolk: Reformierter Protestantismus und Judentum im Europa des 16. und 17. Jahrhunderts*, edited by Achim Detmers and J. Marius J. Lange van Ravenswaay, 105–36. Wuppertal: Foedus, 2005.

Bornkamm, Heinrich. *Luther and the Old Testament.* Translated by Eric W. and Ruth C. Gritsch. Edited by Victor I. Gruhn. Mifflintown: Sigler, 1997.

———, ed. *Luthers Vorreden zur Bibel.* Göttingen: Vandenhoeck & Ruprecht, 1989.

Brooks, Peter Newman, ed. *Seven-Headed Luther: Essays in Commemoration of a Quincentenary 1483–1983.* Oxford: Clarendon, 1983.

Burmeister, Karl Heinz. *Sebastian Münster: Versuch eines biographischen Gesamtbildes.* 2nd ed. BBG 91. Basel and Stuttgart: Helbing and Lichtenhahn, 1969.

Burnett, Stephen G. "A Dialogue of the Deaf: Hebrew Pedagogy and Anti-Jewish Polemic in Sebastian Münster's Messiah of the Christians and the Jews (1529/1539). *ARG* 91 (2000): 168–90.

———. "Calvin's Jewish Interlocutor: Christian Hebraism and Anti-Jewish Polemics during the Reformation." *BHR* 55 (1993): 117–18, 121–23.

———. "Distorted Mirrors: Antonius Margarita, Johann Buxtorf, and Christian Ethnographies of the Jews." *SCJ* 25 (1994): 275–87.

———. "Jews and Anti-Semitism in Early Modern Germany." *SCJ* 27, no. 4 (1996): 1057–64.

———. "Reassessing the 'Basel-Wittenberg Conflict:' Dimensions of the Reformation-Era Discussion of Hebrew Scholarship." In *Hebraica Veritas? Christian Hebraists and the Study of Judaism in Early Modern Europe*, edited by Allison P. Coudert and Jeffrey S. Shoulson, 181–201. JCC. Philadelphia: University of Pennsylvania Press, 2004.

———. "'Spokesmen for Judaism?' Medieval Jewish Polemicists and Their Christian Readers in the Reformation Era." In *Reuchlin und seine Erben: Forscher, Denker, Ideologen und Spinner*, edited by Peter Schäfer and Irina Wandrey, 41–52. Pforzheimer Reuchlinschriften 11. Sigmaringen: Jan Thorbecke, 2005.

Carlebach, Elisheva. "Jewish Responses to Christianity in Reformation Germany." In *Jews, Judaism, and the Reformation in Sixteenth-Century Germany*, edited by Dean Phillip Bell and Stephen G. Burnett, 451–80. SCEH 37. Leiden: Brill, 2006.

Chazan, Robert, ed. *Church, State, and Jew in the Middle Ages*. New York: Behrman, 1980.

———. *Medieval Stereotypes and Modern Antisemitism*. Berkeley: University of California Press, 1997.

———. "The Condemnation of the Talmud Reconsidered (1239–1248)." *PAAJR* 55 (1988): 11–30.

Cohen, Jeremy, ed. *Essential Papers on Judaism and Christianity in Conflict: From Late Antiquity to the Reformation*. New York: New York University Press, 1991.

———. *The Friars and the Jews: the Evolution of Medieval Anti-Judaism*. Ithaca: Cornell University Press, 1982.

Cohen, Mark R. *Under Crescent and Cross: The Jews in the Middle Ages*. Princeton: Princeton University Press, 1994.

Coudenhove-Kalergi, Heinrich Johann Maria. *Anti-Semitism throughout the Ages*. Edited by Count Richard Coudenhove-Kalergi. Translated by Angelo S. Rappoport. Westport: Greenwood, 1972.

Coudert, Allison P. and Jeffrey S. Shoulson, eds. *Hebraica Veritas? Christian Hebraists and the Study of Judaism in Early Modern Europe*. JCC. Philadelphia: University of Pennsylvania Press, 2004.

Detmers, Achim. *Reformation und Judentum: Israel-Lehren und Einstellungen zum Judentum von Luther bis zum frühen Calvin*. JC 7. Stuttgart: Kohlhammer, 2001.

Deutsch, Yaacov. "Von der Juden Ceremonien: Representations of Jews in Sixteenth-Century Germany." In *Jews, Judaism, and the Reformation in Sixteenth-Century Germany*, edited by Dean Phillip Bell and Stephen G. Burnett, 335–56. SCEH 37. Leiden: Brill, 2006.

Diemling, Maria. "Anthonius Margaritha on the 'Whole Jewish Faith:' A Sixteenth-Century Convert from Judaism and his Depiction of the Jewish Religion." In *Jews, Judaism, and the Reformation in Sixteenth-Century Germany*, edited by Dean Phillip Bell and Stephen G. Burnett, 303–33. SCEH 37. Leiden: Brill, 2006.

Ebeling, Gerhard. "Die Anfange von Luthers Hermeneutik." In *Lutherstudien*, 1–68. Tübingen: Mohr, 1971.

———. *Evangelische Evangelienauslegung: Eine Untersuchung zu Luthers Hermeneutik*. 3rd ed. Tübingen: Mohr, 1991.

Eck, Johannes. *Ains Judenbüechlins verlegung: darin ein Christ gantzer Christenhait zu schmach, will es geschehe den Juden unrecht in bezichtigung der Christen kinder mordt. Durch Joh. Ecken zu Ingolstadt*. Ingolstadt, 1541.

Edwards, John, ed. *The Jews in Western Europe 1400–1600*. Manchester: Manchester University Press, 1994.

Elukin, Jonathan. *Living Together, Living Apart: Rethinking Jewish-Christian Relations in the Middle Ages*. Princeton: Princeton University Press, 2007.

Flannery, Edward H. *The Anguish of the Jews: Twenty-Three Centuries of Antisemitism*. New York: Paulist, 1985.

Fraenkel-Goldschmidt, Chava. *The Historical Writings of Joseph of Rosheim: Leader of Jewry in Early Modern Germany*. Edited by Adam Shear. Translated by Naomi Schendowich. SEJ 12. Leiden: Brill, 2006.

―――, ed. *Sefer ha-Miknah [me-et] Yosef Ish Ros'heim*. Yerushalayim: Meḳitse Nirdamim, 730 [1970].

Fraidl, Franz Sales. *Die Exegese der Siebzig Wochen Daniels in der alten und mittleren Zeit*. Graz: Leuschner and Lukensky, 1833.

Frey, Winfried and Andrea Frölich. *Das Judenbild in den Flugschriften des 16. Jahrhunderts*. CD-ROM. Herzberg, 2008.

Friedman, Jerome. "Jewish Conversion, the Spanish Pure Blood Laws and Reformation: A Revisionist View of Racial and Religious Antisemitism." *SCJ* 18, no. 1 (1987): 3–29.

―――. "Sebastian Münster, the Jewish Mission, and Protestant Antisemitism." *ARG* 70 (1979): 238–59.

―――. "Servetus and the Psalms: The Exegesis of Heresy. In *Histoire de l'exégèse au XVIe siècle*, edited by Olivier Fatio and Pierre Fraenkel, 164–78. Geneva: Librairie Droz, 1978.

―――. "Sixteenth-Century Christian-Hebraica: Scripture and the Renaissance Myth of the Past." *SCJ* 11, no. 4 (1980): 67–85.

―――. *The Most Ancient Testimony: Sixteenth-Century Christian-Hebraica in the Age of Renaissance Nostalgia*. Athens: Ohio University Press, 1983.

―――. "The Reformation and Jewish Antichristian Polemics." *BHR* 41 (1979): 83–97.

Funkenstein, Amos. "Basic Types of Christian Anti-Jewish Polemics in the Later Middle Ages." *Viator* 2 (1971): 373–82.

Gleason, Randall C. "'Letter' and 'Spirit' in Luther's Hermeneutics." *BibSac* 157, no. 628 (2000): 468–85.

Gow, Andrew Colin. *The Red Jews: Antisemitism in an Apocalyptic Age 1200–1600*. SMRT 55. Leiden: Brill, 1995.

Gritsch, Eric W. "Martin Luther and Violence: A Reappraisal of a Neuralgic Theme." *SCJ* 3 (1972): 37–55.

Güde, Wilhelm. *Die rechtliche Stellung der Juden in den Schriften deutscher Juristen des 16. und 17. Jahrhunderts*. Sigmaringen: Jan Thorbeke, 1981.

Hagen, Kenneth. *Luther's Approach to Scripture as Seen in His "Commentaries" on Galatians 1519–1538*. Tübingen: Mohr, 1993.

Hägler, Brigitte. *Die Christen und die 'Judenfrage': Am Beispiel der Schriften Osianders und Ecks zum Ritualmordvorwurf*. Erlangen: Palm and Enke, 1992.

Haile, H. G. *Luther, an Experiment in Biography*. Garden City: Doubleday, 1980.

Hailperin, Herman. *Rashi and the Christian Scholars*. Pittsburgh: University of Pittsburgh Press, 1963.

Headley, John M. *Luther's View of Church History*. New Haven: Yale University Press, 1963.

Heil, Johannes. "Antijudaismus und Antisemitismus: Begriffe als Bedeutungsträger. *JA* 6 (1997): 92–114.

Helmer, Christine. "Luther's Trinitarian Hermeneutic and the Old Testament." *MT* 18, no. 1 (2002): 49–73.

Hendrix, Scott H. *Ecclesia in Via: Ecclessiological Developments in the Medieval Psalms Exegesis and the Dictata Super Psalterium of Martin Luther.* SMRT 8. Leiden: Brill, 1974.

———. "Luther against the Background of the History of Biblical Interpretation." *Int* 37, no. 3 (1983): 229–39.

———. "Toleration of the Jews in the German Reformation: Urbanus Rhegius and-Braunschweig (1535–1540)." *ARG* 81 (1990): 189–215.

———. *Tradition and Authority in the Reformation.* Aldershot: Variorum, 1996.

Hobbs, Gerald. "Martin Bucer on Psalm 22: A Study in the Application of Rabbinic Exegesis by a Christian Hebraist." In *Histoire de l'exégèse au XVIe siècle,* edited by Olivier Fatio and Pierre Fraenkel, 144–63. Geneva: Librairie Droz S.A., 1978.

Holmio, Armas K. E. *The Lutheran Reformation and the Jews: The Birth of the Protestant Jewish Missions.* Hancock: Finnish Lutheran Book Concern, 1949.

Homolka, Walter, Walter Jacob, and Esther Seidel, eds. *Not by Birth Alone: Conversion to Judaism.* Herndon: Cassell, 1997.

Horbury, William. *Jews and Christians in Contact and Controversy.* Edinburgh: T&T Clark, 1998.

Hsia, R. Po-chia. *The Myth of Ritual Murder: Jews and Magic in Reformation Germany.* New Haven: Yale University Press, 1990.

Isaac, Jules. *Jesus and Israel.* New York: Holt, Rinehart, and Winston, 1971.

———. *The Teaching of Contempt: Christian Roots of Anti-Semitism.* Translated by Helen Weaver. New York: Holt, Rinehart, and Winston, 1964.

Johnson, Luke Timothy. "The New Testament's Anti-Jewish Slander and the Conventions of Ancient Polemic." *JBL* 108, no. 3 (1989): 419–41.

Junghans, Helmar. "Interpreting the Old Luther (1526–1546)." *CurTM* 9, no. 5 (1982): 271–81.

———, ed. *Leben und Werk Martin Luthers von 1526 bis 1546: Festgabe zu seinem 500. Geburtstag.* 2 Vols. Göttingen: Vandenhoeck & Ruprecht, 1983.

Kaiser, Jürgen. *Ruhe der Seele und Siegel der Hoffnung: Die Deutungen des Sabbats in der Reformation.* Göttingen: Vandenhoeck & Ruprecht, 1996.

Kammerling, Joy. "Andreas Osiander's Sermons on the Jews." *LQ* 15, no. 1 (2001): 59–84.

———. "Andreas Osiander, the Jews, and Judaism." In *Jews, Judaism, and the Reformation in Sixteenth-Century Germany,* edited by Dean Phillip Bell and Stephen G. Burnett, 219–47. SCEH 37. Leiden: Brill, 2006.

Kaplan, Benjamin J. *Divided by Faith: Religious Conflict and the Practice of Toleration in Early Modern Europe.* Cambridge: Belknap, 2007.

Kaplan, Debra. *Beyond Expulsion: Jews, Christians, and Reformation Strasbourg.* Palo Alto: Stanford University Press, 2011.

Karant-Nunn, Susan C. *The Reformation of Feeling: Shaping the Religious Emotions in Early Modern Germany*. Oxford: Oxford University Press, 2010.

Katz, Jacob. *Exclusiveness and Tolerance: Studies in Jewish-Gentile Relations in Medieval and Modern times*. New York: Schocken, 1961.

Kaufmann, Thomas. "Das Judentum in der frühreformatorischen Flugschriftenpublizistik." *ZTK* 95 (1998): 429–61.

————. *Geschichte der Reformation*. Frankfurt am Main: Weltreligionen, 2009.

Kisch, Guido. *Erasmus' Stellung zu Juden und Judentum*. Tübingen: Mohr, 1969.

————. *The Jews in Medieval Germany: A Study of Their Legal and Social Status*. New York: Ktav, 1970.

Kittelson, James M. "Luther der Mensch." *CJ* 17, no. 4 (1991): 384–92.

Klein, Ralph W. "Reading the Old Testament with Martin Luther—and without Him." *CurTM* 36, no. 2 (2009): 95–103.

Kleiner, John W. *The Attitude of the Strasbourg Reformers toward Jews and Judaism*. Ph.D. Thesis. Temple University, 1978.

Kooiman, Willem Jan. *Luther and the Bible*. Translated by John Schmidt. Philadelphia: Muhlenberg Press, 1961.

Krause, Gerhard. *Studien zu Luthers Auslegung der Kleinen Propheten*. BHT 33. Tübingen: Mohr, 1962.

Krauss, Samuel. *Das Leben Jesu nach jüdischen Quellen*. Berlin: Calvary, 1902.

Krey, Philip D. W., and Leslie Smith, eds. *Nicholas of Lyra: The Senses of Scripture*. SHCT 90. Leiden: Brill, 2000.

Kusukawa, Sachiko. *A Wittenberg University Library Catalogue of 1536*. Medieval and Renaissance Texts and Studies 142. Binghamton: Medieval and Renaissance Texts and Studies, 1995.

Levinson, Nathan P. *"Ketzer" und Abtrünnige im Judentum: Historische Porträts*. Hannover: Lutherisches, 2001.

Levy, Leonard Williams. *Treason against God: A History of the Offense of Blasphemy*. New York: Schocken, 1981.

Liechty, Daniel. *Sabbatarianism in the Sixteenth Century: A Page in the History of the Radical Reformation*. Berrien Springs: Andrews University Press, 1993.

Limor, Ora and Stroumsa, eds. *Contra Iudaeos: Ancient and Medieval Polemics between Christians and Jews*. TSMEMJ 10. Tübingen: Mohr, 1996.

Lindberg, Carter. "No Greater Service to God than Christian Love: Insights from Martin Luther." In *Social Ministry in the Lutheran Tradition*, edited by Foster R. McCurley, 50–68. Minneapolis: Fortress Press, 2008.

Lohse, Bernhard. "Die Bedeutung Augustins für den jungen Luther." In *Evangelium in der Geschichte: Studien zu Luther und der Reformation*, edited by Leif Grane et al., 11–30. Göttingen: Vandenhoeck & Ruprecht, 1988.

Lowenthal, Marvin. *The Jews of Germany: The Story of Sixteen Centuries*. Philadelphia: Jewish Publication Society, 1936.

Lubac, Henri de, S.J. *Medieval Exegesis: The Four Senses of Scripture.* Vol. 1, translated by Mark Sebanc. Vols, 2–3 translated by E. M. Macierowski. Grand Rapids: Eerdmans, 1998, 2000, 2009.

Luther, Martin. *Lectures on Romans.* Translated and edited by Wilhelm Pauck. LCC 15. Philadelphia: Westminster, 1961.

———. *Martin Luther Wolfenbütteler Psalter, 1513–1515.* 2 vols. Edited by Eleanor Roach und Reinhard Schwarz. Frankfurt am Main: Insel, 1983.

Marcus, Jacob R. *The Jew in the Medieval World: A Source Book.* Cincinnati: Sinai, 1938.

Marius, Richard. *Luther.* Philadelphia: Lippincott, 1974.

———. *Martin Luther: The Christian between God and Death.* Cambridge: Belknap, 1999.

Martin, Ellen. *Die deutschen Schriften des Johannes Pfefferkorn: Zum Problem des Judenhasses und der Intoleranz in der Zeit der Vorreformation.* Göppingen: Kümmerle, 1994.

Marty, Martin. *Martin Luther: A Life.* New York: Penguin, 2004.

Mattox, Mickey L. "From Faith to the Text and Back Again: Martin Luther on the Trinity in the Old Testament." *Pro Ecclesia* 15, no. 3 (2006): 281–303.

Maxfield, John A. *Luther's Lectures on Genesis and the Formation of Evangelical Identity.* Kirksville: Truman State University Press, 2008.

McGinn, Bernard. *Visions of the End: Apocalyptic Traditions in the Middle Ages.* New York: Columbia University Press, 1979.

McLean, Matthew. "Between Basel and Zurich: Humanist Rivalries and the Works of Sebastian Münster." In *The Book Triumphant: Print in Transition in the Sixteenth and Seventeenth Centuries,* edited by Malcolm Walsby and Graeme Kemp, 270–91. Leiden: Brill, 2011.

McMichael, Steven J. *Was Jesus of Nazareth the Messiah? Alphonso de Espina's Argument against the Jews in the Fortalitium Fidei (c. 1464).* SFSHJ 96. Atlanta: Scholars, 1994.

Meinhold, Peter. *Die Genesisvorlesung Luthers und ihre Herausgeber.* FKG 8. Stuttgart: Kohlhammer, 1936.

Mellinkoff, Ruth. *Outcasts: Signs of Otherness in Northern European Art of the Late Middle Ages.* 2 vols. Berkeley: University of California Press, 1993.

Nestingen, James A. *Martin Luther: A Life.* Minneapolis: Fortress Press, 2009 (2003).

Oberman, Heiko A. "Discovery of Hebrew and Discrimination against the Jews: The Veritas Hebraica as Double-Edged Sword in Renaissance and Reformation." In *Germania Illustrata: Essays on Early Modern Germany Presented to Gerald Strauss,* edited by Andrew C. Fix and Susan C. Karant-Nunn, 19–34. Kirksville: Sixteenth Century Journal, 1992.

———. "Facientibus quod in se est Deus non denegat gratiam: Robert Holcot, O.P., and the Beginnings of Luther's Theology." *HTR* 55, no. 4 (1962): 317–42.

———. *The Reformation: Roots and Ramifications.* Translated by Andrew Colin Gow. Grand Rapids: Eerdmans, 1994.

———. *The Roots of Anti-Semitism: In the Age of Renaissance and Reformation.* Translated by James I. Porter. Philadelphia: Fortress Press, 1984.

———. "Three Sixteenth-Century Attitudes toward Judaism: Reuchlin, Erasmus, and Luther. In *Jewish Thought in the Sixteenth Century*, edited by Bernard Dov Cooperman, 326–64. Cambridge: Harvard University Center for Jewish Studies, 1983.

———. *Wurzeln des Antisemitismus: Christenangst und Judenplage im Zeitalter von Humanismus und Reformation.* Berlin: Severin und Siedler, 1981.

———. "Zwischen Agitation und Reformation: Die Flugschriften als 'Judenspiegel.'" In *Flugschriften als Massenmedium der Reformationszeit*, edited by Hans-Joahim Köhler, 269–89. Stuttgart: Klett-Cotta, 1981.

Ocker, Christopher. "German Theologians and the Jews in the Fifteenth Century." In *Jews, Judaism, and the Reformation in Sixteenth-Century Germany*, edited by Dean Phillip Bell and Stephen G. Burnett, Pp. 33–65. SCEH 37. Leiden: Brill, 2006.

Pakter, Walter. *Medieval Canon Law and the Jews.* Abhandlungen zur rechtwissenschaftlichen Grundlagenforschung 68. Ebelsbach: Gremler, 1988.

Parkes, James. *The Conflict of the Church and the Synagogue: A Study in the Origins of Antisemitism.* London: Soncino, 1934.

Parvis, Sara, and Paul Foster, eds. *Justin Martyr and His Worlds.* Minneapolis: Fortress Press, 2007.

Pauck, Wilhelm, ed. *Lectures on Romans: Martin Luther.* LCC 15. Philadelphia: Westminster, 1961.

Pelikan, Jaroslav. *Luther the Expositor: Introduction to the Reformer's Exegetical Writings.* Luther's Works: Companion Volume. St. Louis: Concordia, 1959.

Poliakov, Léon. *The History of Anti-Semitism: From the Time of Christ to the Court Jews.* Translated by Richard Howard. New York: Schocken, 1976.

Posnanski, Adolf. *Schiloh: Ein Beitrag zur Geschichte der Messiaslehre.* Leipzig: Hinrichs, 1904.

Preus, James Samuel. "From Promise to Presence: The Christ in Luther's Old Testament." In *Encounters with Luther*, vol. 1, edited by Eric W. Gritsch, 109–25. Gettysburg: Institute for Luther Studies, 1980.

———. *From Shadow to Promise: Old Testament Interpretation from Augustine to the Young Luther.* Cambridge: Belknap, 1969.

———. "Luther on Christ and the Old Testament." *CTM* 43, no. 8 (1972): 488–97.

———. "Old Testament Promissio and Luther's New Hermeneutic." *HTR* 60, no. 2 (1967): 145–61.

Raeder, Siegfried. *Das Hebräische bei Luther, untersucht bis zum Ende der ersten Psalmenvorlesung.* Tübingen: Mohr, 1961.

———. *Die Benutzung des masoretischen Textes bei Luther in der Zeit zwischen der ersten und zweiten Psalmenvorlesung (1515–1518).* Tübingen: Mohr, 1967.

———. *Grammatica Theologica: Studien zu Luthers Operationes in Psalmos.* Tübingen: Mohr, 1977.

———. "The Exegetical and Hermeneutical Work of Martin Luther." In *Hebrew Bible/ Old Testament: The History of its Interpretation*, vol. 2, *From the Renaissance to the Enlightenment*, edited by Magne Sæbo, 363–406. Göttingen: Vandenhoeck & Ruprecht, 2008.

Renner, Johannes Theodore Erich. "Some Thoughts on Luther and the Old Testament." *LTJ* 25, no. 3 (1991): 157–65.

Reventlow, Henning Graf. *History of Biblical Interpretation.* Vol. 3, *Renaissance, Reformation, Humanism.* Translated by James O. Duke. RBS 62. Atlanta: Society of Biblical Literature, 2009.

Roper, Lyndal. "Martin Luther's Body: The 'Stout Doctor' and His Biographers." *AHR* 115, no. 2 (2010): 351–84.

Rowan, Steven. "Ulrich Zasius and John Eck: 'Faith Need Not Be Kept with an Enemy.'" *SCJ* 8, no. 3 (1977): 79–95.

Ruderman, David B. *Early Modern Jewry: A New Cultural History.* Princeton: Princeton University Press, 2010.

Ruether, Rosemary Radford. *Faith and Fratricide: The Theological Roots of Anti-Semitism.* New York: Seabury, 1974.

———. "The *Adversus Judaeos* Tradition in the Church Fathers: The Exegesis of Christian Anti-Judaism." In *Essential Papers on Judaism and Christianity in Conflict: From Late Antiquity to the Reformation,* edited by Jeremy Cohen, 174–89. New York: New York University Press, 1991.

Rummel, Erika. *The Case against Johann Reuchlin: Religious and Social Controversy in Sixteenth-Century Germany.* Toronto: University of Toronto Press, 2002.

Schäfer, Peter. *Jesus in the Talmud.* Princeton: Princeton University Press, 2007.

———. *Judeophobia: Attitudes toward the Jews in the Ancient World.* Cambridge: Harvard University Press, 1997.

Schoeps, Hans-Joachim. *The Jewish-Christian Argument: A History of Theologies in Conflict.* Translated by David E. Green. New York: Holt, Rinehart and Winston, 1963.

Schöner, Petra. "Visual Representations of Jews and Judaism in Sixteenth Century Germany." In *Jews, Judaism, and the Reformation in Sixteenth-Century Germany,* edited by Dean Phillip Bell and Stephen G. Burnett, 357–91. SCEH 37. Leiden: Brill, 2006.

Schreckenberg, Heinz. *Die christlichen Adversus-Judaeos-Texte und ihr literarisches und historisches Umfeld (13.–20. Jh.).* Frankfurt: Peter Lang, 1994.

Schreiner, Stefan. "Jüdische Reaktionen auf die Reformation: Einige Anmerkungen." *Judaica* 39 (1983): 150–65.

Shachar, Isaiah. *The Judensau: A Medieval Anti-Jewish Motif and Its History.* London: Warburg Institute, 1974.

Smith, Preserved, ed. *Luther's Correspondence and Other Contemporary Letters.* Vol. 1, *1507–1521.* Philadelphia: Lutheran Publication Society, 1913.

———, and Charles M. Jacobs, eds. *Luther's Correspondence and Other Contemporary Letters.* Vol. 2, *1521–1530.* Philadelphia: Lutheran Publication Society, 1918.

Stegemann, Ekkehard. "Luther's Bibelübersetzung und das jüdisch-christliche Gespräch." *EvTh* 44 (1984): 386–405.

Steinmetz, David C. "Luther and the Blessing of Judah." *Lutherjahrbuch* 71 (2004): 159–78.

Stern, Moritz. *Andreas Osianders Schrift über die Blutbeschuldigung.* Kiel: Fiencke, 1893.

Stern, Selma. *Josel of Rosheim, Commander of Jewry in the Holy Roman Empire of the German Nation.* Translated by Gertrude Hirschler. Philadelphia: Jewish Publication Society, 1965.

Stern-Taeubler, Selma. "Die Vorstellung vom Juden und vom Judentum in der Ideologie der Reformationszeit." In *Essays Presented to Leo Baeck on the Occasion of His Eightieth Birthday*, L. G. Montefiore, 194–211. New York: East and West Library, 1954.

Swidler, Leonard. *After the Absolute: The Dialogical Future of Religious Reflection.* Minneapolis: Fortress Press, 1990.

Synan, Edward A. *The Popes and the Jews in the Middle Ages.* New York: Macmillan, 1965.

Trachtenberg, Joshua. *The Devil and the Jews: The Medieval Conception of the Jew and Its Relation to Modern Antisemitism.* 2nd ed. Philadelphia: Jewish Publication Society, 1993.

Trautner-Kromann, Hanne. *Shield and Sword: Jewish Polemics against Christianity and the Christians in France and Spain from 1100–1500.* TSMEMJ 8. Tübingen: Mohr, 1993.

Walton, Michael T. *Anthonius Margaritha and the Jewish Faith: Jewish Life and Conversion in Sixteenth-Century Germany.* Detroit: Wayne State University Press, 2012.

———. "Anthonius Margaritha: Honest Reporter?" *SCJ* 36 (2005): 129–41.

Wengert, Timothy J. "Philip Melanchthon and the Jews: A Reappraisal." In *Jews, Judaism, and the Reformation in Sixteenth-Century Germany*, edited by Dean Phillip Bell and Stephen G. Burnett, 105–35. SCEH 37. Leiden: Brill, 2006.

Wenzel, Edith Wenzel. "The Representation of Jews and Judaism in Sixteenth-Century German Literature." In *Jews, Judaism, and the Reformation in Sixteenth-Century Germany*, edited by Dean Phillip Bell and Stephen G. Burnett, 393–417. SCEH 37. Leiden: Brill, 2006.

———. "Christliche Hebraisten der Renaissance und Reformation." *Judaica* 30 (1974): 78–135.

Willi, Thomas. "Hebraica veritas in Basel: Christliche Hebraistik aus jüdischen Quellen." In *Congress Volume Basel 2001*, 377–97. VTSup 92. Edited by André Lemaire. Leiden: Brill, 2002.

Williams, A. Lukyn. *Adversus Judaeos: A Bird's-Eye View of Christian Apologiae until the Renaissance.* Cambridge: University Press, 1935.

Williams, George H. "Protestants in the Ukraine during the Period of the Polish-Lithuanian Commonwealth." *HUS* 2 (1978): 41–72.

Wolf, Gerhard Phillip. "Osiander und die Juden im Kontext seiner Theologie." *ZBK* 53 (1984): 49–77.

Wolfthal, Diane, ed. *Peace, Negotiation, and Reciprocity: Strategies for Coexistence in the Middle Ages and the Renaissance.* Turnhout: Brepols, 2000.

Zambelli, Paola, ed. *"Astrologi hallucinati": Stars and the End of the World in Luther's Time.* Berlin: de Gruyter, 1986.

Zimmer, Eric. "Jewish and Christian Hebraist Collaboration in Sixteenth Century Germany." *JQR* 71, no. 2 (1980): 69–88.

Additional Background Literature

Archer, Gleason L., Jr. *Jerome's Commentary on Daniel.* Grand Rapids: Baker, 1958.

Augustine, St. *Expositions of the Psalms.* 6 volumes. Edited by John E. Rotelle, O.S.B., et al. Translated by Maria Boulding, O.S.B. The Works of Saint Augustine 3/15–20. Hyde Park: New City, 2000–2004.

Becker, Adam H. and Annette Yoshiko Reed, eds. *The Ways That Never Parted: Jews and Christians in Late Antiquity and the Early Middle Ages.* Minneapolis: Fortress Press, 2007.

Berger, David. "Christian Heresy and Jewish Polemic in the Twelfth and Thirteenth Centuries." *HTR* 68 (1975): 287–303.

Boyarin, Daniel. *Dying for God: Martyrdom and the Making of Christianity and Judaism.* Palo Alto: Stanford University Press, 1999.

Boys, Mary C. *Has God Only One Blessing? Judaism as a Source of Christian Self-Understanding.* SJC. New York: Paulist, 2000.

Bunte, Wolfgang. *Rabbinische Traditionen bei Nikolaus von Lyra: Ein Beitrag zur Schriftauslegung des Spätmittelalters.* Frankfurt am Main: Peter Lang, 1994.

Burnett, Stephen G. "Christian Hebrew Printing in the Sixteenth Century: Printers, Humanism, and the Impact of the Reformation." *Helmantica* 51 (2000): 13–42.

———. *From Christian Hebraism to Jewish Studies: Johannes Buxtorf (1564–1629) and Hebrew Learning in the Seventeenth Century.* Leiden: Brill, 1996.

———. "German Jewish Printing in the Reformation Era (1530–1633)." In *Jews, Judaism, and the Reformation in Sixteenth-Century Germany,* edited by Dean Phillip Bell and Stephen G. Burnett, 503–27. SCEH 37. Leiden: Brill, 2006.

Carroll, James. *Constantine's Sword: The Church and the Jews.* Boston and New York: Houghton Mifflin, 2001.

Chazan, Robert. *Barcelona and Beyond: The Disputation of 1263 and Its Aftermath.* Berkeley: University of California Press, 1989.

———. *Daggers of Faith: Thirteenth-Century Christian Missionizing and Jewish Response.* Berkeley: University of California Press, 1989.

Cohen, Amnon. *Jewish Life under Islam: Jerusalem in the Sixteenth Century.* Cambridge: Harvard University Press, 1984.

Cohen, Shaye. "'Anti-Semitism' in Antiquity: the Problem of Definition." In *History and Hate: The Dimensions of Anti-Semitism,* edited by David Berger, 43–47. Philadelphia: Jewish Publication Society, 1986.

Davies, Alan T. *Anti-Semitism and the Christian Mind: The Crisis of Conscience after Auschwitz.* New York: Herder and Herder, 1969.

Delius, Hans-Ulrich. *Die Quellen von Martin Luthers Genesisvorlesung.* BET 111. Munich: Kaiser, 1992.

Dillenberger, John. *God Hidden and Revealed: The Interpretation of Luther's Deus Absconditus and Its Significance for Religious Thought.* Philadelphia: Muhlenberg, 1953.

Dunn, Geoffrey D. *Tertullian's Aduersus Iudaeos: A Rhetorical Analysis.* PMS 19. Washington, DC: Catholic University of America Press, 2008.

Francisco, Adam S. *Martin Luther and Islam: A Study in Sixteenth-Century Polemics and Apologetics*. HCMR 8. Leiden: Brill, 2007.

Frederiksen, Paula. *Augustine and the Jews: A Christian Defense of Jews and Judaism*. New York: Doubleday, 2008.

Gager, John G. *The Origins of Anti-Semitism: Attitudes toward Judaism in Pagan and Christian Antiquity*. New York: Oxford University Press, 1983.

Geiger, Ludwig. *Das Studium der Hebräischen Sprache in Deutschland: Von Ende des XV. bis zur Mitte des XVI. Jahrhunderts*. Breslau: Skutsch, 1870.

Gerrish, B. A. "The Word of God and the Words of Scripture: Luther and Calvin on Biblical Authority." In *The Old Protestantism and the New: Essays on the Reformation Heritage*, edited by B. A. Gerrish, 51–68. Chicago: The University of Chicago Press, 1982.

Hilberg, Raul. *The Destruction of the European Jews*. New York: Holmes and Meier, 1985.

Holder, R. Ward, ed. *A Companion to Paul in the Reformation*. BCCT 15. Leiden: Brill, 2010.

Kaminsky, Joel S. *Yet I Loved Jacob: Reclaiming the Biblical Concept of Election*. Nashville: Abingdon, 2007.

Katz, Steven T. *The Holocaust in Historical Context*. Vol. 1, *The Holocaust and Mass Death before the Modern Age*. New York: Oxford University Press, 1994.

Klein, Ralph W. "The Origin and Nature of Our Estrangement." In *The Significance of Judaism for the Life and Mission of the Church*, 19–39. Geneva: Lutheran World Federation, 1982.

Klepper, Deeana Copeland. *The Insight of Unbelievers: Nicholas of Lyra and Christian Reading of Jewish Text in the Later Middle Ages*. Philadelphia: University of Pennsylvania Press, 2007.

Koenig, Richard E. "With Love and Respect for the Jewish People." *ADLIF* 2, no. 1 (1995): 19–27.

Langmuir, Gavin I. *Toward a Definition of Antisemitism*. Berkeley: University of California Press, 1990.

Lazare, Bernard. *Antisemitism: Its History and Causes*. Translated from the French. Lincoln: University of Nebraska Press, 1995.

Lindemann, Albert S. *Esau's Tears: Modern Anti-Semitism and the Rise of the Jews*. Cambridge: Cambridge University Press, 1997.

Littell, Franklin H. *The Crucifixion of the Jews*. New York: Harper and Row, 1975.

Marcovich, Miroslav, ed. *Iustini Martyris Dialogus cum Tryphone*. PTS 47. Berlin: de Gruyter, 1997.

Mildenberger, Irene. *Der Israelsonntag—Gedenktag der Zerstörung Jerusalems: Untersuchungen zu seiner homiletischen und liturgischen Gestaltung in der evangelischen Tradition*. SKI 22. Berlin: Institut Kirche und Judentum, 2004.

Reed, Annette Yoshiko, and Adam H. Becker, eds. *The Ways That Never Parted: Jews and Christians in Late Antiquity and the Early Middle Ages*. Tübingen: Mohr, 2003.

Schilling, Heinz. "The Reformation and the Rise of the Early Modern State." In *Luther and the Modern State in Germany*, edited by James D. Tracy, 21–30. SCES 7. Kirksville: Sixteenth Century Journal, 1986.

Siemon-Netto, Uwe. *The Fabricated Luther: Refuting Nazi Connections and Other Modern Myths.* 2nd ed. St. Louis: Concordia, 2007.

Siker, Jeffrey S. *Disinheriting The Jews: Abraham in Early Christian Controversy.* Louisville: Westminster John Knox, 1991.

Simon, Marcel. *Verus Israel: A Study of the Relations between Christians and Jews in the Roman Empire (135–425).* Translated by H. McKeating. New York: Oxford University Press, 1986.

Singer, Howard. "The Rise and Fall of Interfaith Dialogue." *Commentary* 83, no. 5 (1987): 50–55.

Smalley, Beryl. *The Study of the Bible in the Middle Ages.* Oxford: Blackwell, 1952.

Smith, Lesley. *The Glossa Ordinaria: The Making of a Medieval Bible Commentary.* Leiden: Brill, 2009.

Soulen, R. Kendall. *The God of Israel and Christian Theology.* Minneapolis: Fortress Press, 1996.

Steinmetz, David. "John Calvin and the Jews: A Problem in Political Theology." *PT* 10, no. 3 (2009): 391–409.

Stendahl, Krister. "Judaism and Christianity: A Plea for a New Relationship." *Cross Curr.* 17 (Fall 1967): 445–58.

Stern, Menahem, ed. *Greek and Latin Authors on Jews and Judaism.* 3 vols. Jerusalem: Israel Academy of Sciences and Humanities, 1974–1984.

Stolt, Birgit. "Luthers Übersetzungstheorie und Übersetzungspraxis." In *Leben und Werk Martin Luthers von 1526 bis 1546: Festgabe zu seinem 500. Geburtstag.* 2 vols. Göttingen: Vandenhoeck & Ruprecht, 1983.

Uffenheimer, Benjamin and Henning Graf Reventlow. *Creative Biblical Exegesis: Christian and Jewish Hermeneutics through the Centuries.* JSOTS 59. Sheffield: Sheffield, 1988.

Wengst, Klaus. "Perspektiven für eine nicht-antijüdische Christologie: Beobachtungen und Überlegungen zu neutestamentlichen Texten." *EvTh* 59, no. 4 (1999): 240–51.

Wyschogrod, Michael. *Abraham's Promise: Judaism and Jewish-Christian Relations.* Edited and introduced by R. Kendall Soulen. Grand Rapids: Eerdmans, 2004.